Frontiers

Adam Nicolson

FRONTIERS

From the Arctic Circle to the Aegean

Weidenfeld and Nicolson · London

For James Magan

First published in Great Britain in 1985 by
George Weidenfeld & Nicolson Limited
91 Clapham High Street, London SW4 7TA

Copyright © by Adam Nicolson, 1985

Maps by Richard Natkiel

ISBN 0 297 78709 8

Printed and bound in Great Britain by
The Bath Press, Avon

Contents

And what do the dogs defend behind the high wire fences?
  What home needs fury on a running lead?
Why did the Prince require those yellow walls?
  These private landscapes must be wealth indeed.

JAMES FENTON, 'Children in Exile'

*Pour éloigner tout sujet de discorde, toute occasion de querelle,
on doit marquer avec clarté et précision les limites des territoires.*

EMMERICH DE VATTEL, *Le Droit des Gens* 1758

Der Grenzraum ist das Wirkliche, die Grenzlinie die Abstraktion davon.

FRIEDRICH RATZEL, *Politische Geographie* 1897

We had fed the heart on fantasies,
The heart's grown brutal from the fare;
More substance in our enmities
Than in our love . . .

W. B. YEATS, 'The Stare's Nest by My Window'

On the boundary between Kenya and Tanganyika, three of the
critical place-names by which the border was to be aligned – Sonyo,
Atorigini and Olotoiboiologunya – were the Masai equivalent for
Thingumabob, I forget and *Your boy has gone on ahead.* I cannot even
now be certain that some of my place-names are accurate.

G. E. SMITH, 'From the Victoria Nyanza to Kilimanjaro'

This coronet part between you.

SHAKESPEARE, *King Lear*, Act I, scene 1

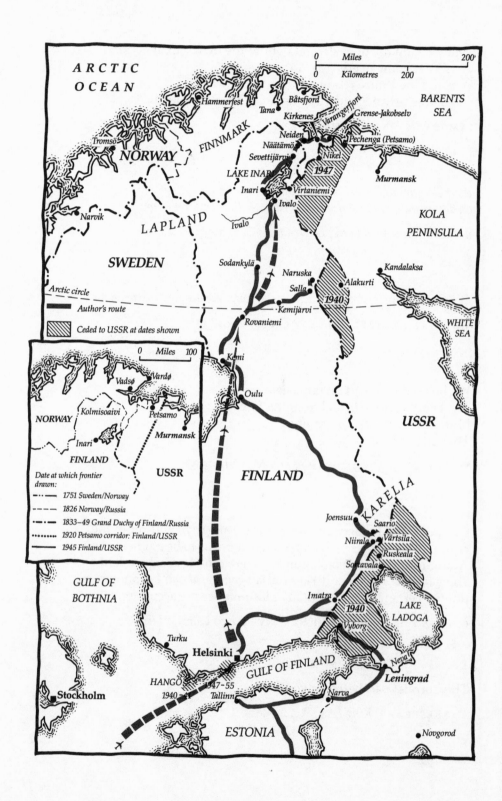

ARCTIC
OCEAN

Hammerfest   Båtsfjord
Tana   Kirkenes   Varangerfjord   BARENTS
Neiden   Grense-Jakobselv   SEA
Tromsö   Näätämö   Pechenga (Petsamo)
NORWAY   FINNMARK   Sevettijärvi   Nikel
LAKE INARI   1947   Murmansk
Narvik   Inari   Virtaniemi
LAPLAND   Ivalo   KOLA
SWEDEN   Ivalo   PENINSULA
Sodankylä   Naruska   Kandalaksa
Arctic circle   Salla   Alakurti
Author's route   Kemijärvi   1940
Ceded to USSR at dates shown   Rovaniemi   WHITE
SEA
Kemi

0   Miles   100   Oulu
Vadsø   Vardø
Kolmisoaivi   NORWAY   Petsamo   USSR
Inari   Murmansk
FINLAND   USSR   FINLAND   KARELIA
Date at which frontier   Joensuu   Saario
drawn: Niirala   Värtsilä
1751 Sweden/Norway   Ruskeala
1826 Norway/Russia   Sortavala
1833–49 Grand Duchy of Finland/Russia   Imatra   LAKE
1920 Petsamo corridor: Finland/USSR   1940   LADOGA
1945 Finland/USSR   Vyborg

GULF OF
BOTHNIA   Neva

Turku   Helsinki   GULF OF FINLAND   Leningrad
HANGÖ   1947–55
Stockholm   1940–4   Tallinn   Narva

ESTONIA   Novgorod

Miles   200
Kilometres   200

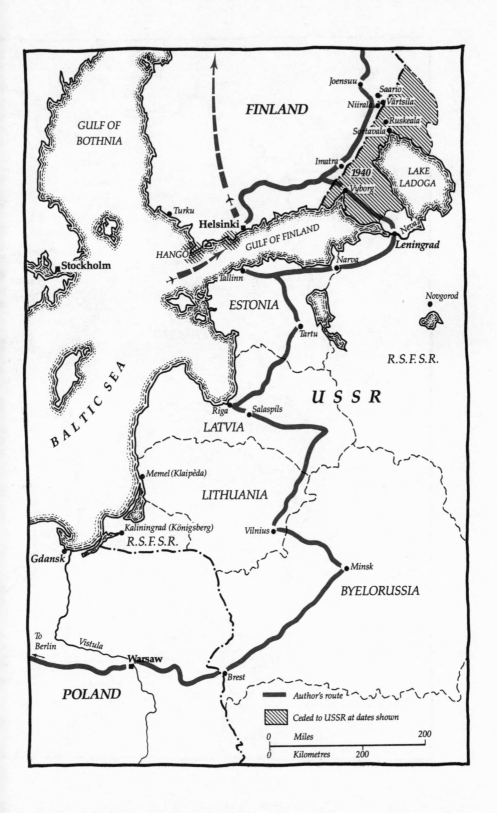

GULF OF
BOTHNIA

FINLAND

Joensuu
Saario
Niirala
Värtsila
Ruskeala
Sortavala

Imatra

1940

LAKE
LADOGA

Vyborg

Turku

Helsinki

GULF OF FINLAND

Neva

HANGO

Leningrad

Tallinn

Narva

Stockholm

ESTONIA

Novgorod

Tartu

BALTIC SEA

R.S.F.S.R.

U S S R

Riga *Salaspils*

LATVIA

Memel (Klaipèda)

LITHUANIA

Kaliningrad (Königsberg)

Vilnius

R.S.F.S.R.

Gdansk

Minsk

BYELORUSSIA

To
Berlin   *Vistula*

Warsaw

Brest

POLAND

━━━━━ *Author's route*

▨▨▨ *Ceded to USSR at dates shown*

0   Miles   200

0   Kilometres   200

Miles 0 — 200
Kilometres 0 — 200

Author's route

Pre-war German Sudetenland

AUSTRIA
Vienna

Miles 0 — 30
Km 0 — 30

USSR

Devín (Theben)
Bratislava
(Pressburg, Pozsony)

Hainburg

March

Leitha

Gattendorf

Danube

Eisenstadt
Siegendorf   Rust   Neusiedler
Klingenbach   See
Sopron   KIS. ALFÖLD
Transferred to   Abda
Hungary, 1921   Nagy Cenk   **HUNGARY**   Győr

ansk

Vistula
Warsaw   Brest

POLAND

ań

AVIA   CARPATHIAN

CHOSLOVAKIA
SLOVAKIA   UKRAINE   USSR

ratislava   Pacin
Győr   Miskolc   Dombrád   Barabás
Esztergom   Tisza   Debrecen
Budapest
ALFÖLD   Oradea
UNGARY   BALATON   TRANSYLVANIA
                        ROMANIA
        BANAT   Arad
        Sinpetru German
        Timişoara   TRANSYLVANIAN ALPS
        Oravaiţa
        Orsova
        Drobetu/Turnu-Severin   **Bucharest**

Belgrade

YUGOSLAVIA   Calafat   Danube

                                BLACK
        BULGARIA   SEA

        Sofia   Svilengrad
        Plovdiv   Edirne
                Orestiás   (Adrianople)
                            Istanbul
Tirana
ALBANIA   **GREECE**   Alexandroúpolis
                        TURKEY

Introduction:
Touring in the Crush Zone

'You only need look at two occasions really,' the professor said, chewing his meerschaum. 'They encompass the whole subject.' He had puffed his hair into a quiff and frothed it up like boiled milk. 'The Sheldonian in 1907 and Teheran thirty-six years later.' The air squeaked in the pipe as he sucked it and his shoes had worn orange in scuffed patches. His face peaked in odd humbug corners. The rain had flattened half the barley in the field outside and a man was felling elms in the wood, where his chain saw whined and relaxed.

The professor had two sheets of paper, one on each velveteen arm of his chair. He shunted himself up and back and then swung his crossed leg in thought. I could see the beginnings of a sock suspender around the hanging calf.

'I always do a Miss World on this one,' he said. 'Reverse order OK with you?' He read out the typed page with a paternal preciousness, treating the episode like a sweet he had already sucked so that it shone and glossed in the light of his own appreciation.

'One. The evening of 28 November 1943 in Teheran.' The professor can be heard on the tape coughing something up and then swallowing it. 'There were about ten to dinner. Roosevelt was the host. Stalin was on form. Churchill reckoned there were between twelve and fourteen hundred million people represented around the table. He had a sore throat. After dinner he led Stalin to a sofa and suggested that they talk a little about events after the war was over. First Prussia (to be dealt with more severely than other parts of the Reich) and then Poland. "Personally," Churchill wrote, "I thought Poland might move westwards like soldiers taking two steps *left close*. . . . I then demonstrated with the help of three matches my idea of Poland moving westwards. This pleased Stalin, and on this note our group parted for the moment." Three matches. The type of match used is not known for certain. It may well have had antimony sulphide in the head mixed with an oxidizing agent such as potassium chlorate. The

1

striking surface on the box next to them on the table would have contained red phosphorus.

'Poland followed Churchill's matches across the mahogany. The one on the right moved and Poland lost 69,290 square miles to Russia. The one on the left moved and Poland gained 39,596 square miles at the expense of Germany. About eight million Germans – we cannot be more precise; the situation was inimical to measurement – fled or were expelled westwards. Königsberg was absorbed by the Soviet Union and renamed Kaliningrad.'

The professor adjusted his quiff and the sheet went down on the velveteen arm. Another denuded elm fell in the wood. It was the preliminary flourish of knives over the body of Europe. The professor uncrossed and recrossed his legs the other way.

'Two. In 1907 the Romanes Lecture at Oxford was given by Lord Curzon. He spoke on "Frontiers". It was the classic imperialist statement. He showed no interest in matching frontiers to ethnic niceties, had no conception of the frontier as a contract between nations and made no mention of self-determination of peoples. The man who once said that he had never experienced more real power than when in Pop blandly assumed that the time had come in the world when "the feebler units are either neutralized, or divided, or fall within the undisputed Protectorate of a stronger Power". The modern frontier was the leading edge of the *imperium*, its defining organ. The British Empire had land frontiers of 21,000 miles – India alone 5,700 – and "outside of the English universities, no school of character exists to compare with them. Character is there moulded in the furnace of responsibility and on the anvil of self-reliance. I am one of those," said Curzon, "who hold that in this larger atmosphere, where the machine is relatively impotent and the individual is strong, is to be found an ennobling and invigorating stimulus for our youth, saving them alike from the corroding east and the morbid excitements of western civilization." Eton, Oxbridge and a few miles of frontier: what more could a man ask of the world?'

The professor knocked his pipe on his heel, put his fingers into the bowl of rose petals and smelled them.

'Curzon did not distinguish between the two senses of frontier. Remember Herr Ratzel: "The borderland is the reality, the borderline its abstraction." But in Curzon's mind the frontier was both the limit of rule and the meeting and mingling of that rule with whatever lay beyond it. The romance, the peculiar wholesomeness of his twentieth-century Marcher Lords, was their role as pioneer-defenders, pushing out and holding off at the same time, combining all the virtues of responsibility to territory with a contempt for home life and its comforts. It is a beguiling picture of a perfect and privileged moment.

'Their frontier was not a line, no trivial string of barbed wire. Curzon had pooh-poohed the fencing of a large stretch of the Swiss border by the Italian Government a few years before – wire-netting, gates connected to alarm bells and a cordon of customs-house officers armed with rifles. This seemed quite funny in 1907, like the first pathetic attempts at aeroplanes or television. No, the boundaries of Empire needed more bottom, more *gravitas* than a cow-fence with bells on the gates. Curzon's Scientific Frontier was not to be "a ridge or even a range, but a tumbled mass of peaks and gorges, covering a zone many miles in width. Within this area the inhabitants may be independent or hostile. It unites natural and strategical strength and by placing both the entrance and the exit of the passes in the hands of the defending Power, compels the enemy to conquer the approach before he can use the passages." The Romans, the Galla states in the Horn of Africa and the Russians have all used the technique. Strategists call it a Crush Zone.'

A schooner or two of Olé amontillado and the professor moved off into less well-rounded areas. Nothing had been worse at the Paris Peace Conference in the spring and summer of 1919 than the stuffiness of the rooms on the Quai d'Orsay. Stuffiness, impatience,

3

doodling: all these had nursed the drift into fallibility. The triple-lined curtains in the masculine rooms had thickened their own kind of claustrophobia in which only the most arbitrary swipes and sweepings could clear a space and sort the random material into separate boxes. In this air, while the Allied blockade had allowed Germany, Bulgaria and Hungary to starve, while Northcliffe ranted 'The Junkers will have you yet', while the French press attacked Woodrow Wilson as a misguided theologian, as the air solidified into opinions and maps, as the ethnographical charts began to merge into the lobes and enclaves, the panhandles and plebiscite zones of the puddles on the pavements, the map of Europe was redrawn. 3,000 miles of new frontier were created, 1,000 of old were abandoned. The reparations were added up; the spirit of vengeance presided and 230,000 Tyrolese were placed under the government in Rome. Three million Germans were included in Czechoslovakia, and three million Hungarians shut out of a truncated Hungary. And then tea and macaroons.

Olé lubricated abstraction. I was ready to set off, but the professor talked and talked about zero-sum games and divided markets, Smart Target-Activated-Fire-and-Forget weaponry, throw-weight, communicativeness and 'friendship'. Hobbes was the patron saint of frontiers, hung over them like the preacher in Ecclesiastes. The two paths were quite distinct, whatever they were. We had Emmerich de Vattel and Herr Ratzel again. The professor saw the *mille-feuille* sheets of trust swallowed in the great gape of suspicion. The Star Wars armouries were a monstrous futuristic Maginot, sequins on the skin of supernationalist isolation, withdrawn from the brink of mutual destruction to the enhanced super-hedges of territoriality, fig-leaves for fools, behind which the blocists could nurture their fears. *But*, he had to admit, he wasn't really decided. He relit the pipe again and played with the matches on the table.

1

Furthermost Outsentinels

The jet did not circle above Ivalo. The airport was the end of the line and, as though driving a train into a country terminus, the pilot simply continued the flight down on to the runway and stopped. It was −32 °C, three in the afternoon, night, two hundred miles north of the Arctic Circle early in January. The padded edge of things.

A gaucheness set us off true: we wore too many clothes – hats, caps, Michelin jackets, flippered gloves. It was a planeload of private saunas. A small notice at Rovaniemi – a miniature traffic sign of a rifle crossed out in red – had banned guns on the plane. Knives were apparently allowed.

The queue to leave was made twice as long by the clothes. The man sitting next to me continued to read a paper on the fragmentary in art. We'd had Rodin's emergent matrons, Svevo's ridicule of them, the Golden Bowl and the Visible Grid. Now we had the Workshop Myth as the passengers queued to leave.

The airport building was a sort of log cabin. Split logs were bolted on to the concrete structure and left unplaned. There was an open fire next to the check-in desk. The signs on the loo doors: two schematic Lapps, male and female, with curving-out hair and bonnets of the four winds. Notional real red candles were lined up on the raw pine bar.

Two Lapp woman waited on the forest seats. Sioux in pioneer photography holding between them one plastic boarding pass, nylon anoraks and Lapp hats, the residue of a dress now worn in its entirety only by Finnish dentists at the meetings of Sodankylä Rotarians. Wolverine fur and felt tabs stuck up along the Brontosaurus crests. Below the hats and untouched by the anoraks, the jug faces themselves, boiled trophies from one world in the fingertip grip of another. 'Enjoy the heartfelt welcome of the wilderness,' I read in a brochure to snowmobile tours which, if time was tight, could begin at the airport itself. 'Lifesee among the Lapps,' it said in creamed-off unction.

Olivia and I took a taxi into Ivalo. This was no arrival, but a series of

5

insulations and contrivances in which the landscape had shifted away unnoticed, leaving only its polarities in the dark.

Ivalo was a frontier town in the eighteenth century. A small gold rush in the hills to the south of it attracted pioneers and produced nothing of lasting value. The traditional market of the Lapps, forty kilometres to the north-west at Inari, is the older, more natural centre for the region while Ivalo has always belonged to the less rooted pioneers from the south. It is on no political boundary, but is a frontier town in the American sense, full of people who think of themselves as out on the edge. The others, the Lapps further out than they are, for whom this is the familiar landscape of the fixed middle, are effectively ignored.

It's a skeletal place. Flesh has never thickened on its needs and purposes. It's a Meccano version of a town in which everything is ergonomic structures. Six gas stations lined up along the Arctic Highway, its spine. A hospital, some banks, the State Employment Agency, which shares a building with the State-run Alko store. Lapps come in from their communities on the road north at monthly intervals, pick up the dole, visit Alko and make a festive trip of it back home in the post bus. Across the river the Lutheran church and a school. None of the buildings join up. There's a sense of gratuitous randomness in their arrangement. Each is coherent in itself, designed in isolation somewhere else and put down like bricks in sand.

The snowploughs and mechanical shovels clear the snow from the streets all day and into the night to keep the slight character of the place unmuffled, free from the iced elephantiasis with which the surrounding forest is diseased. Early in January, with new falls almost daily, one sank up to the waist in the sugary semi-liquid of the uncleared snow – not drifts, but the simple accumulation since October.

On the outskirts of the town, across the frozen river used as a highway for snowmobiles, Ivalo begins to merge with its winter surroundings. The snow is cleared there only in the narrowest of access tracks. It obliterates the divisions of ownership. Pale wooden houses stand in a communal snow garden. No fences are to be seen and no trespass is possible.

Olivia and I went into the TL Grilli Bar. Grained plastic walls of imitation pine, bald tinsel looped across the windows, polythene baubles slung from the door frames in testicle pairs. On the television, fixed eight feet above the floor, cleaned up Italians sang carols in English. The children wore stetsons with sequins around the brim, and unseen session men slid bottlenecks on steel guitars. The set was above the doorway and the audience in the Grilli Bar faced us as we came in. It was male, repetitive, silent and drunk. On the tables in front of it stood smeared empty beer glasses and the empty poly-styrene traylets in which the Rovaniemi-packed hamburgers had been served. The heartfelt welcome of the wilderness. The men wore greased overalls and stared at Olivia. On her head was a rather motheaten fur hat found in a loft somewhere, the earflaps folded down but curving outwards like the bottom of a graph. Most of her face was hidden by a check scarf. Below that, with no break between them, an army surplus anorak last worn by a Marine sergeant at Pnom Penh, which curved out and then in to accommodate the eight-month-old unborn child. And then, emerging about half way down her thigh, a red-and-white striped dress of remotely Gujarati allu-sions, coming to a pair of blue Wellington boots with white soles and white lace-up tops intended for the fore-deck of a yacht in Porto Ercole. I was in grey.

'*Snouw on Snouw, Snaaaaaarwansnar,*' went the Italian cow-children.

The eyes turned from Nashville to us and stayed there. We moved up to the counter to escape them, but with a deep smeared shuffling of bottoms on moulded plastic they moved with us. Pregnancy in public in Ivalo in January was something to be seen.

'Are you doing right?' Matti Loppina asked me. His ears were enormously red. Like butterfly spots, they drew attention away from his blank eyes. 'She is too big for here. How many?'

'Eight.' The lateness of the day was explained in Finnish and the room whistled inwards.

'You must not dominate,' Matti said. 'She is almost perfected. We have said "done-up".' He ordered some food for her, 'the best in the time'. His mother had eaten nothing else while Matti was gestating. It was sliced pink frankfurter in water served by the prim, hysterical woman behind the counter. She was the source, I realized, of the strangled tinsel and see-through balls. Perhaps she had also chosen the plastic pine, deciding against plastic mahogany and plastic beech because they would not fit in with the surrounding forest. She knew her Grilli Bar was nice, never mind its occupants or their raw, spent poverty. Here was the frontier in the bar: polarized men and women, set apart from each other, nurturing their separateness behind the double doors. Outside in the evening – it had been night for eight hours – the occasional passers-by looked the same, unsexed by the cold and dark. We had brought some of this in with us and, as far as the *patronne* was concerned, Olivia, despite her condition, was, as a customer, male.

But not for Matti. He was twenty-two and bony. His brother was in the frontier guard and had found him a job in the Ivalo Esso station. The family came from the south and his father worked in the state employment office in Hangö. It was another world in the south of Finland. 'Here it is free air. I come up,' he said. Two years in Ivalo with only a week last summer in the south – thick Finland he called it – and that one week was enough. He was straining in the family ties by the second day. 'And the girls down there all think they're Miss Europe.' The real Finnish woman – he swallowed at the words like a gout of sherbet – her qualities are *inside*. Matti wavered between swank and shyness, suddenly awkward in his bravura passages. His free world out in the north was hedged around with alien strangers. The Swedes were arrogant, the Lapps lazy, the Russians no more than foreign. These peoples and the Finns in the south of the country were the polar coordinates of his world. He manoeuvred on the graph between them, nosing out their promontories, veering from their failures. Not arrogant, not lazy, not smug, not foreign, not hostile: Matti charted his wilderness with negatives. There in the blank space of the Lapland Esso station he could indulge the peculiar geographical psychology of a frontiersman.

Logging convoys shook down the Arctic Highway at intervals past the reflected Finns and the quadrupled lines of tinsel in the glass. The molecular snowdust danced up into eddies and then lasted in swirls. Until 1945 the road had led to Finland's only year-round, ice-free port at Petsamo (Pechenga), along a narrow corridor of Finnish territory awarded by the Treaty of Dorpat in 1920.

Outside the bar a Lapp sat against a lamp-post. The cold made us choke, as if another substance was mixed with the air. It pulled at any open skin like the pressed-on nozzle of a hoover. The Lapp knew nothing about it. His body was incompetent with drink. He lay propped up in the circle of the street lamp as helpless as a neonate. On his head a hat of the four winds flopped at the corners, and his face had collapsed inwards at the nose. His silver one-piece zip-up suit was rubbed and tarnished at the bottom and knees. It had flaked in places and been patched. A logging truck banged down the highway past us and its snow wake washed over him. He turned over in a foetal cramp and nuzzled the snow where a dog had peed.

Matti led us back to the bare room we had taken. The Lapps get 85% grant, he said, on anything they want. He was full of contempt for skiving stay-at-homes, even for those to whose homeland he had come. He was openly racist.

He talked to Olivia in a chaos of enthusiasm and sadness, looking at her for reassurance between his outbursts. She soaked it up, prepared to be the mother he wanted her to be. Floating behind us down the road was the real Mrs Loppina, absent in Hangö, worried that her sons were wasting away in Lapland. Olivia was everything she could not be: convenient, ignorant, passing through, a disposable mother. Every time Matti rang home his real mother asked him to come back. Once it was weekly; now may be twice a month, if that.

So he talked on: about the road, cut off at Virtaniemi by the Russian frontier a few miles to the east; the cold and the dark, Finnish complementaries and mutual reinforcements. But he loved the cold and hated the dark. There had been no sun since November. On 15 January for two minutes a tangerine slice of it would edge up over the horizon, eaten into by some of the forest trees. You could see it best – that is *longest* – from the bridge over the frozen river, and half the town would be there like spectators at a football match to watch it as the tipped world began to swing back into light. From then until the equinox the days would grow in five-minute nudges, half an hour a week, nearly two and a half a month. No balance out here. Either everything, nothing or a hurried trip between them. The year explodes and implodes in Lapland. It is enough to make anyone phlegmatic, self-contained, contemptuous of weakness, ready to imitate the global indifference of the sun itself.

The orange post bus to Kirkenes was full of hats. A small theatre of furred cartwheels and encrusted pompoms was all you could see from the gangway. They formed a weird sort of geological layer where clams, cockles and ice-cream-cone shellfish had come to rest on a stratum of grey sandstone, the faces of the passengers themselves. It was as though the character of the Finns, shut in by their zipped-up duvet jackets, had siphoned up and out of them, bypassing their faces and flowering into hats and caps. No one needed to talk. The bus was already full of a millinery babble.

I said goodbye to Olivia at the small brick bus station. She was going south to a log cabin she had rented on the Russian border near Salla. I would meet her there in a few days' time. The last I saw of her she was playing 'Gorilla' on a video machine, watched by a Lapp with his hands in his pockets. She was watching the screen and he was watching her.

The blunt-nosed post bus swung out of Ivalo. It was just after two in the afternoon. A six-hour ride to Kirkenes. I had yet to reach a frontier, but this was the zone. This corner of Europe, where states cram in and adjust in the emptiness, it was all frontier territory, somehow critical and unimportant at the same time. On the map each of the national outlines had been distorted in the struggle. Finland a stag-headed oak, its stubbed arms reaching up to the Arctic Ocean, but falling short; Norway bent into a leprous hand in this corner, its rubbed-off fingers hooked around Finland; and to the east the mass of Russia, damaged only in its margins, bruised and splintered like the bulwarks of a trawler, marking collisions.

The day had turned green in the south and the light had shifted marginally rightwards. That is all there was to the day, the baffled cashmere light moving in another room. As the bus drove north on the iced roads, stopping to drop passengers at random in the forest, that modest, aged version of day sifted off in a departure as slight as its arrival. Within half an hour of leaving Ivalo we were in unconditional dark, layered by the two-dimensional cut-out trees in the headlights.

I had expected the exuberance of the hats to leak downwards as the journey wore on, but I was mistaken. This was not a long-distance bus with all its possibilities of confidences and exposures, but a succession of local buses which happened to be strung together like a train. I sat alone in the double seat and looked out of the window. Lapland wheeled along in a flickering kinetograph. One of its frames would have been beautiful: anonymous forest, bulked out and clogged with snow, the arms bent round and folded inwards to make pretzels against the night – more a block of cheese that had rotted into columns than a pine forest in the midwinter drought. Repeated endlessly in the communal TV-room air of the bus, it was sickening. I lurched into sleep: the frontiers were neon-lit for miles across the tundra, triple barriers of wires and mines, chained dogs on runs that were now incised into the snow around them, barks ghosting up from the trenches. Steve McQueen on a skidoo coasted the scrolled barbed wire, the rolling hugs at the bottom of a sister's letter, and landed in the stale fur of the carpeted bus seat.

Repeated ads for sofas on offer in an Ivalo shop were flung out into roadside nylon baskets by the driver's mate. The driver slowed and quickened between these places, delivering mail to the Lapps.

The Sevettijärvi bar was full of Skolt Lapps in one-piece quilted suits, foresters with soft woollen scarves round their necks. The leather tongues of their belts lolled out beyond the buckle. One small man took a note from his wallet and laid it on the table in front of him. His young neighbour was inexperienced in this diplomacy and began to put the debt away, then – loss of face – refused it.

An old woman in transparent spectacle frames adjusted a tall, curving hat like a Byzantine bishop's. She retied the scarf that held it there. It was silk, printed with a Goyan harvest scene.

The young Lapp stood up, suddenly enormous in his quilts, a mussed-up red head balanced on top of them, and walked out. We all bought beers.

I stayed in the bar when the bus moved on. The Skolts are a borderland people. They probably followed the shrinking of the ice-sheets and the movement of the reindeer from somewhere deep in Asia two or three thousand years BC. By the ninth century AD they were paying tribute to Viking chieftains down the Norwegian coast. Harald Fairhair claimed everything as far as the eastern end of the Kola peninsula in 872. The Russian for 'Norman' is Murmansk.

For nearly a thousand years this northern Skolt corner was disputed territory. Throughout the Middle Ages there was regular feuding between royal Norwegian agents and the Karelian deputies of Novgorod in Russia. A treaty in 1326 between Norway, Sweden and Novgorod recognized vast common districts in which collectors from all three states could raise tribute from the Lapps, but the fighting and confusion continued. By the late sixteenth century Moscow-Novgorod, Sweden-Finland, Norway-Denmark and the Russian Orthodox monastery at Petsamo were all attempting to raise some kind of tax from the Skolts, caught in a dangerously shaded part of the map.

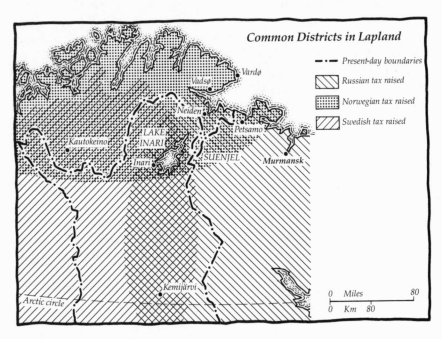

Common Districts in Lapland

— · — *Present-day boundaries*

Russian tax raised

Norwegian tax raised

Swedish tax raised

From the early seventeenth century this political crowding of Lapland began to sift out. Sweden-Finland abandoned any pretensions to the Arctic coast, acknowledging no more than the logistical realities of the time: the cross-country route to the ocean from the Gulf of Bothnia was infinitely more difficult than the journey around the coast itself. But it was a measure of Lapland's marginality that the border between Sweden-Finland and Norway was not finally agreed until 1751 and not marked out with cairns until fifteen years later. Even then, that left the huge Norwegian-Russian 'common areas' unresolved. Until 1813 the Norwegian bailiff of Varanger made a yearly visit to his Tsarist counterpart in Kola. It was the high point of the year. In his gilt-thick uniform and with an entourage around him in diminishing depths of golden Turkey work, he came to enquire if he could collect taxes in Murmansk for the Norwegian king. Each year the Russian said no, not as far as he was aware, but he would certainly send the request on to St Petersburg. Meanwhile, the Skolts were double taxed.

In 1809 Sweden ceded Finland to Russia. It became a Grand Duchy in the Russian Empire, theoretically autonomous, but with the Tsar as Grand Duke. This strengthened the Russian hand in the frontier zone. When Norwegian and Russian frontier commissioners met in 1825, it was confidently expected in Helsinki and St Petersburg that Norway would be squeezed out of the contentious area and the Russian frontier brought up almost to the end of Varangerfjord. But in the negotiations, finally settled in a convention signed in May 1826, the Norwegians did extraordinarily well. They scooped a great boot of territory reaching down almost to Lake Inari along the valley of the Pasvik, and instead of accepting the mouth of that river at Kirkenes as the place where the divisions of Europe should reach the Arctic Ocean, Norway was allowed to balloon out another forty kilometres to the east, as far as the Jakobselv, a tiny Arctic river that joined the ocean at a settlement now known as Grense-Jakobselv. It was to that furthest, undusted corner of Europe that I was now heading.

The Russian commissioner was accused of venality: he had accepted a small gold casket studded with diamonds from the Norwegians. Why had the Finns not been represented at the convention? Why was the Orthodox chapel at Neiden left deeply embedded in the Lutheran state of Sweden-Norway? Throughout the rest of the century the Russians nurtured revanchist schemes for expansion westwards across the top of Norway, fixing on Varangerfjord as an ideal naval base and looking further to Tromsö and Narvik as outlets into the Atlantic unconstrained by the narrow corridor of open water between the North Cape and the winter pack-ice. Palmerston arranged a naval treaty in 1855 with Sweden-Norway to protect the gains of 1826, but any need for protection evaporated after 1904, when the Russian fleet was virtually destroyed by the Japanese.

After the 1826 agreement the Skolts were no longer double taxed, but the convention had taken no account of their own divisions into *siidat*. Each Skolt *siita* was a self-contained group of herders and fishermen, not all of them blood-related, who lived a semi-nomadic life within well-defined boundaries, most of which followed the watersheds. They migrated each year to summer pastures and fishing sites from a central winter village and then back again. These ancient patterns were mutilated by the new international arrangements. The Lapps, one traveller wrote, were treated like dogs. When the borders were closed in 1853, the reindeer continued to migrate across them, but their owners were forbidden to follow.

The movements and limitations of Lapland frontiers in this century have been the most destructive of all. What remained of the *siita* system was thrown into chaos by the First World War. In 1914 the Skolt Lapps had 8,000 reindeer. By 1918 there were only 1,500 left, the others slaughtered for emergency food. The frontiers arranged in the Treaty of Dorpat, Finland's Brest-Litovsk, sliced through Skolt territory. The *siidat* of Muetke, Kild and Nuett'jaur were left in the Soviet Union; the others divided between Norway and Finland. Little is known of what happened to the Lapps left in Russia. They were probably removed from their frontier zone. For those in the Petsamo corridor it was a golden time, as the Finnish Government poured money into the harbour installations, the nickel mines and the Arctic Highway which connected them to the south.

In 1944 the Russians repossessed the port and the whole of the corridor. The Skolts living there were allowed to choose whether to remain in their home territory, now part of the Soviet Union, or to live in Finland. Almost unanimously they voted to live in Finland and leave their home *siita*, the Suenjel.

The people – there were under three hundred of them – were moved to German barracks near Ivalo and then, in the spring of 1949, resettled at their own request in a place more suitable to reindeer herding. The Government chose a remote string of lakes north-west of Inari. It was almost uninhabited and the Government built fifty-one tiny wooden houses in clusters along their shores. At the edge of one lake, Sevettijärvi, they built a school, a church and a health clinic. This became the capital of the reserve and I was now in the bar of the trading centre there.

No television. Instead, at each table, a slapping down of card after card, raised up like a threat and thumped to the formica. I was ignored and smoked a cigarette.

The girl at the bar wore the kind of jersey you could make a nest of, the wool somehow fluffed up into a breast-enhancing haze. Arja said hallo in a demure, self-projecting way. She was a Finn. Her father owned the shop and bar, and was the forest warden. He employed every man in the room. She sat at the end of my bench for half a minute at a time, sloping up to work at the men-filled tables, while I picked at the polyurethane veneer on the pine. She was as pleased to see me as I was to see her. I was the South, everything she felt cut off from in a place that was dark all winter, tourists all summer. Tourists didn't come in January. She was going to learn English in Turku in the spring. Turku: a magic place of pavements and professors; no greased overalls rubbed shiny at the elbows. 'They are these dirty men,' she said loudly, knowing their ignorance cut them off from her insults. Dirty inside and outside. We smiled in the conspiracy of English, her common blue eyeshadow a stain on her face. She was thinking of Turku, its steel-rimmed professors in black silk polo-necks, and of her own clothes, her tapered black trousers and blurred-vision jersey. In her mind at least she was already down there. How long would it take her to notice that the same game was played in Turku, her professors wrapped in woollens and with ragged hair, concerned for the survival of the minority culture to whom she was now serving beers?

Was there a Lapp I could talk to, one who would remember life in Suenjel?

'Where? . . . Before the war? . . . After work.'

Laiso looked inwards. His face was thick with flesh and a lick of hair sat on his square, fawn head. A padded wooden armchair in the wooden house, a large brown ox-bow clock on the table next to him and on the wall behind them both a tapestry in which the Monarch of the Glen dominated in browns. Was I from the Human Adaptability Section? The Skolts had been the subject of something called the Scandinavian International Biological Programme for many years. Various departments of it came to measure and interview them from time to time. Physical Determinants had been here in November. Human Adaptability was due any day. Social Constructs would be coming in the spring. He and Arja said these names like botanical specimens.

Coffee in the brown room, his framed sons as soldiers on the sideboard, and, through Arja as the interpreter, he told me how life had changed. His wife was dead and he had never been to look at the border. It was another country now, but things had been better then.

There had been none of these snowmobiles which hurried the reindeer into the corrals. They used to drift in on long migration strings in Suenjel. The grazing was richer over there, the winter lichen thicker. Over here you couldn't slaughter an animal after March. There was no meat on it, nothing to sell. *There* and *then* floated in and out of each other. He fingered the curled corners of postcards stuck in the window frame: from a cousin in California, a creased and ruptured Golden Gate Bridge and a newer unruffled Big Sur.

'But if you put me back in the spot and took a cloth off my eyes I could find the way anywhere,' Arja said for him. He had heard of a German who had come back to Ivalo, who had been there in the war, in the garrison, and he couldn't find his way around the place. Too much of it had been destroyed for him to remember, returning to a multilated past. But Laiso could feel his way around his own perfected memory with ease. He could remember his house, which they had returned to in 1940, after the first evacuation. All that was left of it was the brick chimney and the stone oven as its plinth around the bottom. Even this had been held in his memory as a symptom of a more perfect world. Arja scarcely hid her impatience with this lugubrious nonsense.

At the second evacuation in 1944, when the Finns were forced by the Russians to expel the 200,000 German troops in Lapland, the Skolts were rushed to Ostrobothnia in trucks down the Arctic Highway. Their reindeer were lost or shut off behind the new frontier. The Government provided the Skolts with replacements in 1949 but they were from other parts of Lapland and got lost on the new Sevettijärvi territory. This is what the Skolts were like themselves, Laiso said, and Arja lifted her eyes to the ceiling.

Did he ever dream of Suenjel? Now and then, but there were never any houses or tents in his dreams. Just the reindeer, the lakes, his family, the rocks and birches.

The report of the Scandinavian International Biological Programme (Interim) was in the Ivalo Library. The peak had come in 1969 when eighty investigators – one to every four Skolts – from nine countries, both East and West – had measured the Lapps (anthropometry it was called) at the rate of forty a day. The scientists decided that the Skolts were 'naturally irrational and have a child-like mentality'. Their aversion to the investigators was considered a symptom of psychic abnormality. They were also thought not, on the whole, to be happy.

I stayed the night in one of the forest warden's tourist rooms. Static with electricity and filled to the ceiling with debilitating dry air, it was half warehouse, half cell. The brick walls painted white, the blue beds only six inches off the ground, their structure invisible. Blue carpet, orange doors, rounded orange plastic coat-hangers. Heavy round spotlights hung from a rack in the ceiling. Washing about in this sterilized solution, leached of all germs, I fell into a freakish sleep.

Laiso's grandson drove me to Neiden in Norway in the morning. He and his family lived in a house like his grandfather's along the lake. It was what the anthropometrists called 'a gene cluster'. His Datsun was ten years old and the catch on the passenger door didn't work. We tied it shut with string from the inside. He spoke a little English and had painted the letters GTX on the side of the car at the back. A small sticker next to it said PAKASTA ELAMAA DUNLOP above a woman in a bathing-suit holding a tyre.

He had never known Suenjel, but had a conventional and pious attachment to it. Suenjel – he called it Suonikylä, the name of the winter village – was the place where the Skolts were Skolts. Sevettijärvi was 'a bad mixing' by comparison. 'This is not our place,' he said, waving at the butter-yellow tundra going past at 94 mph. 'Helsinki, Suenjel and London are places where you are not mixed.'

His prelapsarian vision of isolated innocence left us in silence in the mid-day dawn light watching reindeer high-stepping in the snow. He wouldn't stay here. All the girls went first. Two of his uncles would never marry. They were on their own in their forties. 'You see old men in Näätämö at the dancing, looking for the Norwegian girls coming with the boys.' We slid past Näätämö, a gathering of supermarkets and a couple of bars in the tundra, their interiors fluorescing in the dusk, the scene of Lapp desire and cross-border shopping. A silver four-wheel-drive Daihatsu jeep was parked outside the shops, N on its bumper.

He was going to Australia, where he would have a car with a shut door and a shut woman. 'I must go to the army and then I will go.'

We slowed at the frontier. He waved at the Finnish border guard in his box, a single pale room in the Arctic. The man waved back with a cigarette between his fingers and looked at his paper again. The first frontier. A sign by the road said 'Norge'. Pennines low-browed soufflé gone cold. No division in the snow, the 1826 line cutting away to the south-east and north-west unregarded.

He dropped me outside the bar in Neiden and said goodbye without interest or affection. He was already on Bondi, where men were men and doors had catches. Olav Ostvedt was drinking sour coffee and clipping bobble links off a chain with an all-in-one manicure set. He was nineteen and had a small moustache which failed in places. At the edges it went too blond to be visible, except from the side. Olav was in the army and had missed the bus. He would have a hell of a time when he got back to Tromsö. No one would believe he had spent fifteen hours in the Neiden Handel, rationing himself to a drink every twenty-five minutes and carefully moving up and down the menu. 'Control!' he laughed. 'I should be a general!'

Last night the chain had held the ID disc. But there were only forty-three days left in the army and he had decided to make it a diary. A bobble off a day until there was one left and that one he would give to the sergeant.

Olav wouldn't be a soldier when the Russians came. They had 200,000 troops across the border. 'We have very few.' But what about his allies? This was the Norwegian strategy: nominal trigger force to roll in the Nato juggernaut. Olav brought it down a level. 'Have you seen *The Heroes of Telemark*? They think they're the heroes of Telemark. They get dressed up in white clothes, freeze in the mountains and think they are real men. Every year the English marines freeze.' Olav felt the hole in his moustache, appalled at the vision of his allies immobile in ice-cubes: the terror of a frozen Thermopylae.

My bus arrived and I left Olav rummaging in his kitbag, waiting another seven minutes for the next beer. The day had failed again and the Norwegian bus slicked towards Kirkenes, the Three Degrees on the stereo, carpet on the floor.

The buses explained a national difference: the Finns are glad to be out on the edge; the Norwegians pretend it's the middle. The Finnish bus is plastic and lino, a lorry made tolerable for human beings, while the Norwegian bus is a drawing-room on wheels. The Finnish one rattles, the Norwegian hisses pneumatically. The Finnish driver (a man) holds on to the Bakelite wheel as if on the bridge of a trawler; the Norwegian (a woman) swivels with one looping automatic hand the padded power steering on the bends. The front wheels of the Finnish bus (which is painted a straightforward orange) are in an obvious way right up at the front and the bus steers like a big car. In the Norwegian bus (an altogether more ambiguous claret) the front wheels are set well back under the third row of seats and the suspended body slides in and out of wide spirographics on the corners, its gyrations only distantly related to the movement of the wheels below. The Norwegian bus is a Finnish bus puréed.

The bus dropped me at the Turisthotel in Kirkenes. It was Reading in Lapland, viscous with comfort. The woman in reception wore a silk blouse and tailored skirt. The carpet repeated bouquets of tan carnations. She asked me to pay in advance and took my dirty knapsack to the room. All the little signs: a give-away chocolate wafer biscuit in two wrappings, paper and silver; control of the one TV channel from the bedside; the manager extending his welcome in pop-up cardboard silhouette – something looked odd about the shape of his head. In ugly-textured zero-country: longitude had slipped, latitude meant nothing.

I rang Olivia in Naruska, in the house of the people who owned her cabin. The journey, she said, had been hateful. The buses had not run to their advertised schedule and she had endured a five-hour wait in the bus station at Kemijärvi. It was the local rendezvous. Drunken Finns at the shiny pine tables and fruit machines. She had tried to escape to the loo to read there, but was followed in and the men peered over the plastic partitions. Crouched in the loo-cell and looked down on by taunting drunken adolescents, she had cried. She went out again into the café. It sold, oddly enough, baby equipment and she bought a rattle. There was a man there, a thirty-year-old, who shooed away the boys and began on scarcely subtler invitations of his own. He had a house in the mountains. He rather liked pregnant women. In fact, he liked all shapes and sizes. A shrivelled drunk began to push obscene biro drawings on to the table in front of her, adding random English words in between the anatomies – 'disco' . . ., 'whisky' . . ., eventually 'fuck' – looking up into her face at each new one for reactions. At last the police had come on a routine patrol and rescued her in a car that smelt of aftershave. She had spent the last two hours in the comfort of a cell with its door wide open.

I read my map in the scarlet dining-room of the hotel, shifting it sideways on the table when the waitress huffed at the inconvenience. 'Pliss,' she said every time she came to the table. The other single diners had paperbacks lined up beside their plates, but I was absorbed in the spreading map, hooking it into the horseradish and later finding bits of herring dried on to Varangerfjord. 'Pliss.' It was called Joint Operations Graphic (Ground), and had been drawn up by the US Department of Defense. Any corrections, it instructed me, I was to refer to 'Commanding General, US Army Topographic Comm [glob of butter] DC 20315'. I had bought it in a map shop in Helsinki. 'Be happy,' the woman had said. 'Pliss.'

The military map describes the frontiers between Norway and the Soviet Union, and of both with Finland. The purple boundaries loop across its surface, a dotted black line embedded in the ribbon. The mapmaking conventions are the same on either side of the frontier and there is none of the blanching of Russia that you find on the Norwegian maps. 'Swit?' asked the waitress. There the roads, mountains and buildings all turn white across the border – only the lakes and bogs stay blue. On domestic Norwegian maps, whatever is important stops at the closed frontiers. Even the drawing of the contours turns a little sloppy past the line. Territory, but not meaning, continues across it.

The Pentagon map wasn't like that. An attempt at description continues right across it. At first glance the border appears no more significant than any administrative line, but closer inspection reveals the division it marks. 'Limits of reliable information', the American cartographers have printed, sometimes along the border itself, sometimes a few kilometres into the Murmanskaya Oblast. The railway line from Pechenga (Petsamo) to the nickel mines at Nikel is followed by the legend 'approximate alignment'. Many places are bracketed 'approximate location'. It is the experience of anyone in unfamiliar territory, where objects – houses, railway tracks, airfields – are obvious and definite in themselves, but strangely disconnected, half loose in a framework of ignorance. It is a map that has got half lost itself. Looking for fixed points in a foreign world – 'Thank you' – the mapmakers have labelled tiny places in the Russian wilderness that would have gone unnoticed on home ground. 'Fisherman's hut' and 'Cabin' in the middle of nowhere; in the border zone itself many 'Ruins', '*Rantas* (ruins)' – the archaeology of eviction. The dotted lines that are marked 'Vinterveg' in Norway become 'Winter Roads' in Russia. It is common, hostile territory beyond the line, common because hostile, which can be described in the allied *lingua franca*. Finally, in the mass of hints and legends at the bottom appears a note: THE REPRESENTATION OF INTERNATIONAL BOUNDARIES IS NOT NECESSARILY AUTHORITATIVE. Room for error at 1:250,000. On the ground itself, I guessed, there could be no doubt.

'Slip vill, pliss,' she said.

I walked around Kirkenes in the morning, waiting for the light. I had arranged for a taxi to take me to the Russian frontier, only seven miles out of the town. Meanwhile, in the dark morning, Kirkenes was very beautiful. The ironworks were above the town, on the nose of a ridge called Toppenfjellet, and out of scale with the houses they dominated. A railway ran to the black buildings along the ridge from the iron ore mines at Björnevatn a few miles to the south. Seven million tons of iron pellets were manufactured in the works each year. But on this morning they looked like a giant toy. I had once owned something like it: a black plastic space station with ladders and platforms and small hollows in which dials controlled the movement of parts. A crew of plastic uniformed figures could be arranged on its black chrome surfaces. I set light to it one day with stolen firelighters, but it didn't burn well. I wanted the crewmen dripping in the flames and the whole structure exploding in the heat. But the extruded plastic whitened and bent slightly. The crewmen fell off into the dirt. I had wanted a Viking burial; I got a half-charred toy.

But the ironworks fulfilled the dream. A huge stalk of smoke stood up out of the one chimney and bloomed into a ceiling of cloud that roofed Kirkenes. It mottled at the edges and revealed the stars. Diagonal elevators dropped from the black hangars towards the quay, all of them stagelit in isolated white arcs.

The rest of Kirkenes is a sweet wooden arrangement of identical houses in different colours. Stars of Bethlehem in the windows, a snow-caked bandstand crowned in metal cusps, and everywhere, like a sap, the irrepressible domesticity of Norway. Girls wore strappy high-heeled slingbacks on the iced pavements, skipping between the cafés and chemists. I fell over in my sure-grip boots with a thump. Smiles from the shopping women. It can only be a question of getting used to these things: the frontiersman stands upright on ice in stilettos.

Kirkenes had been a hinge in the northern war. On 15 June 1940, as France collapsed, and on the day that the Russians occupied Lithuania, the German flag was raised in Kirkenes. The nickel mines just over the frontier in the Petsamo corridor and the iron at Kirkenes itself made it a valuable prize. But even in 1940 the Germans had their eyes on Murmansk, a hundred miles to the east, Russia's principal ice-free port. As the northernmost fragment of Operation Barbarossa in June 1941 the German Mountain Corps pushed in towards Murmansk, but never penetrated more than fifty kilometres beyond the start-line.

Seven thousand Norwegians and some imported slave labour worked the iron mines and serviced the German troops concentrated on the town, 70,000 of them, a fifth of all the Germans in Norway. After Malta, it became the most bombed place in Europe: 328 air raids, most of them Russian. When the Red Army at last counter-attacked in the summer of 1944, the battle of Kirkenes lasted three weeks. In the tunnels of the mineral railway 3,500 civilians hid and starved. The town was destroyed by the Germans before they left, leaving the chimneys standing in the summer ashes.

Christian, the taxi-driver, was frankly nonplussed. A shaved blond head and vacuumed eyes. We established the fare to Skafferholet before setting off: about £9 for the return trip to a place of complete unimportance. Why should I pay good money to see a nowhere? I tried to explain that the border itself – closed by the Russians in 1946 – was some kind of baseline, the first closed frontier. But our minds were out of tune. 'Nutting,' he said, 'nutting atoll.' I said that I was a 'middle' man, someone not from a frontier. He thought I was trying to do a deal about the fare.

We drove out of town in the feathery half-light, slipturning off the main road to Neiden, and again off the road to Grense-Jakobselv, moving up a thin climbing track to Skafferholet. Christian stopped the car at a snowdrift in the road. He pulled up the handbrake and left the engine running. The headlights buttercupped the drift in front of us. Christian stayed inside and I got out into the twilight. This was a Tsarist cut-off. Alexander I, who died before the negotiations were complete at the end of 1825, had insisted that the tiny orthodox chapel dedicated to Saints Boris and Gleb on the *west* bank of the Pasvik should be included within the territory of the Empire. It is the only Russian bridgehead on to the Norwegian bank of the river, which is deeply trenched, a moat for Kirkenes. The chapel is now ruined, and the site invisible from Skafferholet.

The frontier alone made the landscape significant, asterisked and italicized it, an icon of a place. The dark light continued the shadow-less outlines of the hills upwards, with the same mutuality at the horizon as sea and air. The diesel of the taxi burbled in the silence, its headlights twin apricots. Bleached timber huts half sunk in the snow. The reindeer fence looped down to the river, thickened and hung with frost. Reindeer can jump it in winter and the Lapps collect them from over the border. The Russians corral the escaped animals once or twice a season. Empty flagpoles in the drift at the end of the road, their cords rigid in the quiet. A vacant observation tower on Russian stilts. I stared across at it, gauging nothing. All one can do is look across, voyeuristic, impotent.

Back in the heated car Christian said: 'Nut much. It is always fucky in England.'

'Fucky?'

'In London. Always fuck like this.' He had watched me staring into the fog ('mutuality') for ten minutes while the clock gathered kroner, feeling, he guessed, at home from home. Perhaps this is what I had come here for. Kirkenes must have been too Norwegian. Out on the Soviet frontier I could imagine I was back in foggy England. 'It used to be,' I said.

The manager of the Turisthotel had never been to Russia. 'There is so much stuff over there,' he said, flicking his thumb at the smorgasbord. 'Kola is very strong. In 1962, in the Cuba crisis,' he said with confidence, 'they brought the tanks up to the border here. We heard the noises in this room.' The waitress arranged the knives and forks next door. He had suddenly become animated. 'We were in the shit. So high. You know the bridges are already undermined? Up with the balloon, up with the bridges. There are not enough soldiers in here and Kirkenes will poof.' Kirkenes poofed in his outstretched hand. 'They'll be at Tana in the afternoon.'

One look at the map confirmed the manager's strategic sense. The ragged peninsula of Norway that stretches east of Tana is indefensible. The Russians only have to curve in through northern Finland to isolate it at Tana and throttle the neck. But this is an unrealistic picture. It is inconceivable that Russia would ever attack in Finnmark without a general war. The loss of Kirkenes or the battle of Tana will be small incidents in the world conflagration. But the manager himself hadn't acknowledged this. He could still hear the Cuban tanks, or whatever they had become, massing beyond the reindeer fence. He too was still back with the Heroes of Telemark. He was only thirty, but shared the kind of traditionalism which the Falklands – or Entebbe, or Grenada – had so reassuringly satisfied: the imagined past comfortably re-enacted as modern. He liked the role of frontiersman, to think of himself as a professional and slightly amused brinksman, so used to being on the edge of terror that he could play in the face of it. There could be no question of his ever going to live in the south, in safer Norway. That would have filleted his life and rendered it invertebrate. He gave an alarming picture, south of Trondheim, of a landscape peopled with spayed Norwegians.

In the summer he used to take his guests out to Grense-Jakobselv to show them the border there. (The strong dollar had doubled the business.) The Russian guards run a little farm the other side of some rocks. Pigs and cows wander down to the riverside. 'We use them for a little show,' he said. The trick was to arrive on the edge of the Jakobselv valley as quietly as possible, with the wind blowing away from the frontier and the Volvos no more than ticking over. And then, as they dropped down to the river at the bottom – the frontier itself – to rev the engines like a squadron of personnel carriers. The Russians would come hurrying out, guns in hand, to repel the invasion, only to find a platoon of giggling tourists fumbling behind their Nikons. Joke villains, harmless as Punch, convenient butts for practical jokes. It was no more of a tease than putting vodka in a girl's drink. A form of

self-congratulation. 'They're only people like us,' he said with all the
complacent, slack-lipped luxury of a man belching in a high wind.

Pinned up next to his reception desk was a quarto-sized sheet of
plasticized paper which said in Gothic blackletter:

This is to certify that

– – – – – – – – – – – – –

has stood at the furthermost outsentinel of
NORWEGIAN LAND
and has personally confronted without
FEAR or ALARM
the hostile territory of
USSR
And that – – – – – – – – – –
IS HEREBY WITH THIS DOCUMENT
appointed an Honorary Member of the
Honourable Company of Bear Tamers.
This – – – – day of – – – – – – 19 – – – AD

You could get it in German, English and Norwegian. It had a drawing
of a pair of frontier monuments, one Norwegian, the other Russian,
with a bear prowling about on the other side. It cost fifty kroner.

I spent the rest of that day – it was already night – with the border
commissioner. Brigadier Inge Torhag picked me up from the hotel. He
had just been cross-country skiing. Genuinely cross-country. He
didn't like the neon-lit track that spooled out for a few kilometres from
the town and back. I had noticed it the night before from the bus, small
figures flipping along it like anxious marionettes. The brigadier said
he felt like an electric hare on that circuit. He always made his own
tracks through the forest.

Mrs Torhag had prepared cakes. They were both in their fifties. Her
Donegal tweeds sheltered a rather more fragile person. She was
English and was more than welcoming in the hesitant boxed-in
English way. Her husband wavered between uncle and officer. His
face was screwed up as if clamps on either side of it were giving him
pain. She lit a red candle and we had the cake and thick coffee around
the low table. The night filled the plate windows. It seemed to have
been there for hours. It was four in the afternoon but this strange
teaparty was like biscuits and cocoa after a midnight fire-practice at
school. 'You have to get winter on your side,' he said. 'It can get
through to you and overtake you, but by then it's probably too late to
do anything about it.' I already felt staled by the daylessness and the

endlessly recycled air. Hence his langlauf and the children playing ice hockey under neon outside.

He had come north the previous November to spend the last three years before he retired as *Grense* (border) *Kommissar*. Kirkenes was still new to them. 'It's like a layer-cake,' Mrs Torhag said. She hadn't yet pushed beyond the outermost sponge. He had been in the air force and at Nato and in the security services. He could have had another soft job in the south, but he loved Finnmark. It was the size of England, but only 78,000 people lived there, the population density of the New Stone Age. Bears, wolves, salmon, emptiness, eagles, skiing, everything that was remote and primitive. From this perspective the frontier was almost a sideline, no more than the edge of the court on which the commissioner could play in freedom. We began to talk about his job, but he would always bring us back to this idea of Finnmark as a playground where, if officially he was one of the linesmen, he was also the freest of players, wheeling across the surface in a sort of private skaterly delirium. It was Thoreau on Ice.

'My decisions are binding on central government,' he said. 'I am a plenipotentiary.' When the Border Commission was set up with the Soviet Union in 1949 it was decided that any protocols established here should have the force of law from the moment they were signed. 'But I'm bound to confess, having said all that, that my current opposite number – Matila, he's a colonel in the KGB – is not really quite as independent as all that.' There was a hint of pulled rank. 'I think you'll find quite a lot of it has to go back to Leningrad.' Last time they had met, Matila had brought a young woman with him. Exceptionally well briefed. There to keep tabs. Almost certainly the political section. There were 300,000 KGB border guards between here and Siberia in an arc around what he called the Crush Zone. It was one of the great hidden symbols of the Soviet Union that the KGB should guard both the geographical and the ideological frontiers of the state, Russia in the mind as much as Russia in the world.

Torhag and Matila met once a month on alternate sides of the border. Each brought a deputy, an interpreter and a secretary. There would be a small meeting and they would sign a protocol. The business was always mundane. That, in a way, was the point of it. They would discuss water agreements on the Pasvik, or the running of the four hydroelectric stations on the river, built by the Norwegians in the 1950s. There was a very small trade across the border in butter and salami, and some paperwork over that. And they had just finished a revision of the 196-kilometre frontier, where sandbanks in the Pasvik had shifted and left the old line nearer one side than the other. It was all deliberately undramatic. The whole purpose was to relax any tension.

In the 1950s things had been a little sharper. Norway had joined Nato in 1949 in the face of severe Russian warnings about destabilization. There had been several shooting incidents during the following years. Norwegian soldiers had been awarded medals even for shooting *at* Russians. He said this with a snort, like a young man remembering the days when he was frightened of girls. There was no shooting here now, but the Turks still did it. A couple of 'poor Turks' had been shot dead last year for wandering over the line in Armenia, Nato's only other frontier with the Soviet Union. All that was well left behind.

The Russians used to send spies over, posing as refugees. One man had arrived with an overcoat stuffed full of names in little bottles. Some of them were true but insignificant, the rest false. He was sent back. Perhaps he had been genuine and trying too hard, I suggested. 'Perhaps,' the commissioner said, 'but it wasn't worth the risk. They're great ones for trying it on. Last year we had a letter from the Women of Murmansk addressed to the Women of Kirkenes.' He said this through his nose. 'It was asking them to campaign for Norway's withdrawal from Nato.' He looked anxious. 'Of course I wouldn't have anything to do with the thing. They had sent it via Colonel Matila and of course I sent it straight back. There was no doubt it was a little test for me, to see how the new boy performed.'

This was the sort of official paranoia of which the Russians themselves are so often accused, but it seemed to have more to do with not failing in front of one's colleagues than any sort of fear. Fear does not come into it. The letter was rejected out of confidence, not fear, as a signal to those in the Justice Department in Oslo that their new Grense Kommissar wasn't soft. But this sort of behaviour *en masse*, when officials repeatedly conform to the expectations of their colleagues – a planing off process, a destimulant – can look like and have all the effects of fear.

The brigadier decided to drive his wife Jane and me to his conference house at Storskog. 'I haven't heard half of this,' Jane whispered while her husband was in the loo. With the commissioner refreshed everything returned to its more official plane. He drove like a Milanese teenager on the iced roads. Jane held the upholstery. It was all part of the backwoodsman's elastoplast attitude to axing off one's thumb. The first law of survival: indifference towards it.

Across the Pasvik at Elvenes the commissioner could see over to the lights at Boris Gleb, around the Russian power station there. Khrushchev had come to visit the site when the Norwegians were building it and was impressed more than anything else by the solid pine doors they had fitted to the administrators' houses. He ordered one to be unscrewed from its hinges and flew back to Leningrad with it. The Norwegian manufacturers 'rubbed their gloves', as the commissioner said, at the prospect of the contract to come. For two years they heard nothing, then, one day, the managing director went on a trade mission to Sverdlovsk and stayed at a hotel in which his own doors hung in every doorway. Khrushchev had given the original to the Central Commissariat (Doors) with the instruction to copy it. Arguments were now finished from Kaliningrad to Petropavlovsk-Kamchatsky according to Norwegian design. 'You've got to stay one step in front,' the commissioner said. 'They play chess.'

The conference house was a tiny Hansel and Gretel cottage in the forest, weatherboarded and painted yellow. Lanterns hung from the walls outside. In the dark the frontier was nowhere to be seen. The commissioner explained in the snow. Jane stamped about. 'It's always rather a performance when we come here.' He enriched the 'a' in rather. 'There's always rather a lot of us and we solemnly process around this stone before going into conference.' His interpreter was making a study of Russian Communism and of the pervasive influence upon it of Orthodox Christianity. This solemnity of ritual was only a small example. The Lutheran Norwegians played up to the full.

The house was lived in by two very young members of the border guard. They kept it awesomely clean and had a television set the size of an altar in the corner of an otherwise naked room. Beyond the living-quarters – the house is arranged in a line like a submarine – was the communications centre. A white board on the wall is divided in two: 'From USSR' and 'To USSR' with a black line between them. Both sides are blank. The focus of the room is on the other side. A large desk is lit with a fluorescent tube under a red shade. In its operating-theatre light there is a red telephone without a dial and without any numbers. As if in a hotel room, all you have to do is pick it up and a receptionist – a Russian – will answer. At the other end of a landline across the frontier they had a green one. It is the only direct contact between a Nato and a Warsaw Pact base in the world. The Moscow–Washington hotline is now a sophisticated telex on which pictures and diagrams can be transmitted as well as words. There is no contact between the Turks and the Russians in Armenia. Before Andropov fell ill, there were plans to bring Sakharov out through Storskog to avoid publicity. Some of the tentative arrangements were made on this telephone. Since then nothing more has been heard.

Beyond the telephone is the conference room itself. It's like a sauna. Various woodcuts of Norwegian life and culture have been hung on the raw pine. One shows the people of Kirkenes leaving their refuge in the mines in 1944 after the battle was over. It is a tactful choice: the liberators were Russian. The conference table itself, covered in baize, runs down the middle of the room. It has two small flags on it and a model piece of landscape with boundary posts: yellow with black cap for Norway, green and red stripes for the Soviet Union. The two delegations sit either side, the Soviets on the *far* side of the table from the Soviet Union only a few yards away in the snow. The commissioner said this was not significant.

The meeting may last for an hour, sometimes less, and 'Then,' Inge Torhag said, 'we move in here.' This was the inner sanctum. The doors were folded back and we entered the last room of the house. Here, after the protocols are signed, the party moves on to some drinking. It usually lasts four or five hours. 'The Russians are rather old-fashioned about these things,' the brigadier said. 'They don't know about social drinking as such.' Before Khrushchev, half-pint mugs used to be provided for the vodka, but since then they have made do with ordinary wine glasses. It's all great fun. As the afternoon wears on everybody relaxes. The short speeches that accompany each new round get a little longer. They become a little franker about troop movements and strengths. The brigadier teases the colonel with little gobbets gleaned from the satellites, the colonel the brigadier with little titbits picked up by one-man submarines. It could be seen as a form of vodka-verification. 'It's what we call a CBM,' Torhag joked. This is détente jargon. Not to be confused with ICBM, it means Confidence Building Measure. Initials reify. They give each other kitsch presents like twinned mayors: a china jug in the shape of a chicken, a small wooden bear from whose jaws you can hang slippers, egg-cup boxes from Byelorussia and straw ukuleles from Uzbekistan. In summer they have fishing or shooting expeditions and in winter visits to the camera shop in Kirkenes. At the end of the day the happy party marches down to the frontier, salutes goodbye in another ritual: salute – twenty paces – salute – slightly diagonal – straighten – goodbye – and waits for the next month.

'We don't let the international situation affect us,' the commissioner said. I asked if I could see the frontier itself. One of the conscripts was sent off into the dark while Inge, Jane and I stood on the verandah like some *ante bellum* extras outside Jamestown, Virginia. We waited a few minutes. Inge Torhag explained how the KGB had a thousand men, give or take, on the 120-mile frontier, while the Norwegians had a company – about 120 men – until out of the dark a string of neon lights began to glow. They were cold and took time to reach full brightness, moving through all the colours of a postcard dawn. The lights illuminated nothing but themselves, a gap-toothed string of plastic gig-lamps stretched between Nato and Russia. But at the near end they threw a pair of wrought-iron gates into silhouette. The gates were closed and looked like the entrance to the ten-yard-long drive of a retired mouth surgeon in Walthamstow. Next to them was an orange sign, pointed at the eastern end. It said: 'Sovjetunionen'.

Beyond the last light was the biggest concentration of military power there has ever been in peacetime. (Hobbes: 'The nature of War, consisteth not in actual fighting; but in the known disposition thereto, during all the time there is no assurance to the contrary.') In the Kola peninsula there are twenty-five airfields, with 300 warplanes, and 50,000 troops, including two motorized infantry divisions at Pechenga and Alakurti. One regiment of marines, the 63rd, is named the 'Kirkenes' after its exploits in the last war. But this garrison and this arsenal are not there to fight the last war. They are there to protect the Soviet Arctic Fleet in Pechenga and Murmansk. In the revised geography of superpower rivalry the Kola peninsula has become one of the front lines, matching Sakhalin at the far end of the continent. (Brigadier Torhag asked Colonel Matila at one of their parties if the Russians would shoot down an airliner that wandered over Murmansk by mistake. They would.)

Norwegian recognition of the sensitivity of this area has led them to ban any Nato aircraft from crossing the 24°E meridian (just the Russian side of Hammerfest) and any Nato vessels from calling at ports east of the same line. These, like the absence of both nuclear weapons and foreign bases on Norwegian soil, are self-imposed, one-sided limitations. They recognize in part that the Kola Peninsula arsenal is pointing in another direction, across the North Pole. There are nearly 200 submarines in the Soviet Arctic Fleet, half of which are nuclear. This is about two thirds of all Soviet nuclear submarines. They are concentrated here because Russia's other naval outlets are severely restricted. The Black Sea and the Baltic could both be pinched shut in a moment, with military – if not political – ease. American monitoring equipment on submerged towers in the Greenland–Iceland–United Kingdom gap now means that 70% of all Russian submarines trying to get into the North Atlantic would be destroyed in a war. The Arctic is a refuge. The ice itself makes too much noise for good surveillance by sonar. Submarines can cruise in relative safety under the ice canopy, navigating by satellite fixes and by inertial navigation systems which allow them to travel for more than a month before accumulating an error of one nautical mile. This is good enough to be sure of hitting cities, even if the destruction of American missiles in their silos cannot be guaranteed.

Skylights – or polynyas – of ice no more than a metre thick cover up to 8% of the Arctic Ocean even in midwinter. They can be torpedoed or nosed through by the submarine itself before firing. Imagine that in the dark at the opening of the war. All over the Arctic, Soviet submarines breaking through the thin ice. SS N 18 missiles have a range of 5,530 miles. Cities anywhere in North America can be destroyed from submarines in this ocean. It is not surprising that Colonel Matila has to refer his decisions to Leningrad.

The only other guest at dinner with the Torhags was the garrison commander. He was forty and Nordic, pure Viking. He wore a tweed jacket of the same angularity as his jaw, and his blond hair was arranged in a way I have seen only in portraits of the generals at Borodino: it was blown forward along the side of his head into cirrus wisps and somehow held there. But he was a disappointed man. He had applied to join the Norwegian forces in the Lebanon, but had not been accepted. So here he was commanding snowmen with his wife 900 miles away in Hönefoss and feeling sad.

We discussed Jane's literary career. She wanted to write a book about a nineteenth-century opera singer. She had already chosen the singer – a year or two ago in fact – but she wasn't sure about the background. How do you find out about the background? Books took so long to get to the library at Kirkenes and it was so difficult to get the background without the books. We all examined the candles. The Viking cleaned a perfectly clean fingernail with the point of his knife. Perhaps she'd write a book about Kirkenes. 'It's layered like a cake,' she said again for the benefit of the garrison commander, who hadn't been there earlier in the day. Someone had in fact already written a book about the opera singer, but it was a very bad book. The Viking put a hand on his hip, from where it stuck out like a derrick.

I tried to get them to talk about strategic issues, but this was a failure. It was probably a reluctance to talk shop, but at the time all that I registered was a general closing down of the mind. All the brigadier's tactical playfulness, his amused ingenuity in the game, all that fell away. His flexibility froze as the questions grew larger. He said that human nature had not changed; that Nato was an extraordinary achievement; that the Common Market was an extraordinary achievement; that trust was important between allies. The peace movement –

'really no more than a peace feeling' – was self-deluding and sponsored by the Russians; Kekkonen had been a dictator; the neutrality of
Finland was a bogus and cosmetic transparency. Balance of armaments was the only possible guarantee. You have to negotiate from
strength. All of this as though he were discussing the colour of a
postbox.

I said something about a deterrent being an anxiety-building measure – no response – and about the psychological stupidity of imagin-
ing that to threaten a powerful enemy would make him cower. Nothing. But I was in embarrassingly full flood and quoted something:
the idea that the struggle for power is the prime mover of politics
persists in an age when the renunciation of the struggle has become a
prerequisite of survival. I was a tape-recorder. The dinner-party had
effectively collapsed. Hopeless earnestness, way outside any sort of
Carrington-style sophistication, the accepted model.

The brigadier repaired it with a story. I played with a Kazakh napkin
ring and holder set. A CIA coordinator recently, after visiting the
many listening-posts here that monitor the movements of the Soviet
shipping out of Murmansk and Pechenga, told his Norwegian hosts
that he wanted to go hunting reindeer as a break from Russians.
Laugh. The Norwegians didn't dare admit that there are no wild
reindeer in Lapland or tell him that he might as well hunt heifers in
Gloucestershire. Smile over at Jane: Jane came from Gloucestershire.
They paid a Lapp to neglect his herd for a day, and subtly directed the
agent towards the browsing animals. Everything went well. The
American guessed nothing. Hesitant expectation. And eventually he
bagged a vast Hemingwayan buck with large furry antlers. When the
carcase came to be picked up it was found, unfortunately, to have a
little bell around its neck attached by a neat piece of Lapp embroidery.
Shouted relief, laughter and drinking. The anglepoise colonel, who
had originally told the brigadier this story, said that American confidence in the Norwegian defence posture had never been quite the
same since.

When I got back to England I discovered that a high-ranking official
in the Norwegian Foreign Office had been charged a week after the
dinner-party with spying for the Russians. I thought of Brigadier
Torhag and the blow-dried colonel and wondered why they had both
been so very amused at their own old story. Had the diplomat been
found with a bell around his neck too?

It was sixty kilometres from Kirkenes to Grense-Jakobselv. The road
was blocked after twenty. The rest would have to be by snowcat. It
was a day's journey into the furthest corner I could find, a diplomatic

concession, an ice-cream scoop out of Russia, swopped 150 years ago for a diamond-studded box.

The day was too good to last and after eleven it worsened and dirtied. Snow thickened the sky like flour in a sauce. Visibility dropped and I thought of Olivia so very pregnant in her log cabin. Christian picked up some diesel for the snowcat at an unmanned petrol station and we soon came to the end of the road proper. A man had stuck his car in the terminal drift there and we pushed him out of it. By now it was snowing hard and the falling snow had cancelled the light. We went into the one house at this place, Vintervollen, and Christian telephoned to Grense-Jakobselv to ask about the snow conditions. I was left alone with the house's lonely occupant. A human goat, six and a half feet tall and hunched over his immense height. Slightly mad. He talked in an endless creamy gurgle about his family history in a German I could scarcely understand. He was a milk farmer and the house smelt of it. There were buckets and pails everywhere. His Guernsey breath blew all over my face as he shouted about Schleswig-Holstein – or were those the cows? – and the timber exports from Jakobsnes. The *Eisenbahn* to Trondheim came into it. His liquid hysterical laugh caught up with itself and then burped globules. Over the basin in the kitchen were expensive skin preparations, but he was structurally pocked. His skin was as patchy as the sideboards. It was his uncle's farm, his mother's sister's husband's farm, Oskar's it had been. Did I like cows? I loved cows. But Grense-Jakobselv – had I heard of the man-eating fish there, the walrus? A terrible disappointment began in his face, my German failing under the onslaught, his loneliness closing in. Christian came back, the snow was all right and we could go. He said goodbye to the milk farmer as if to a senile aunt, gently and dismissively. Only the final message registered on the poor man's face.

The snowcat was half-hidden in the snow. A heating element was stuck under its bonnet like a thermometer. The cat was in two parts, tractor and trailer, joined by a thick universal joint. It was built by Volvo, designed as a tracked personnel carrier for northern armies. Nine soldiers are carried about in the back half. There were stretched nylon covers on the seats patterned in brown and mauve dahlias. It smelt deodorized, but you couldn't hide the real smell. The lurching made the passengers sick. I sat in front, in the officer's seat in the tractor where things were more stable. The machine did a kilometre to a litre or three miles to the gallon, and never topped 30 kph. Usually it was more like 15 in bad snow. Sickening slow motion snow war.

It started first time, we climbed in through the windows and for three hours the view did not change. The journey was a dark invisibility as we lurched over the snow bumps from one road stick to the next. At times the two square frog-eyes of the machine pointed at nothing but the yellow specks of the falling snow. The velcro tearing of the gears and the clacking of the tracks under the van. I kept thinking of something the commissioner had said in a sort of litany rhyme. The Russians want

> Finland to be like Poland
> Sweden like Finland and
> Norway like Sweden.

You could turn it upside down in another revisionist dream:

> Poland like Finland
> Finland like Sweden
> Sweden like Norway.

But that last line dangled and it did not have the logic of geography. I had tried to talk to the commissioner about this. It was, after all, a commonplace of détente thinking. Somehow in Scandinavia a low-level balance had been achieved. Norway and the Soviet Union were confirmed members of the opposite camps. They held hands here at the top. Under the shelter of that fingertip meeting Sweden and Finland maintain a neutrality on either side of a gentle apex:

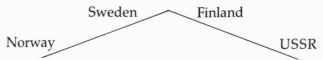

It was an example for Europe. It could worsen without becoming disastrous. The triangle could steepen, the camps could polarize, the Iron Curtain could be drawn up the Gulf of Bothnia and there would be no world war. But in Central Europe worse means disastrous. The only directions possible there are war and détente. Scandinavia has the enviable option of pure bloodless hostility. But then we had veered off to the CIA reindeer hunt. My schemes for a great swathe of neutrality through Europe – Denmark, West Germany and Greece; Hungary, Czechoslovakia and East Germany – had belly-landed in Jane Torhag's creation Bananas Kirkenes. No one would ever again believe in *cordons sanitaires*. The metaphor had changed, the hospital had become the breaker's yard, and sterilizing fluid the jaws of a vice. Central Europe had become Eastern Europe and the sanitary belt – no wonder they never translated it – was now part of the Soviet crush zone.

Christian stopped the snowcat in the middle of nowhere, and out of the snow appeared a man on a snow scooter. A rifle was slung across his chest. His moustache was frozen and he pushed his goggles up on to his hat. He had been delivering a microwave oven.

We moved off and the wind blew moiré spirals of spindrift in the headlights. We drove straight across the top of a frozen lake and arrived above the valley of the Jakobselv. There was a sickle moon. We dropped down past the lights of a Norwegian border post and then a four-man ski-patrol, white clothes, red faces. The border itself is a small scrubby brook with full-sized versions of the Storskog border markers on either bank. Some joker had stolen a Russian one the year before and erected it in Oslo as a peace protest. The Soviets had complained. It was not, they said, conducive to peace.

On the far side the land sloped upwards and away like upper Wensleydale. In Norway there was a cliff. Ice turned it grey and on top, 300 feet above the valley floor, a radar boom was revolving. It is the most obvious of the Nato ears with which this corner is stuffed. The Russians had nothing like it, only a leggy observation tower and – Christian had to point it out to me – the makings of a new camp. It was here that some of Brigadier Torhag's men had been able through binoculars to read the motto already over the main gate. It says: 'Our borders are inviolate.'

But the division receded. What mattered about the place, about the one valley, was its northernness, its end of any road. After two hours in the metal cab of the snow tractor we arrived on the shores of the Barents Sea. Ten-foot rollers bowled in from the darkened north. The day had lightened, the land was white and the cliffs skinned in ice, but the sea itself – part of that family of vast forgotten northern seas, the Laptev, the Kara, the Chukchi, the Beaufort, the White, the Canadian island waters that fringe the Arctic Ocean – this sea, warmed by the last ghost of the Gulf Stream, was a deep colourless black. It washed the ice-coat from the rocks to a line. I stood in the unlit day staring north, forgetful of borders, listening to the bumbling of the diesel and the sucking of the polar waves.

I wanted to talk about the undivided sea, free of human interference. But it would not have been true. In 1869 a stone Lutheran chapel with a little spire was built in Grense-Jakobselv to sanctify the furthest corner of Sweden-Norway and to act as a sea mark for fishermen off the coast. It is now supplemented by two large dayglo orange lozenges, lit at night, which like start-line marks for yacht races indicate the frontier when, from out at sea, they come into line. Nevertheless, the frontier they establish is challenged by the Russians and a large grey triangle of Barents Sea is in dispute. The concern now is sea-bed minerals rather than fish. Brigadier Torhag refused to discuss the point, either at dinner with me or with Colonel Matila at any time.

The driver turned the Volvo round as I watched from the stubby breakwater. An orange sign said 'Kirkenes 60'. Now the journey to the Aegean could begin to unroll.

We went twenty yards. Christian stopped outside a tiny house with the snow drifted thigh-high in front of it. A tiny old woman called Frū Kasereff lived there as if in a nursery rhyme. She was eighty-five and Russian. She cannot have been more than four feet tall and everything surrounding her was equally tiny. There were lots of little crocheted carpets on the floor, little china objects on the tables, a small icon in the corner furthest from the door. She gave us little cakes with little cups of coffee. There were only two anomalies: a giant box of Kellogg's Smacks on the larder shelf and a thick gold ring, scarred and notched, on the wedding finger of her hand. In this grand extremity, inside her miniature frontier cabin, Frū Kasereff maintained a Lilliput. She rushed around it arranging the landscape of tartlets and napkins on the table, sorting out the photographs of those grandchildren in Sydney from those in British Columbia. There was nothing precious about her. She spoke in a tough, rubbed-down way like a gamekeeper. As a child she had lived in Murmansk and in 1917, in the winter after the Revolution, her new husband – a teacher – had escaped from Russia by skiing for two days and nights over the unmarked tundra. He became a fisherman in Norway, while by stages she made her way westwards, staying with relations and their friends and sending clandestine messages to her husband across the border. After a year a rendezvous was fixed and the Norwegian fishing boat came secretly to a remote quay on the Russian coast near Tsyp Navolok where she was waiting.

He took her away and, after a series of jobs in Vadsö and Vardö, they had come to live here in this tiny house within sight of the homeland. They had brought up eight children. He was dead now and she showed me his photographs, young and old. There were no regrets. She scampered around the room lighting candles. Her firewood and the unplaned logs that formed the beams for the ceiling had drifted on to the storm shore outside. She would never leave. One son still lives with her for part of the year and a daughter who has gone south to live in Stavanger (a sort of lush Gauguin fantasy in vermilion and magenta – it's on the same latitude as the Orkneys) cannot bear the fleshpots of sub-Arctic life and is coming back to Grense-Jakobselv to live in purity on the frontier.

This was wonderful, the sort of discovery I had wanted, with the snowcat outside in the dark, its headlights pointing back along the track we had made. But then the truth. Ksemé Kasereff was famous. She was, in fact, the most famous person in Finnmark. A Dutch television crew had made a documentary about her. There had been an Italian radio programme and a couple of short biographies, one in Swedish and one published in Melbourne called *Arctic Whirlwind: The First Lady of the North*. I was only the latest in a queue of pilgrims. The edge, it seemed, had been folded over, like blankets on a bed, and the furthest corner turned out to be the most familiar of all.

2

A Generous Smile of Ruined Teeth

Frank was good at 'Gorilla'. He could avoid the thrown-down electronic time devils and expanding jaws of hell fire with enviable ease. Already four maidens were lined up in the cell at the bottom. He had been packing fish all winter in Båtsfjord and was fed up with it. Frank, too, was going south to see his girl. He had driven to Ivalo, but the extra petrol was too much and we were both waiting for the midnight bus. But it was obvious that with petrol shared the price halved, and the prospect of arriving early at his girlfriend's flat – he showed me the key, a masonic pass – made it worth driving. We travelled for three hours in his old Volvo at eighty down the straight and empty highway, the vertebral cord of Dorpat Finland. The white road at intervals turned caustic in the sodium village lights.

Frank wanted to go to Australia. He had an uncle there, next summer perhaps. It depended on the girl. She was a nurse in Rovaniemi and he would go as soon as she was free. But what did Australia mean? For Frank, for the Lapp in Sevettijärvi, for Stano in Bratislava, for the young men in the crush zone, it had come to represent everything that America had been for their great-uncles and great-great-uncles. No matter the true nature of these distant continental countries; the way in which they were seen by their would-be immigrants had changed. It was partly sheer distance. Australia was two oceans and an America away, while America itself was now so involved with Europe as not to seem removed or different from it. It had become a Europe with shortcomings, a Europe that had failed by simple reproduction. The strain of anti-Americanism that is now shot through these young Europeans is a contempt for the shared faults, inherited by one, transmitted by the other. To emigrate there now is no more than to move to another part of one's own country, the same colour in the mind. But Australia was golden for Frank at two in the morning. Its name meant the south. It was still the land of opportunity, while America, trammelled, had turned out to be the land of repetition. Australia is still a blank. To go there is to become yourself. To go to America is to become an American.

Frank's future was a simple recipe of escape in which no cold and no fish factories were included; only his girl in the warmth by the warm sea in the warm, a-historical bath of physical, moral and geographical freedom. All the age of Europe, the father-like restrictions of Båtsfjord – where he had yet to possess a Boston whaler of his own – all that would drop away. It was an old dream.

He left me at the bus station in Rovaniemi and went off to his nurse's bed. I curled up on the plastic benches in the smoked air of the taxi office and waited for the morning bus to Kemijärvi and Salla. Olivia's cabin was within four miles of the Russian frontier in the commune of Naruska, near Salla. The eastern side of Finland kinks and buckles on its way south from Näätämö, but centred on Salla, in a front 240 kilometres long, the line swerves westwards in one smooth scalpel slice. It is one of the impositions of the Treaty of Moscow in 1940, after the Russians had defeated the Finns in the Winter War. It is a fossilized military salient, which pushes Russia thirty kilometres nearer the Gulf of Bothnia. Just over 5,000 Finns were expelled westwards from the annexed territory. The flanks of the salient are secure, shallow enough to prevent the famous Finnish tactic of encirclement. The line of the frontier gives the Soviet Union a head start in any future Scandinavian war. With Russian ships in the Baltic, a strike across the waist of Finland to Kemi would give them control of the country.

The Russians included in the 1940 treaty a demand that Finland should build a railway from the existing head at Kemijärvi through Salla and Alakurti to join the Leningrad–Murmansk line near Kandalaksa. The Soviet Government claimed that the purpose of the railway was to open Russian trade with Scandinavia. Finland was required to allow transit rights for Russian goods. This was a transparent lie. Its purpose was military.

There was a long-standing belief in Russia that the 'natural frontier' of the country lay along the Gulf of Bothnia. (The most revealing fact about the history of 'natural frontiers' as a political theory is that no country has ever *withdrawn* to a frontier that it recognizes as natural. The theory has always been an excuse for expansion.) The railway would be the artery by which that furthest front line could be fed – or at least these were the Finnish fears. There was always the example of the Baltic states across the Gulf of Finland, which had been annexed, absorbed and destroyed as countries.

The Salla railway has never yet been put to the test. There was one irony over its construction. The Finns were naturally reluctant to complete it and, despite an undertaking that it would be finished by the end of 1940, it was not finally built until the autumn of 1941. By then it had become the all-important supply line for the German divisions operating against the line to Murmansk.

Past Kemijärvi and Olivia's bus station there, the road swung in and out of the Salla railway, a primitive single-track line blown over with snow and frosted. There is no passenger traffic east of Kemijärvi and no more than occasional wood loads crossing in from the Soviet Union. It is a railway in storage, waiting in the charcoal blur of the forest for its only real outing.

I left the bus at Kotala, a couple of wooden houses, and bought groceries at the store. The women in the shop were angry. I politely picked up bundles of American Red Devils from the shelves and figs from Izmir, and some Dutch chocolate with a smile. No break in the hard-nosed reception. I moved on towards tagliatelle and pear-shaped tomatoes in a tin from some Calabrian *latifundium*. Granite. Vastly overpriced chestnut purée from the Maures picked up and thrown into the basket. Nothing. I had done something wrong. I began to behave with all the estuarine charm of a Jane Austen villain, unctuously allowing the other women to go ahead of me, half privately admiring the wealth of produce in the desert, murmuring amazement at the fertility of the Finnish supply system. But none of this had the desired effect either. I began to suspect that I was known in Kotala. The bundled-up women were now openly examining me, hands on hips, their faces a collective tut. I smoothed my hair, but ranged by the cash-desk was a bastion of shared morality from which I was somehow excluded. I got out the phrase book in an attempt to bridge that particular moat. Your woman here, it told me. Maternity ward. You are not here. Sin dawned. I tried to explain all the subtleties of the marriage, how independence and interdependence fed off each other; how love was not the same as physical proximity; something about liners berthing and flames leaping together; how it was actually Olivia's *choice* to come here first. But it didn't work. I had ordered my wife, who was eight months pregnant, to spend three days alone in an isolated log cabin without a telephone and a hundred miles from the nearest hospital all because I didn't want her on my skiing holiday in Sweden. And everybody knew about Sweden. Next to the till the women of Kotala were unassailable, quietly occupying a fat and questionless heaven.

The post taxi dropped me on the road opposite a small wooden signpost pointing west to Kuopsimaja. This was Olivia's cabin. To the east the ground rose towards the distant forest heights, which Russia had included within the salient. The postwoman waved goodbye. She was off to arrange an emergency obstetrics class for the Naruska first aid club.

I walked downhill through the quilted trees and across the frozen river. A snow-caked dinghy lay hull up on the bank and the cabin was on the far side. Olivia was baking bread. I waded through the mess of occupation to hug her and the child stirred about inside. The cabin was a basement flat in St John's Wood, a sort of triangular Toblerone chip laid flat in the snow with a flat roof. The walls alternated orange and beige, the ceiling was a diagram of the Polish railway system, and between the sauna and the outside air you could cross 80 °c of circumambient temperature in three bemused paces. Under these circumstances snow feels hot.

The border post was a mile down the road. Another little cottage in the forest and inside it the brutalized half vacuum of military life. We waited for the warrant officer to return from patrol. Posters advertising the border guard were stuck on the walls. Jolly young men sat around a camp fire elaborating future reminiscences. Their helmets shone. An armoured personnel carrier prodded out of some spruces as if endorsing roll-on deodorant. This was the advertising. The reality, or part of it, appeared in the photographs of the Finnish generals stuck up over the desk. The two in command of the border guard had been loyally outlined in red felt-tip. They were bureaucratic and thin-lipped men, their uniforms only faintly more substantial than the bodies they contained. There was none of the puffed-up worsted of Russian marshals, of the sheer *stuff* of Russian uniforms. The Finnish generals and their clothes – they command an army which, by the Treaty of Paris in 1947, must remain below 41,500 men – are fussy and lank at the same time. They wear the disappointment of rather tired commissionaires outside an Oban department store, keeping their end up by oiling their hair and shining their shoes.

Lounging on the tables were some Finnish magazines, slack and grey from use. Imagine these weird waiting-rooms all over Europe, the men turning through magazines they have turned through eight times before, everything slack in lives that consist of this permanent and dreary expectation. The advertising poster was a lie. It portrayed the frontier as a threat cheerfully borne; in fact it is another article about Sophia Loren's rumoured hysterectomy.

The warrant officer returned from the ski-patrol red, tired and angry. His forehead had bumped up into anxiety scarps. He kept flicking his hairlick back. No, we could not go to the frontier. There is a frontier strip three kilometres wide which foreigners can enter only with permission from the Security Police in Helsinki. He showed us the map. It was beautiful, full of brown curled contours and deep river trenches, the few hayfields around Naruska in caramel squares. Cutting across it from south-east to north-west the raspberry line drawn in Moscow one night in early spring of 1940. The perfect cartography of Finland came up to this pink line, moved half a centimetre beyond it with every detail complete, every waver in the contours represented, and then stopped. Beyond it was nothing but white paper overlain with the national grid of Finland also in pink and the letters SNTL, meaning USSR.

A thinner pink stripe marked the 'back border line', the edge of the exclusion zone. It is defined on the ground with yellow rings around the trees. 'If you do go to the border area,' he said, 'we will take you and give you to the security police. If you want to see a border, the border with Sweden has no exclusive stripe.' This was a joke, so we moved on to other things. He hated journalists. 'They paint stories too much. They are true, but not so true.' An American journalist had said that the Finnish border guard was 'effectively part of the Soviet Security system on its western borders. Its record of returning would-be refugees to the Soviet authorities is unenviable.' This was too much, the warrant officer thought. 'There *is* a border there,' he said. 'These are two countries.'

I asked him if the straight swords on his jacket badge were really meant to signify, as I had heard, the arms of the West set against the invisible Eastern scimitar. He didn't know and turned cagey, spending a long time feeling his hairlick between answers. Was it ever boring, Olivia asked. And then he was angry. He told a subordinate to ring the security police in Helsinki. 'How is it boring? It is important, good work.' The effrontery of our coming to his office and asking silly questions was made clear.

Olivia asked why his wife lived in Rovaniemi. Were the living quarters nasty? He had heard a jumbled version of something else Olivia had asked in the shop at Kotala and said: 'You thought there were Russian soldiers here? That we could drive you around in tanks like your husband in Norway?' Full contempt. His biro doodle punctured the Munich Olympics. We were given a sheet of paper called 'Instructions Concerning Movement and Stay in Frontier Zone' and we read it on our stools like schoolchildren. The Soviet Union was never mentioned in the document. 'In order to secure peace of the frontier', it said, 'and to maintain and emphasize general order and safety, a special frontier zone has been formed at the south-east and eastern frontier of Finland.' Like the map, the document was coherent up to the line and no further. And, like courtiers in ancient Peking, this printed sheet could refer to the great presence, but never to its name. But there was no avoiding the fact that the frontier had two sides to it and towards the end the Soviet Union becomes 'the neighbouring country'. Once the subject is mentioned, there is no holding it. Three times in one sentence: no shouting at, no photography of and no light thrown upon 'the area of the neighbouring country'.

This, of course, is self-Finlandization. There is no such zone in Austria. It is the self-limitation of a neutral intended to quieten the anxieties of a powerful neighbour, anxieties which, if left unchecked, might lead to closer control or Polonization. It is a real *cordon sanitaire*, preserving hygiene in a political microclimate. Anyone violating the law in the frontier zone will be fined or imprisoned for up to two years.

Back in the log cabin I read some of the speeches of Urho Kekkonen, the President of Finland from 1956 until 1981. Throughout them he repeats the words 'necessity', 'tragedy', 'reality', 'destiny'. 'Facts have a gravity which goes beyond wishful thinking,' Kekkonen says with the rational obviousness that was his hallmark. Again and again the President quotes the great saws of *Realpolitik* from the past. Napoleon: 'Politics is the assessment of circumstances and the calculation of possibilities.' The nineteenth-century Finn, Gripenberg: 'Blind adherence to what is right in abstract terms without thinking of the consequences, without thought to what is wise and possible in the prevailing circumstances, leads to disaster in real life.' And himself: Egotism, self-preservation, is the only dependable foundation for a small state. . . . There is no justification for allowing ideological likes or dislikes to influence this policy. . . . If we look around us, we can see in every quarter things which ought to be protested at in the name of humanity. But we do not. We cannot.' This is courageous honesty. Unlike his civil servants, Kekkonen can name the Soviet Union without blanching. It is part of the straightforwardness, the anti-emotionalism on which his successful treatment of Russia depended. He advertised clean open rationalism.

It is this that sets off his idea of Finland from the pre-war heroic posturing, and from all the old attempts at playing between the Russian and German rivalries in the Baltic. Those, for Kekkonen, were emotive years and policies that stemmed not from reason but from desire. He throws contempt on those western writers who have talked about Finlandization in terms of 'a small and weak neighbour, awed by the might and political ruthlessness of a totalitarian superpower, making shameless and embarrassing concessions of its sovereign liberties'. That, says Kekkonen, is 'an ingrained and prejudicial image', based on rigid and emotional ideas of the nation as a self-reliant unit, a political virgin, perfect inside her unbroken frontiers and independent of the political and strategic reality outside them. That is not the nature of an interfolded world.

Understandably, in his collected essays and speeches, he does not mention the Night of Frost in 1958, when, under Russian pressure, he effectively dissolved a Finnish government that contained no Communists; nor his calling of parliamentary elections five months early in 1961 in order to throw the Opposition into disarray; nor his torpedoing of the Scandinavian Free Trade Area in 1970 at Russian insistence; nor the financially disastrous purchase of Russian railway engines, power stations and oil (the price of which is a state secret); nor the arrangements by which the Finns have totally refurbished the Saimaa canal in Russian Karelia, of which they make very little use themselves; nor the ceilings imposed on the Finnish armed forces; nor the self-censorship by which newspapers may not properly discuss foreign policy; nor the Finnish failure to condemn the invasion of Afghanistan in the UN. These things too are an aspect of political reality, of a perforated frontier.

Saunas in the triangular cabin – 'you must tease yourself' – the baby shifting in the womb and the animal creaking of the house as the thermostat relit the boiler and the water percolated down from the roof.

We walked a mile the other way to visit some farmers called Moilanen. Hilkka was a nurse in Kemijärvi, her younger sister Seija was learning Russian at university in Turku. Their father had thirteen cows and a few tall wooden buildings – hayloft, byre, garage, workshop, house – standing randomly about on the edge of the forest and the snowed-over fields. Photographs of the summer, furry blotched Herefords browsing in the forest and the orchid clover. Two cuts a year. Hilkka shone and Seija froze with intellectual pretensions. Mr Moilanen was nearly toothless. He placed a sugarlump between two of the Hoy stumps and sucked at it in a wide smile. The mother knitted a white sock. The head of a moose stuck out of a wall and a pair of blue plastic aeroplanes hung from an antler. Its nose was the front of a bomber. The soft milk soup of domestic joy. The border had been shorn off, the maps had gone blank and the Moilanens could only turn westwards. The frontier zone excluded them too and they knew nothing beyond the line in the forest where the trees are marked with flashes. It is living with a mirror and, whichever way you look, there is only one view.

We had sweet cakes and coffee, and I told them about the brigadier in Norway. They listened seriously to how other people treated the thing. But it was no game down here, only a cut-off. It marks another part of the world, the place where 'here' becomes 'there'. It is the scar left by the cutting edge of *Realpolitik*, a caesarean section, only to be understood with the seriousness they instinctively bring to it.

We left the cabin early in the morning. As we crossed the frozen river with our bags, the ice shot an echo downstream. The same route in the bus, through Kotala, Salla and Kemijärvi to the train at Rovaniemi. The pattern of the roads made it impossible to go south along the frontier itself and the time was approaching when, for safety's sake, Olivia should return to England. I would fly back from Berlin to be with her.

At Oulu we changed trains. The Helsinki express went south into the yellow evening with its cargo of half-calf boots intact. The new train was more basic. The sourceless fluorescent wash of light was now a dim urine glow. A straggled-haired woman changed her mouth into a mannerist tyre and painted it red. Seams stretched. A man opens his legs, leaves one on the floor and puts the other on a seat beside him. We were travelling back to the frontier and the cloth covers on the headrests had gone grey in the middle.

From Joensuu I went to Niirala alone. On the map near by, on either side of the frontier, was a place called Värtsila. 'Värtsila' and 'Värtsila' in two different types. The one-carriage train ran down through the forest. The ballerina branches of the pines held down by the snow, collapsed at the end of a performance. I looked out through the back window to watch the lines converging in a single slow metallic clap. A negative wake through the window of the cab which the driver would occupy to return. His hidden gestures in the front were repeated on the instruments in the rear. He flicked at the levers and pulled the knobs, and the levers twitched and the knobs turned. A push-me-pull-you Newtonian world, each half matching. At intervals, outside, the dead ringing of automatic bells.

The road past the station was barred in the forest. Three red lights along the pole. A straight kilometre away another red pair shone up. A border guard watched me from a gantry across the road. An Ascona was parked at the bottom of the ladder. The sidings were packed with Russian steel containers on flats. A man was digging snow from between some points.

The guard came down from the gantry. He took my details and I signed a paper. Would he take me to the frontier? I only wanted to see the frontier, to see what it was like.

'No.'   *The frontier an explicit geographical negative.*

'Why not?'   *It makes one direct, unsubtle, unscheming.*

'Because it is so.'   *Not susceptible to individual questioning.*

'Surely it is because the Russians require it, don't they?'

A generous smile of ruined teeth.

I walked from Niirala the few miles to Värtsila. The right-hand verge of the road became the back-frontier itself. There was no fence along it, only the notional yellow splashes along the telegraph poles, and I toyed with the idea of crossing over into the zone in the empty fields between the two places. But after an hour, when the buildings had become roofs, an orange Volvo passed me with a guard and a dog in it. The car stopped a hundred yards in front of me, turned round and drove back. Alsatians evaporate freedoms and I stayed on the road. It was lovely. Duvet meadows with small wooden farmsteads set apart, all of them painted in vegetable colours. It was Massachusetts in 1730. But this was Karelia, in many ways the heartland of Finnish national consciousness. It was from scattered villages like these that Elias Lönnrot began to collect the folksongs in the nineteenth century which he amalgamated into the national epic, the Kalevala. Across the border, the hills of what is now Russian Karelia rise in the forest. It was wonderful walking along the hard white road past the little cross-laced balconies and the fretted bargeboards on the eaves. There was nothing brutal in the landscape and I sang Irish songs about love of one's country and the sash my father wore. A weathercock on a stable said 1749 and a café in Värtsila sold me hot chocolate. I was thinking about asking for houses to rent.

But the frontier will always intrude and here the anomaly was an observation tower. These black girdered structures dot the frontiers of Europe. Värtsila was a community cut in half in 1940 by the frontier imposed at the end of the Winter War, by which Finland lost most of Karelia. Some 420,000 Finns, a ninth of the nation, came over into the torso of the country as refugees. But Värtsila is so scattered, like the islands in the Pacific divided by the International Date Line, that there is no image here of a rural Berlin. The frontier is all but invisible. The houses dot eastwards across it without interruption and only an observation tower, like a heron in a pond of coots, reminds you of the imposed divide. The tower is pure political architecture, poking above normality and embodying a soulless, ugly inquisition. They are invigilators hung over your shoulder as you write, loathsomely and literally superior. The towers are everything a fence is not and yet they twin to fences exactly, the x and y axes of the modern frontier.

Perhaps there is a delusion in all of this. It was too easy here to adopt a mild internationalist stance, to say with Isherwood's Mr Norris: 'All these frontiers ... such a horrible nuisance. They ought to be done away with.' The look of frontiers offends. Without them, one imagines, the landscape – the human and physical landscapes – would be so much better, the same but better. One would have a picture entirely of rust- and mushroom-coloured farmhouses. The black girders would go and no one would miss them.

But, if Kekkonen meant nothing else, he meant that the tower guaranteed the farmhouse, the invigilator the exam and the Berlin Wall, however horrible an object, some sort of peace in Europe and the world. There is an ecology here which universalist dreams could only disrupt and destroy.

The Tikkas ran the shop in Värtsila. It sold abrasives and face cream, hatchets, firelighters and saw blades, butter, yoghurt and contraceptives. Helena left the shop to her mother. She knew little about old Värtsila, but took me to see her uncle. We drove for twenty minutes. Helena, who was seventeen, had the same extraordinary style on the iced roads as other Finns. There was simply no fear of slipping off the edge into a ditch. She had the sf disc on the back of the car and told me she had heard that foreigners thought it stood not for Suomi, but for Soviet-Finland. She wasn't allowed into the border strip to fish or collect cloudberries. Even those who farmed it or delivered goods to houses there needed a special pass with a photograph. She didn't mind. 'The Russians have said that it must be and we must accept.' *We must accept.* That meant two things: Finland must accept and Finnish people must accept. There was a formal connection between the two. Finland bore the same relation to the Soviet Union as private citizens to their government anywhere.

$$USSR: Finland = Finland : Helena\ Tikka$$

Or in general: Finlandization is the necessary resigning of freedoms to a higher power. It was nothing but Hobbes, the patron saint of frontiers. Finland was doing no more than was every citizen in the world who stopped at red lights and didn't murder. Paasikivi and Kekkonen had turned *Realpolitik* on its head by extending social obligation into the international sphere. Realism became, in their hands, the understanding of power in order not to fulfil one's ambitions, but to reduce them.

This frontier that divided Värtsila, which reduced Dorpat Finland by 12%, which deprived it of 30% of its power stations, 20% of its railways, 30% of its sawmills – the primary industry – this mutilation of national integrity was in fact the natural political frontier. Anything nearer Leningrad – and between 1809 and 1940 the Finnish frontier came within thirty-two kilometres of the city, easy artillery range by 1900 – would be artificial and out of equilibrium. Or, as Helena said, 'We must accept.'

Her uncle lived in Saario. He was a victim of this reality. (Throughout Europe, on this journey, the same pattern emerged: rural victims of urban perceptions. The shock of Berlin is at least partly that of a policy coming home to roost, the most ferocious of divisions edging by the reconstructed back parts of the Reichstag.) Onni Tikka and his wife Aino had lived in Ruskeala, due south of Värtsila and now in the Soviet Union. He wore a thick jersey with reindeer walking from side to side across it and played with the ends of his fingers. His grey hair spoked up where it had been cut short near the crown. Mrs Tikka, as small as Frū Kasereff, held the edges of her apron and listened.

When the war had been going for 125 days they were given one week to leave. A new border was drawn and they were forced to go to the other side of it. They had to leave behind whatever they were unable to carry and shoot the animals. Some had been hitched to the back of carts, but the terrain was difficult and the journey was hard in March at the end of the winter. The Tikkas came with two horses and two colts. One of the colts was sold on the journey. In theory it was a voluntary evacuation, but no one wanted to stay, except for a woman from Sortavala, who went to work on the radio and used to broadcast to Finland, persuading the others that Soviet Karelia was all right. The evacuation was calm at first, but the people had hurried when they heard the Russian soldiers were coming over the ice of Lake Ladoga towards them. The Tikkas burnt nothing themselves, but the Finnish soldiers burnt it after they left. Or so they had heard, and Aino bowed to confirm it.

They had gone back in 1941, at the start of the Continuation War against Russia, as the Germans besieged Leningrad, and they had found their house virtually intact, with a few holes in it, standing almost alone in the ruined village. They smiled at each other at the memory. But in 1944 they had left again, this time in a great hurry, and had begun, with the hundreds of thousands of other Karelian refugees, a series of forced moves around southern Finland from camp to camp, while the government and parliament struggled with the repeated national trauma.

People wept openly as the news of the second armistice was posted in Helsinki. The fatherland was diminished, actually and spiritually. 'Ours is a hard fate,' Marshal Mannerheim said over the radio, 'when we are compelled to give up to a strange race, with a different world outlook and different moral values, land which we have worked for centuries with sweat and suffering.' This was the background to the Paasikivi–Kekkonen line.

Finland's independence was bought with Karelia. The new frontier, near enough, was the line established in 1721 after Peter the Great had defeated Sweden in the Great Northern War. Finland was a foreign country to many of the Karelian refugees. The dialects differed, there was a tendency to regard Karelians in Finland as backward and primitive. There was some cheating of the displaced people. It was, like a family Christmas, a difficult mixture: on the one side a sense of obligation and on the other enforced gratitude, complicated by loss and hurt. Each family was given a smallholding – on average thirty-seven acres of forest and thirty-seven of arable land. Some 40,000 of these farms were created, and three quarters of the Karelian families ended up with more land in 'Moscow Finland' than they had held in Ladoga Karelia. The people from Vyborg and Sortavala went to the cities.

Like many others, the Tikkas waited years for their land allocation. Until the spring of 1951 they lived on a series of vegetable patches provided by the government and intended to keep refugee discontent under control. But at last their turn came and they arrived with their few belongings at Saario. There was nothing but forest here. It was as though they had arrived on that other sort of frontier in the American colonies, weirdly re-enacting the ideal of pioneer life in their little seventy-four-acre government-provided enclave. There was nothing but the forest trees and the neat Thoreau-style economy of the frontier. Mr Tikka cut some of the trees, built a tiny house with the trunks, stacked the smaller branches for firewood and planted the first crop of potatoes in the land he had cleared. He showed me a grey photograph of himself with his wife and son and daughter outside that first cottage. He had been handsome with shone-back hair and the whole cottage had been twelve square metres in area, three by four, with the forest crowding around it. And other photographs of the potato crop, flowering on its ridges in the room of trees.

Since then he had cleared the whole of the seventy-four acres and had rebuilt the house with barns and cowsheds beside it. Every piece of furniture in the house was painted bright gloss green and he had made all of it. The huge stone oven that went through the kitchen wall

47

to heat the sitting-room next to it he had built too. All the dead animals that lined the walls – grouse and capercaillie, a brown hare and a white hare, a weasel, a mink and a lynx, the head of a wolf and the skull of a bear – he had shot them all. The household was pure patriarchy and his wife was his servant. She never sat down at the table with us, but brought the coffee and the cakes, and removed the empty cups. Like the painted, polished used wood that was everywhere in the house, and the arrangement itself of house and barn and fields, the Tikkas were utterly sustained by the patterns into which they had been born. One would have thought that thirty years in this place, literally making it what it was, would have instilled some kind of loyalty towards it, but in Onni's mind Saario would always come second to Ruskeala. The land itself here was all right, but the weather was much worse, colder than over there, because at Saario there were no lakes. Ladoga itself softens the weather, and crops always grew in Ruskeala. Here you could not be so sure and anyway half his land was wet, little better than marsh.

Saario, this courageous and admirable transformation of circumstances, was an exercise in re-creation, in rebuilding the place that had once been lost. Like eighteenth-century hermits at the bottom of a Northamptonshire garden, the Tikkas were living an idea and a memory. But they *had* left in the first place. Whatever he might now say about the fertility of Ruskeala and the sweetness of the Ladoga air, they had left it for some other abstract idea which they could have known only as 'Finland'. In confirmation, and as a parting shot, Mr Tikka told me that *The Times* was printed on Finnish paper and that Churchill used to send Sibelius a cigar every birthday.

The North Karelia Beauty Festival paraded hair-dos in front of a shabbier audience. In the still air of a sequined dining-room the exiled caryatids in a cosmetic haze bore windswept structures with a rigid grace. The word was *permanentin*. A Rotary Club choir in red bow ties sang songs of the borderland, and they smiled. A football player, the wife of the Burgermeister of Hof in Bavaria, last year's winner, the 1927 third place and a television doctor judged them, and they smiled. They made short speeches, seven with bridgework made perfect with flaws. The prettiest said almost nothing and won. And, having won, smiled. You could see why she had left the smile *hors de concours*, as it puffed and flaked the edges. She would go far and was a wise choice, since the competition was intended to select the whole woman. The compère, who edited *Helsinki Vog*, had a different sort of hair-do, which ingeniously reproduced the weather conditions prevailing in

Finland at the time as seen from a Meteosat. The *friseurs* of Joensuu would be enjoying a lucrative year. Everybody agreed that Vog's frosted cyclonic effect was startling.

Professor Heikki Kirkinen appeared the next morning in brown-tinted glasses and a beret. In his youth he had taught at the Sorbonne and he nurtured the whiffs of Left Bank style. A habit of slapping one hand with a plastic ruler held in the other for emphasis. 'Karelia is a *vitrine*', he told me, 'of the laws of history. And it is those laws, my dear young man, to which we are all sub-slap-ordinate. The history of Karelia is the history of division.' Ruler held with two fists meeting in the centre, indicating the history of division. 'You will hear people complain that Karelia was destroyed in 1940 and 1944, that national *intégrité* of Finland was cut*jabup*slap. But the *frontière* between Finland and the Soviet Union now is the same as it was in the eighteenth and also in the thirteenth. Finland is *cloué* – swift downstroke – 'between East and West. One must look at the entire history. In 1617 Sweden dominated the entire Karelia because of war. In 1809 Russia achieved Karelia and Finland because of war and international power *politique*. But these situations are not *équilibre*.' Slap. I looked with concern at his beaten hand. The ball of the thumb had turned a little pink. 'Each time East or West has found itself a little weaker, the situation has returned to where we are now. Cultural Kekkonenism.'

He stroked his pink hand with the blunt head of the ruler. 'It is *axiomatique* that history is not only the recounting of facts but the apparition of the past in the full luminosity of the present. We are slaves of the era. But for me, for 90% of Finns, the present foreign policy is objectively right. Finland can only pursue a *politique d'éffacement*. The *nécessité* dictates. And this is not, as I say, a treachery to the history of Karelia. It is the fulfilment. This has always been the border country, between East and West, between orthodox and western Christianity, whether Roman or Lutheran. We still have 65,000 Orthodox in Finland. There is a church down the road. We are not the bridgehead, as you say, of the West' – spiral waving of ruler – 'pushed out into the East. We are more border people than frontier people. Can you comprehend? We are divided ourselves.'

He went on to explain some of the complexities of the Kalevala to me. He talked about The Plunder of Sampo, The Rune of Lemminkäinen, The Forging of the Golden Virgin, The Knee-Wound of Väinämöinen and The Incantation of the Birth of Iron. There were songs about the sadness of women and children, and also drunk songs and joy songs. But the point was this. (Steady downbeats on to hand, now landing softly.) Finnish scholars have claimed the Kalevala songs were invented in western Finland and mysteriously drifted eastwards to Karelia, where Elias Lönnrot found them in the 1830s and 1840s. Soviet scholars have claimed an eastern origin. And it is true that elements of Russian, Byzantine and even Persian myths are to be found in them, as well as Viking and Germanic influences. But this debate misses the obvious point. The Kalevala songs are the songs of the borderland. They grew up and flowered in the forests of Karelia, the remote borderlands of both Sweden-Finland and Novgorod-Moscow, far away from the centres of culture and church influence to east and west, outside any regular taxation until the seventeenth century. It was ironic that in the nineteenth century Finnish nationalists should have taken the Kalevala to heart as the core of their nationalism, as the songs in essence were eclectic, pre-nationalist expressions of something that was universal. But, the professor said, the irony goes a step further. Unwittingly those nationalists were right to choose the Kalevala, since the character of Finland itself, its geographical and historical destiny, was and is to be a borderland, outside the narrow confines of nationalist self-sufficiency and *amour propre*.

He laid the ruler on the table beside him and showed me a tree trunk standing in the corner of the office. It was a real pine tree, diagonally slashed in chevrons which the pine sap would have run down. The tree had once grown and been marked in Russian Karelia, White Sea Karelia, and, when it had fallen, had floated down the rivers across the border to Joensuu. A member of the faculty had seen it floating in the river, picked it out, cleaned it up and presented it to Heikki Kirkinen as an expression of Karelia, the whole of Karelia, itself.

We went to look at the Orthodox church. The building was covered in demure and dowdy little bits of daring. It was like a very odd translation, Shakespeare in German parsed into English. It could have served as a station whose stationmaster had grand ideas in private about 'oriental inheritance' and had elaborated flourishes on the simple Finnish structure without planning permission. He would have dreaded the coming of the regional supervisor, who would order the removal of the green onion domes, the burning of the lacy gutterboards, the whitewashing of the flashes under the eaves, the dismantling of the golden crosses on the pinnacles, the nailing up of the star-shaped windows and the grand auctioning of the two green copper bells so the station might return to its simple brown utility.

The church was locked up and neglected in the snow. No priests to be seen. I thought of Father Job in St Panteleimon on Mount Athos 1,500 miles away in the Aegean winter, nursing dreams of an

Orthodox revival in Asia, while the great barracks of the pre-Revolution Russian monastery rotted around him, lived in by ten monks, built for 2,000. He used to tell me about the 'fallout of the Soviet Empire' – he came from Cleveland, Ohio – in the plush formal sitting-room of the monastery, where lithographs of L'vov and the Tsarevich hung high up and leaning out from the walls. He dreamt of the day when a gush of young men would come south to the monastery from Russia. It was something that Professor Kirkinen had hinted at too. 'Europe does not end at this border,' he said. 'The East begins in Asia Minor, in the Near East and in Asia. That is the real distinction and this may be significant for the Soviet Union in the future. I will say no more.'

The night train to Helsinki was segregated into male and female compartments. There can be no trans-sexual sharing on Finnish night trains, at least in second class. Separated by a plastic wall, our bunks exactly opposite each other and about an inch apart, we travelled sideways through the night in silence. Olivia devised a code, but the wall turned out to be knock-proof. The line swerves round the south east of Finland, through Parikkala and Imatra in an arc tangential to the frontier and then west to Helsinki. The track had been laid after the war, when the main line through Niirala, Sortavala and Vyborg had been cut off by the new frontier. So we swayed head to foot, foot to head, braking to the left, moving off again to the right, along the new guarantor of Finnish self-sufficiency, the rewiring in a house of which part had been bombed and demolished.

One corner of Helsinki Central was full of Arctic 'shock troops'. Some of them had suitcases with little wheels at the edge and others had violet eyeshadow. This party of mature students from Idaho, group-equipped for the European winter, was waiting for the train to Rovaniemi, the Las Vegas of the north. It was eight in the morning. The colonel had them netted in a loose formation by the left luggage window while she negotiated terms with a porter. One man licked at an ice-cream that matched his wife's eyelids and they were all dressed in the full combat outfit that had seemed necessary in Boise. One or two of the uniforms had been ordered a size tight. Olivia, returned from the front and bowed backwards with her pregnancy, waved at them in reassurance and her own extraordinary Arctic ensemble. I don't think they noticed; Europe – and the colonel – had been hell.

We walked out into the Helsinki streets. Old snow ridged them. We had spent a morning here before flying up to Ivalo and slid straight back into a café called Oh Happy Days Trattoria, like old Helsinki hands. I'd nursed a Len Deighton image of the city, before going there, as a present-day equivalent of wartime Lisbon, Casablanca or Dublin, where the sides met and deals were made. From a bus I saw a house which Michael Caine had walked up to across a frozen lake. It was the CIA nerve-centre for northern Europe. The door had slid open by light sensors. In the film it had looked marvellous: Finnish Gothic, painted yellow and grey, with some spruces a little menacingly around the back, all cut into the ice-edged December light. It was, after all, a cold war and only natural that the CIA should choose a house that looked like a spy-nest on the edge of a frozen lake. It was where defectors, searching around for some place to defect to, would naturally gravitate. The house even *looked* like Robert Vaughn.

A more ordinary Helsinki quickly substitutes. Even the Finns are now a little bored with the monumental centre of the city being used as a replacement Leningrad by western film-makers. Red Russian banners and actors in Soviet uniform were at one stage in the 1970s almost continuously in occupation of Senate Square. The BBC now favours Dundee. But there is some historical irony. When Tsar Alexander I became Grand Duke of Finland in 1809, the duchy had no capital of its own. Stockholm had been the capital of Sweden-Finland and the small university and episcopal town of Turku, across the Baltic from Uppsala, the administrative centre for the province. Old Helsinki was burnt down in the war by which Sweden lost Finland, and after it Alexander created an unprecedently handsome capital for the new duchy, with senate, cathedral, library and university all in the best Leningrad style. Finland was to serve as a model for the liberal ideas Alexander held at the time, particularly admiring the freedom of the Finnish peasants and their representation as one of the four estates in the Diet. He hoped to extend this liberalism through the empire as a whole. Finland's expensive new capital was a grand expression of its independence from St Petersburg, less than 200 miles away across the gulf. But the capital intended by the Tsar to show its difference from Russia is now taken to indicate all the influence of Empire, an imported and superimposed idea of government and culture, translated from Rome, through Paris, Berlin, St Petersburg itself, and dumped here on the shores of the Baltic. It came to serve as an example in the negative for all the later Finnish nationalists. Sibelius lived in a bare pine house with no rugs on the floor, unshaped logs for beams like Frū Kasereff's and no hint of a cornice or a volute. The President of Finland still lives in the Romanov palace, but, when it came to siting the parliament building in 1924, a place was chosen well over on the other side of the city from Alexandersgatan near the National Museum. There you find it today in a rather tough, unstuccoed and slightly pink granite.

Everyone in Oh Happy Days had been bullied at school. They ate microwaved slices of antiseptic pizza in silence. Only Olivia's high, liquid laughter broke it. The style of the place was plastic eclectic out of Knightsbridge Veronese. It was genuinely nowhere. Olivia was going home and we had a last lunch in this space station. It seemed the right choice of venue at the time. She had to be wrapped up in two extra jerseys and a coat to hide the bulge. Airline authorities dislike the idea of pregnant women on planes; it is something to do with air pressure. So I said goodbye to the layered bundle on her airline bus. It would only be three weeks before I, too, got home for the birth and it felt like an emigration.

A thaw started in the afternoon. Wet pools of grey water mimicked the pavement until you sank into them. I booked into a room like a Swedish prison cell with a view of a multi-storey car park filling the window. Ordinary Helsinki. Tea in a place on the *esplanadi* designed to have *fin de siècle* appeal, and full of dead souls in jeans. A boy sailor in black Baltic blue drank tea with a girl. They tidied back the bent-over pages of a magazine on the table between them. Her chin doubled if she looked below the level, and he coughed exactly, bringing a fist up neatly to his mouth.

Late in the afternoon I went to visit Major Saksella in the headquarters of the frontier guard. His office was on the fifth floor of Korkeavuorenkatu 21. It was one of those *Jugendstil* streets where *putti* manhandle logs between the third and the fourth floors, and swallows the size of horses dive three storeys between hermaphrodite caryatids on one side and ecstatic Medusas on the other. But the military office was plain, the grandfather of all those sterile interiors that line the frontier. A cage lift took me up. A Finnish border mark, such as I had never been able to reach, stood in the lino corridor, five feet high in blue and white stripes.

The major was still in a meeting and his secretary showed me into his room. It was scarcely more human. He, too, had a log in one corner and a small axe in the middle of one wall. These were the domestic details. The rest of the room exhibited a rational and inscrutable anonymity.

A prepschool master bounced in. It was Tintin twenty years on, become district commissioner and a little paunchy. Pigeon-eye tweed jacket, creaky black lace-ups with large silver eyelets and a Boy Scout twinkle air. 'Hal*lo*!' he freshed. 'How was Inge Torhag?' I hadn't said a word. 'Such a very charming man, and what an interesting career. And Jane, is it?'

'Yes, Jane.'

'But you know you really should have got in touch. Naruska's all very well, but we could have shown you the lot. But never mind. There we are. Horses for courses, different strokes for different folks, and here we go!' He had been in the room fifteen seconds.

Major Saksella gave me an illustrated talk on the role of the frontier guard in Finland. It lasted three hours. I learnt about the financing (Ministry of the Interior), manning (3,500 paid employees, 1,000 conscripts), organization (cephalopodian) and duties (nationally important) of the frontier guard. But everything was in the asides. Major Saksella *loved* his job, it was the best job in the world. 'We are the national washerwomen,' he said. 'I joined the guard because it was the only way I could get paid to be a Boy Scout at twenty-five and now I find myself working in the national laundry. The frontier keeps the country clean. A clean frontier is a clean country.' I asked him if any codes of conduct had been imposed on the frontier guard in 1944 and 1947. There were, of course, rules: no open fires near the border, no strong light to be shone across it, nothing to be physically thrown over it and nothing to be put in border rivers. 'You must never show your worst side,' he said, and bent over waving his buttocks in the air. 'But we are not going to imitate them. Ah ha!' He suddenly pounced half-way down the room. 'Zoo, wort half wee hair.' This was a Russian accent. 'No, no, no, no. None of that bunkum. We are not reading the orders like the Devil reads the Bible.' Major Saksella beamed at me like Little Jack Horner.

'You are lucky,' he said at one moment. 'Your frontiers are formed by nature.'

'Not in Ireland.'

'Not in Ireland.' He whistled inwards. 'But grossly. We have only this small light strip that is supposed to be holy. Yes, we will always mention the holiness of the border.' He put one hand flat in mid air and pointed with the other at the line where the green carpet met the white lino. It was a familiar prop. 'Do I step over?' He stepped over. 'No.' He stepped back. 'Finns will not enjoy going over the border. It is physically possible. There is no fence. Only the posts like the one in the corridor, and the vistas between them.' He thumped his chest. The three felt-tips in his breast pocket jumped. 'We must in our hearts let the borderline be. We must let it be like the table in church. In summer the guards clear the line from one mark to the next. They must be careful that they cut the trees and the brussels to fall westwards into Finland.'

'Why does the border guard return refugees to Russia?' I asked. An Estonian had been sent back two months before.

'I cannot discuss that question on the record. If you have any understanding of the situation of Finland, you do not need to ask the question.'

We moved on to safer ground. The major talked about the Fates and Destiny, and at length about Bell Jet-Ranger helicopters. But he was not in love with the technology. He preferred the Davy Crockett style.

'It must be private in the frontier zone,' he said. 'I mean silent. We patrol on skis, not the ski-scooters. In summer we go with dogs. They are very clever to snooze your tracks.' I, at least, had been effectively snoozed, dog or no dog. He couldn't resist a final dig. 'So it's tomorrow you go to Leningrad? *Across* the border this time?' How did he know? Not the man at the airport. He hadn't taken the details of the Russian visa. Perhaps the railway company, part of the everyday procedure. I was in the dark. He saw me out as far as the lift. 'Now don't go playing any of this 007 stuff, will you?' he asked.

'Good Lord, no,' I said. 'I wouldn't have the foggiest how to start.'

I spent the evening in O'Malley's, Yrjonkatu 28. No sort of an O'Malley had ever been near the place. There was Guinness and Jameson's for sale; there were mirrors behind the barmaids and mirrors dividing up the bar; a few sombre drunk solitaries watched the froth slide down from the rim to the residue. But it was too clean and the silence too neat to be Irish and *there was no television*. The lights were dimmer-switched down in the suffocating congruity of it all. This indeed was a bad translation. I talked to the ugly bargirl with warts. 'It is a wish to make it Irish,' she said. That much had been clear. I thought of William Blake's pub in Enniskillen, where a man in a fawn wool suit with clocks on his socks talked to the television. He had a high and rather strangulated voice and his legs were wrapped three times around the barstool's. 'You're a jackanapes fool of a boy,' he told Jan Leeming. 'You're wrong, you're wrong. You're mistaken in that ever since you got on there. Are you even Christian? Some of those boys out in the Middle East aren't Christian boys at all. Don't talk to me about Paisley. Are you trying to suggest I'm a Paisley man? Don't you come in here and start talking the fock at me like that. Are you a man or a mouse? If you are I'll marry ya.' He wouldn't have lasted long in O'Malley's.

Jokke Lehikoinen interrupted from beyond the nearest mirror. 'Do you believe in cart?' he asked.

'Cart?'

'Yes, cart. Are you are cartly man?' Jokke meant God. But from that moment of clarity, the conversation followed the froth downhill. He had renounced sex for twelve months yesterday and, somehow connected with it, had just finished as Father Christmas. These two characters – Cart and Santa – became impossibly confused. He could be hired by telephone in Finland for about a hundred marks, Jokke said, and his mother was one of the few people still to believe in him. Only one Christmas in ten was 'black' nowadays. People were never quite sure if they wanted him to have a white woolly beard and all the rest of it. You had to feel sad. I vigorously agreed. He wished me the very best of blessed good luck for the baby. Perhaps I could hire him for the ceremony? I told Jokke he was the first person I would think of. And then, on leaving, he said in a ratty little giggle, 'Have some nice nightmares, please.' I was ready for something different.

3
A Political Mirhab

In the rough-cut granite station, where the ticket offices but not the platforms are roofed over, the snow fell on to my glasses and starred and slurred the platform lights. The Russian train was in. It had five carriages and a large windowless van labelled 'post' in Cyrillic at the end. The whole train was a dull military green with a muddy yellow stripe along the side and an antique solidity in its construction. It was the kind of unglossed train which you or I might design, with obvious parallel constructional ridges running the length of it. Nosed into the smart and understated materialism of the Finnish station, the Russian train looked hopelessly abroad, a ploughman in a wine bar. Metal badges were pinned to the sides saying CCCP with the hammer and sickle superimposed on a silver globe and all of it cupped in sheaves of wheat. Below each globe was a lozenge, where the hammer and sickle appeared again, this time on the lightning zig-zag of electricity. 'Communism', Lenin had said, 'is Soviet power plus electrification.'

Kathrin Elsa Fischer from Göttingen was in the compartment. The lady attendant stood in the passageway door. Her hair emerged from under her forage cap in tufts of cushion-stuffing, and she clucked at the match she had made. Elsa was twenty. The compartment was an operating theatre and she was the anaesthetic. The train jolted off: eight hours to Leningrad. Elsa began to talk about the coming doom for the world and her hopes for Europe. She was a disciple of Egon Bahr and of something she called Tripartite Games Theory, which involved a completely neutralized, demilitarized, defrontierized and integrated Europe from Ireland to the Ukraine, which would somehow guarantee world peace by example. She didn't like Kohl and she didn't like Hitler. 'We need a realistic dreamer as Chancellor,' she said. I thought that might do as a description of Hitler. 'You're too English to speak of. The English only trust someone who looks at the end of his nose.'

We drifted sideways and looked out of the continuous window at the snowed-in huts and the washy brown landscape, at the grey brown and the grey red of the weatherboarded barns. 'Even Petra is getting dirty in the system,' Elsa said suddenly and then smoked. She was studying social work in Helsinki and Leningrad, somehow under the auspices of the German embassy or consulate in each place. She had a red diplomatic passport and her father was an ambassador somewhere, but she didn't like him much. She hugged her knees. 'He lay down two years in front of Stalingrad and never reached it. This is a much more happier way to go to Russia.' Elsa had been to Leningrad before and had views on Russia and the Russians. 'The Soviet system has many economic problems,' she told me. 'The shoes are very bad quality and the dentists are not good. But I like to look in the people's faces and see something there.'

'Apart from the teeth, you mean?'

She pondered. 'The little old women at the markets ... it is a country of long suffering. I don't like the Soviet Union, but I like all the Russian people.' She looked wanly outside. 'They don't like old things. They like everything new. You can get lots of antiques very cheaply. But they really *are* people, you know. Some people just don't understand that.' History was a blank in Elsa's mind. If things were perfect we would all be roaming free on the uninterrupted surface of the planet, in a state of nature that was different from Hobbes's, because people were always *really* people on it and nice to one another. As it was, we were imposed on by regimes of various kinds – the kinds scarcely distinguishable – like a series of magazine diets.

The train had stopped and oil-tankers drew heavily past the forest, squealing on the points. 'It's so like *Anna Karenina* by Tolstoy,' Elsa said and went back to *Shōgun*. The book didn't hold her and so we returned to the philosophy of history. 'I will tell you something very personally,' Elsa said. 'My mother died of crabs.'

'Oh? Did it tickle?'

'*Crabs.*' She meant cancer, but at that moment, from another compartment down the corridor, came the enormously amplified message that someone in Birmingham, Alabama, had the boogie-woogie in his soul and was enjoying the feeling.

'Yes,' I said.

'And once she knew she'd got them, she was very happy. She didn't cook or wash any more, but we were always getting very closer. And maybe the world, if it knew it was going to die, would behave like us.'

'Are you talking about nuclear war?'

'Yes, nuclear war, pollution, AIDS, acid rain, abortions, the forests – do you know that the forests are dying?'

'Do you believe in Armageddon?'

'I must first get myself right before I can think of ideas,' she said. She hated the police, but on New Year's Day in Berlin she had been saved from a drunken mob of men by a squad of policemen. 'It was like a night-club,' she said, and returned again to oriental violence.

In the corridor a Kenyan with perfect teeth and a red leather tie was going home. He had been in Sweden studying paper-making technology for ten months. He had never phoned his wife in Kenya. What was the point? He was going to see her eventually anyway for free.

Next door two old Australians were feeling the cold. I had met them in the London Intourist office in Regent Street, where bored and ignorant English girls had told them that Leningrad was OK for two days, Moscow for four. Mrs Ride had wanted to go in a camper, but Mr Ride knew a train would be more restful. And had he been right? They were slightly bushed, but knew they couldn't have covered the ground in a caravan. They'd really got the travel bug now and this was their fourth trip abroad. They'd done America comprehensively in a camper. He pulled on an extra jersey. AUSTRALIA oxbowed in 72-point across his spreading ex-pectorals. 'It's nice to see the old countries?' he asked.

We were all here to cross the line: the Australians to go over the top, to another sort of place, the trench analogy; the Kenyan to get the cheaper flight home and Kathrin to demonstrate to herself, if nobody else, the universality of her vision. The Eagles played on the train Tannoy and then a Russian imitation of them.

We were passing through the country of the Winter War, where the Finns had held the Russian divisions between November 1939 and February 1940. To the world's surprise, Finland succeeded where Poland had failed the previous autumn. They were preventing the Nazi–Soviet vice from closing. The Finns were pitifully equipped. In the summer of 1939 they had no anti-tank guns and only a couple of dozen tanks, some of which were antiquated, the others unarmed. The Karelian defences were 'hardly more than a sparse string of machine-gun nests, unsatisfactory tank traps, inadequate pill-boxes and trenches hastily dug by schoolboys and students'. That is how Mannerheim described what the Russians, invoking Maginot and Siegfried, called the Mannerheim Line. The title was an excuse to explain their failure to break it until late in February. In fact, the Russians had underestimated the Finnish will to resist. The bloody civil war in Finland, only twenty years previously, had split the country between red and white to its roots, and there was lasting bitterness. But the Russian attack united the country and the Finns were on home ground.

The winter was one of the coldest of the century. A clear blue high settled over southern Finland for weeks on end. It meant beautiful short days, and nights that always sank to between −40°c and −50°c. The Russians were unable to penetrate along a broad front and, attempting to advance in column along the few roads, they allowed the Finns to create massive, vulnerable traffic jams by destroying the first few vehicles, which blocked the road. The Finns then encircled them in a tactic known as *motti*. The word meant the cord with which a bundle of firewood is tied.

Once the line broke at Summa, the Winter War was soon over and Ladoga Karelia surrendered on 13 March in Moscow.

Karelia was recaptured by the end of August 1941, just over two months after the Continuation War had started. Finnish troops stopped at the old border, except in East Karelia, long part of Russia and long considered part of the homeland by Finnish nationalists. None were involved in the German siege of Leningrad, nor in the operations against the Murmansk railway, despite repeated German demands. Mannerheim was adamant that no substance should be given to the longstanding Russian fears that Leningrad was vulnerable to Finnish attack. This may have been the critical factor in Finland's avoiding, at the end of the war, the fate of Estonia, Latvia and Lithuania on the one hand, and of Poland, Czechoslovakia and the Balkans on the other.

In June 1944 the Russians launched their major offensive in Karelia. They were not to repeat the mistakes of the Winter War. They destroyed the Finnish defences before the attack with a barrage from artillery pieces placed on an average every two and a half metres along the whole front.

Night fell as we came to the frontier, into the birches and lion grass like seedlings in the snow. Kathrin said she usually got a redhead at borders and we all felt the generalized guilt. Smokey and Doors had been turned off about fifty miles short and now in the barren, silent train we filled in the forms. 'With me and in my luggage', it was suggested, 'I have':

1. Weapons of all descriptions and ammunition.
2. Narcotics and appliances for the use of.

Emptied into print, it was the interrogator's trick of telling you that he knows you're a criminal, so why not save time. The forms meant nothing. They were to real interrogation what the frontiers themselves are to a real front line, no more than formalized repetitions of an old stance, a creeping barrage in sullen paralysis.

The guards arrived, stars on their lapels, pancake-brim hats, the old-fashioned leather knee boots, like an eighteenth-century hunts-man's, that fall and ruckle at the ankle beneath the greatcoats with a rich, star-pressed button in the vent. These bulked-out young men searched us. It was the most intimate search I have ever undergone. I watched myself and the others in our fallible, modern, train-crushed clothes being felt and prodded by these human icons in their plain uniforms conceived on a scale different from ours with all its civilian affected trivia, its national remarks embroidered on part-woollen pull-overs. No one except a lover would dare come this close. Here was Leviathan with nimble fingers sifting through our clothes and under-clothes as if we were dead or under five, pulling out old sweet-wrappers from pockets, the ends of his fingers encountering that gritty residue, half sand, half fluff, which lines the hemmed-in bottom of a pocket, like a doctor reaching down for memories and feeling between my T-shirt and my skin. It was all done in silence, making obvious what at home – or at least away from the borders of social existence – remains discreet: the power of the state. Perhaps this explains frontier guilt. The only other times at which you come up against state-sponsored intimacy are when you have done something wrong, or when the state thinks you have.

The train moved off into the Karelian Autonomous Soviet Socialist Republic. I had wanted to spend the night in Vyborg, the old frontier town, but in Regent Street they had said it was not an Intourist city and so we passed it in my sleep.

Kathrin's sexless legs were tight up against the seat. The corner of her purple neckerchief was in her mouth. She was in a twit. The train was late and she was worried that the consul would be cross. Lenin-grad began to surround us and the dark patch of Kathrin's spittle began to spread out from the corner of the cloth.

The train stopped, Kathrin disappeared and I never saw her again. This was the Finland Station, where Lenin had arrived on 3 April 1917 to a huge crowd, searchlights and the Marseillaise, and from where he drove in triumph and an armoured car to the Bolshevik headquarters, the ex-mansion of a prima ballerina and ex-mistress of the Tsar. But that was sixty-seven years ago and I had landed on the moon. The soft snow and faerie lights of the scene from the train window had become slush and neon: the football-field square in front of the station, the crowds waiting in fatty nodules for the trolley buses, whose contacts flashed at junctions and which were smeared up the sides in an arc from the wet snow. On the corners of the buildings in the square neon stars and sickles. The frontier was next to my skin and I was completely alone. I moved around the station. Lenin's wood-burning locomotive in a large glass box. If Lenin had been a capitalist revolutionary, perhaps they would have preserved his carriage. But the image of the great prime mover of history boxed up, cleaned up, repainted, unsmudged by use, literally untouchable – there was something in that. Drifting thoughts in a frightened isolation. I tried to remember where I had seen this sort of fear before. It was in Crossmaglen in Northern Ireland, where for safety's sake the army can come and go only by helicopter. I was talking to a soldier through the netting cage that surrounded his sentry post. A Marine corporal from Portsmouth, he was white in the face and very clean. He kept flicking his head round in automatic fear. He, too, was surrounded by the frontier. Like an actor who had expected a proscenium arch – an obvious here creating an equally obvious there – and an audience looking at him from only one direction, he finds himself instead in a theatre in the round. There was no cloth, no cardboard in which the look-out holes could be cut. In fact, he was surrounded by a sort of absence. Only the eye sockets in his skin and the little mouth at the end of the rifle showed that there was an inside and an outside, something to be defended and something to be defended from. The frontier covered his face in a sort of cosmetic, a blanching compact cream that kept him perfect. But there was a paper thinness in it too, as though the surrounding hostility had leaked in through those holes and infected and stained him inside, colonizing those areas of fear and hostility to self which it could rely on for sympathy, leaving this soldier paper thin, a thin mould of a man embedded in the matrix of his fear.

At the information desk there was a large woman in a black uniform. It was undone to show a little of her slip and bosom, with the gold on the uniform flapping backwards and forwards as she denied any knowledge of information. I had no map of Leningrad and no roubles. It was ten at night. I wondered if this was the purpose of being abroad, to test that romantic liberal capitalist bourgeois here-primitive idea that we are all alone anyway. But great provinces of me loved the panic. A beautiful girl walked past with her arm hooked into a soldier's. He couldn't help marching and she didn't look at me. I began to prepare a phrase from the phrase book, and instead found myself accelerating down the story of disaster I found there:

Here it is. Very cheap. Look out. Come in. This way. What's the matter? You are right. You are wrong. It doesn't work. Very well.

Nothing else. By chance. On purpose. What's this? Who's this? Where are we going? Where are you going? I don't know. Leave me alone. Go away. I didn't do it. What must I do? What have I done? When do we get there? In five days' time.

'Good evening, Mr Nicolson.' I had been snoozing again. 'I am here to meet you, but I have no car.' He was a handsome man with a moustache and a jaw and a woollen ski-hat. He told me the way to the hotel. 'We like to meet individual travellers.' No hint of triumph like Major Saksella. Only a dull job done late on a Thursday night, part of the structure of things.

I walked through the dark and the slushy streets of the half-lit city. All the gritty, dampened details of Leningrad appeared marvellous in the night. I passed a steamed-up window where a saxophone was playing and then three squads of midshipmen in ranks of four, marching through the slush puddles with suitcases in their gloved left hands. Over a long bridge across the Neva, where battered ice-floes drifted westwards and out of the light towards the Baltic and where conveyor belts at the back of trucks collected the snow, shoved on to them with broad hardboard shovels. Past a gas flame in a park blown sideways in the wind like a flag, stroking at and melting the snow on that side. A war memorial. Two men in the middle of the night langlaufed between the trees. It was the sort of mood which Kathrin imagined would grip the world once nuclear weapons (and power stations) were banned. It was my own private transitory utopia.

There was dancing in the hotel. A Russian band with blue and red lights that flashed around the drum played western songs. 'Take this badge off of me', they sang, and people danced in front of them, *Nomenklatura* members for all I know. The men were in short suits that stayed buttoned up, the women in ugly electrostatic dresses, all of them kicking their heels and throwing their elbows apart in their fatness and plastered hair. Redemption Day in Cookham churchyard. But I had no partner and I went to bed in my ninth-floor beechwood room.

Chimneys and golden spires stood up out of the dun mass in the morning. Smoke lay across the city and the Neva was lined with palaces and admiralties in colour. It was a show city, playing at being a city like that perspective painting in Urbino in which temples, arcades, roof gardens and entablatures are all conglomerated and disposed to make a street and squares. But there was more here, the toy was a better toy for having the half-mile-wide Neva cut through it. The river is a continental and authoritarian presence in Leningrad.

Everything is in its width. It is not sunk and forgotten like the Spree or the Thames, but flowing and existing on the same flat level as the streets that were built on its marshes. The great river, coming out of the East like the memory of Asia, draining Ladoga, would be enough in itself to create an appetite for Fabergé, for some demonstration that life is independent of the scale of rivers like this and continents. With the Neva on one's doorstep one has to show that geography is not everything and that it is possible to concentrate one's luxuries, even one's values, into the palm of a hand. The Neva models the idea of Russia itself – the continental country the size of South America.

When Peter the Great founded his new capital in 1703 at the bog-ridden and diseased mouth of the Neva, it was still foreign territory, taken from Sweden in the Great Northern War. Not until 1721 did it officially become part of the Empire itself. The choice of site was breathtakingly daring. It was as though the Israelis in 1967 had chosen for their grand new capital a virgin site on the banks of the River Jordan. For the heart of the new empire Peter had taken a place on its most exposed and vulnerable rim. He made a capital out of a frontier post, a listening-post, its antennae tuned to Europe. The strangeness of St Petersburg, its mixture of audacity and vulnerability, its sense of unnaturalness and imbalance stem from that conscious effort of turning an edge into a middle.

In March 1918, only five months after the Revolution, Moscow once more became the capital. It was a return to source, a shrinking inwards to the central blank bastions of the Kremlin, leaving the great strung-out façades of the imperial city, flamboyant in their length and repetitions, to the edge of things, as a fantastic appendix in the body of Russia.

Leningrad is a divided capital, not in the crude and brutal way of Berlin, but more deeply. It has all the readable trappings and structures of power – of centrality – but the power is not there. It is a lived-in Palmyra, a perfect archaeological actuality, beautifully maintained and invisibly decayed. This is not a function of history, but how St Petersburg always appeared to be. Nineteenth-century intellectuals romanticized the life of old Muscovy as 'organic', because the life in St Petersburg was so empty-centred, a city where not only the houses but also the trees and the people were made of stone. Beneath the palaces there was always the ghost of the Ingrian swamplands, the unformed reality which the baroque façades could never efface. The more glorious the structures of the city, the more total the denial and the more bitter the parody of the truth they avoided. But there was always the Neva and for Pushkin the ghastly image of the bogland cemeteries:

> The railings, columns, ornamental tombs
> Beneath which lie the city's rotting dead,
> Crammed somehow side by side into the swamp
> Like greedy guests crowding at some poor table . . .
> Urns which the thieves have twisted off their columns,
> Fresh slippery graves that open in expectation
> Of a new tenant on the following day.

This radical sensation of foreignness-to-itself embedded in Petrine Russia was set against the knowledge of the great mass of Russian people, who were true – in this schematic arrangement of things – to themselves. It is the distance, in effect, between the palaces and the grey river they confront, a meeting of opposites, which was the mainspring of the great Russian culture and of the Revolution it produced. The contradiction reached one sort of emblematic climax in the early morning of 17 December 1916, when the trussed body of Rasputin – his name means debauchee – thick with cyanide and with two bullets in it, was driven in the boot of a Rolls-Royce to the banks of the Neva and pushed through a hole in the ice, where he drowned – the corpse of one Russia floating away unseen on the subglacial current of another.

I walked everywhere in Leningrad. A form of distrust. On one's feet there is no danger of losing touch. All tourists do it. I was absorbed in the crowd. In a multinational state there was no reason why I should be taken for a foreigner. Other people had American jeans like mine, white faces like mine, Finnish anoraks and haircuts like mine, even a sort of wandering tourist air like mine, on the look-out for specifics with their string bags and, instead, coasting about on the empty carapace of the city. Perhaps my fur hat made me look Russian. I was always being waved at by the contents of Intourist buses with that medicinal health visitor look which meant superior pity. It was by turns revolting and pitiable itself. But nobody else had my glasses. After a day I understood why: they looked like Trotsky's.

Frontiers on the mind, and I saw division and unconnectedness everywhere. The constant Communist placards, the wrong set of subtitles in a film. In the great semicircular piazza formed by the green back of the Winter Palace and the curving yellow arms of Rossi's ministries, a low podium had been built in a finely graded hierarchy of shallow levels. It was empty and wet with snow-melt. Ice-blocks in the gutters behind it fell and shattered on the girder tower which carried the badge of state and then down in shards on to the seats themselves. Opposite this bank of empty speakers, a present absence like a political mihrab, was the equally notional audience, slapped on to the austere face of the ministries – the General Staff building – blocking out windows and pilasters over five storeys and forty bays. A panorama of square-jawed heroes and bosomed women were grouped in far-seeing clusters and mutually sustaining solidarities. Like St Petersburg itself, it was a picture of handsome irrelevance. When the meeting was held, the exhortations from the podium would float uninterruptedly over the heads of the real people and arrive at those beautiful painted landscapes across the square. It was a vision of military and industrial pastoral in which communication was perfect. There was no 50% divorce rate, no alcohol in those guts and no abscess in those gums. But seen this morning it was a terrible joke. The ideal people towards whom one was meant to strive appeared, instead, like an impossible upper class, from which everybody in the square, every dun, baggy, atomized human body down there, was cut off. It was like putting up posters of the most beautiful athletes in a home for paraplegics.

If one wants to look beyond the iconographies, to degeneralize the appearance of things, Leningrad does it for you. The official version of pastoral is so continuous that it throws into relief the specifics it cannot include. I had expected to be behind the frontier in Russia, looking out from the inside, but found myself *on* it, seeing it every- where. The thought habits of the borderland are the thought habits of life in an all-encompassing state. The gap between nation and state which is the character of a frontier – the artificial and clumsy matching of an idea to an uncooperative reality – was everywhere in Leningrad, the nation lurking in the corners which the state smoothed over. I walked down the avenues of the city past the grand placards and the grander shops, past the queues and the closed faces of those in them, and would come again and again to openings off the pavement into dark and rutty courtyards where:

an old man and woman bowed and kissed together, the fur of their hats mixing and becoming one hat,. hiding their faces from me; their black cloth arms touching each other's shoulders in symmetry and again the ice cracking down and out of the drainpipe in the thaw behind them;

a young man smoked alone in an archway, the cigarette between the fingers of a thinly gloved hand – they were nylon inners – his elbow cupped in the other and mascara on his eyelashes. He waited for the people to climb on to the bus and then stepped across the pavement and on to it himself without pushing;

there was a hurried transfer of cabbages between bags by an un-marked door, at the head of a queue curving between the puddles in the yard.

There you could slip the point of the knife under the tortoiseshell. It didn't have to penetrate far before the whole slab above it started to lift away. Doing no more than looking in the voyeuristic way of foreigners abroad, one could feel part of it, as foreign to the structures as they were, automatically sharing the status of alien. This was the homeliness of Russia, made homely by the distance from officialdom in which neither I nor the people among whom I circulated could ever hope to share.

There was a squalid tussle at the door of a café. Lena was trying to get inside, the doorman was preventing her. She had a glove on the long, tarnished handle, pulling at it. His old boot was pushed against the bottom corner of the door. 'Why not let her in?' I said in English to myself.

'Because he doesn't want to,' Lena said.

'Let's go to another one then,' I said. And we did.

I spent the rest of my time in Leningrad with Lena. Like students, we floated in the undertow of her unhappy life. It was full of tiny and aimless deceptions. She told me that she was a waitress and that this was her day off, but that was untrue. She was actually a student in the Railway Engineering College. She told me she was twenty-four; in fact she was twenty-five. She told me she had bought her saffron quilted anorak in Helsinki on a trip there; in fact she had got it on the black market through a friend who dealt in these things. She never took me home – that was the most significant cut-off of all – and she could never meet me in my hotel. I could only ring her from a phone box in the street. In the one I used someone had scratched LET IT BE in half-centimetre-high letters on the metal, the only graffito I saw in Leningrad. We always rendezvoused at neutral public points in the city, in the Finland Station, outside the Smolny Institute, where the Decembrists had been hanged, and in the foyer of the Hermitage. I thought these precautions faintly ridiculous at the time, the self-dramatization of an insufficiently diverting life. But when I got home to England I tried to ring her at the Leningrad number on which I had reached her or her parents so often before. Each time – I tried three times – I heard the Russian operator tell her English counterpart that there was no answer. But I knew that her mother was housebound and that she always had the telephone by her. She was one of those people, Lena had told me, who sit by the phone letting it ring four or five times before picking it up so as not to appear 'hungry', as she said. There was no possibility of no answer. The interruption came further up the line. Lena never told me her other names, nor her address, and I have never been able to reach her since.

But this first afternoon we went off together to visit a friend of hers. She stopped a taxi and lit a cigarette. A sign on the dashboard said 'No Smoking'. Lena said, 'Haven't you learnt yet not to understand anything you read in Russia?' The friend was the supplier of anoraks. Valery was 1974. His turtleneck was tucked into his hipsters. He had a Zappa moustache ('tash') and wore a big fur hat all the time. Drunk, his thumbs in a huge belt buckled with a spread eagle, he told a joke about cowboys with long thumbs feeling happy all the time. He was also anxious to get the effect right. 'Can you say "Hey, you guys...",' he asked me, 'to men *and* women?' I thought you could.

'Well now,' Valery said in a voice that came from about ten miles outside Odessa, Texas, 'you jes' get yerself arownd a li'l mite of that.' It was Southern Comfort. 'And let's get ourselves talkin' 'bout that damn fine cinema *Apocalypse Now*.' He had just watched it himself in a 'secret film'.

The staircase to the flat stank like the inside of a dog's ear, and the flat itself was scarcely better. The floor was made of unvarnished herringbone strips, the walls of unpapered hardboard. There was a sofa of boxes with a rug over them. The sleeve of a Rolling Stones album was pinned to the wall, folded out so that one could read the notes ('their own sense of integrity'), and a couple of centre-spreads from a French magazine: Miss Mai with her stockings rolled and Miss Août playing with a kitten. Valery's bravado filled the flat and Lena's unhappiness grouted around it. A silver stereo compact played the Doors. Valery always made sure he had a cigarette in his mouth before changing the tape, so that the smoke could curl up into the half-closed eye as required. Six people of three generations lived in this flat. Valery said he was one of your really great dissidents, the Al Capone of *samizdat* literature. More Comfort. 'How the fuck can you get yourself stuck out in the fucking boondocks?' he performed. And then confidentially: 'Do we say boondocks or Berkshires? Sometimes I have listened *Berkshires*...' I recommended boondocks for the generality. He started up again. 'How the fuck can you get yourself stuck out in the fucking boondocks? There ain't nothing there! Waddya do sept js eat ya gizzard stiff, sleep it off and fuck the woman? Day after every day! You are most borrrd!' And then he slumped back for another slug of Comfort. Torhag reincarnated.

Lena asked me if I could send her a husband.

'Of course!' I said gaily, adopting the Valery style. 'What about a whole football team? You can line them up and take your pick.'

'Does your village have a football team?'

'And cricket. Which would you prefer – football or cricket?'

'We don't play cricket here,' she said solemnly. Valery glazed and I realized through the Comfort that Lena was serious. She wanted a husband. I had been acting the Brigadier with a refugee. Valery went on with the jokes. 'What about these goddam Americans? Whenever I see them I see something a little bit crazy in the eyes.' He was thinking about the secret film and slammed his own fur hat over my eyes. It smelt of the stairwell. 'They're crazy. They only think missles. Let's nuke Lenin! Let's do a trade-off – Minsk for Baton Rouge.'

Lena stared emptily at me thinking of her football team. In a pause – Valery lit a cigarette and took a leak with it in his mouth, shouting abuse about Jason Robards while he peed – I asked her what the plan was for her husband.

'Ah, no, this is too much,' she said. 'You joke too much. We will not talk now.' She pointed at the telephone and waggled a finger. 'We must not talk with the telephone here. They listen to Valery. He does not do enough to be taken, but he is near the line. They don't like him dealing in foreigners.' There was no hint of a smile. She was serious. She wanted a husband from abroad and she wouldn't let my half-afternoon drunkenness endanger that ambition. There was a rigid adulthood here which my own comfortable life and Valery's lunacy could never approach.

Over the next few days Lena's short history emerged. She had been in love with a German student – West German – who was spending a year in Leningrad. They were going to be married. She was nineteen at the time. She would leave Russia to live with him in Tübingen. But at the end of the year he had left for home secretly and quickly. Her desolation had shaped her life. Everything in it was directed towards filling the gap he had left. She kept herself well dressed and well made-up so that westerners might notice her, so that she might remain acceptable to them. She told me this without any self-pity. It was realistic calculation now. She wanted to leave Russia, but she wanted to be able to return to see her mother. Marriage to a foreigner was the only means. I asked her if this ploy wasn't rather transparent to the authorities. 'No,' she said. 'That is one thing they really still do believe in.'

'What?'

'Love. Even if I find it difficult to believe in now. Perhaps you have superstitions about marriage? Perhaps it disgusts you that I wanted to marry someone for myself and not for him?' We were having lunch in a restaurant.

'People do it all the time.' She suddenly reached over and kissed my cheek. I told her about Auden and Erika Mann. 'It makes it even more romantic for us,' I said, and I saw in her face that she thought I was joking again. She never did relax with me over this. It was too holy, too near the centre of her life. The original and criminal deception had turned her life itself into a series of deceptions and anxieties. She looked much neater and cleaner than the other people on the streets, as if it was purity she wanted to display. Purity more than difference.

Lena was no lover of the West. She saw herself as a political virgin. Solidarity was a CIA plot. The Pope was involved. She didn't like Poles anyway. They were the most contemptuous and contemptible of people. Of course the Bulgarians should want to kill the Pope. If Russia was corrupt with imposition, the West was corrupt with its careless treatment of freedoms. There was what she called a High Society here. She didn't know the word *Nomenklatura*, but she used to point out its members in the street. We passed a woman of bearing with expert lipstick and artificially arched eyebrows in an Astrakhan skullcap fringed in mink. Lena reckoned the hat cost 300 roubles, two months' average wages, or the rough equivalent of £1,200 in England. 'Our High Society exists,' she said to me quite angrily, 'but it does not exist to be seen. There is not much ado about it,' she said from her lessons. 'But yours are the heroes and that is bad.'

I wondered where she wanted to go if she could leave. She wouldn't tell me at first. 'It is a little country, like a private country.' So I had to play a guessing game. Andorra? New Zealand? St Kitts and Nevis? But this wasn't funny. She finally confessed that her choice was Switzerland. It glowed neutral in her mind, untarnished with politics and – almost as a result – beautiful and clean. 'There are no rubbish Thatchers there,' she told me. (Lena believed, incidentally, that Mrs Thatcher smokes large cigars in private. 'Everybody knows she does.')

Lena was thinking of a film set. She felt equally betrayed by the life which, in her words, the Communist state had forced upon her and by the cynicism of her German lover. They had become two halves of one Manichaean equation in her mind and she wanted nothing to do with those mathematics. She had retreated into a sort of private hygiene. *Amour propre* was clean self-love. She looked like an advertisement for skin milk. Her whole appearance, her pale clothes in a city filled with dark, winter cloth, was the outward manifestation of an inner and treasured neutrality, a private and dreamt-up Switzerland.

You can imagine how much I wanted to bring her marriage about. It was not less pressing because the same request is made to most foreign men who go to Russia, and no less important because I was unsure what good it would do. I remembered that President Carter had legislated that any country which allowed free emigration of its citizens would become a 'favoured trading partner' of the United States. It is perhaps a core American belief that the free movement of individuals is the definition of happiness, or at least the foundation on which happiness can be laid. But it is an ideal that is complicated by all the real ambiguities of emigration, of the frontiers closing behind you as firmly as they had been in front, of the deprivation that leaving one's own country will always mean. For some Americans, of course, emigration holds no fears. In the simplest terms it is nothing more nor less than release. But to drain off the objectors and the discontents in Communist countries by economic inducements is to strengthen the regime in those countries, both economically and politically. It is to guarantee the continued existence of the repressions and deprivations to which those émigrés object. On a large political plane this is a difficult choice to make, but in detail, with one person, with Lena and her alpine Shangri-La, there could be no doubt. You can imagine how bad it was, after I had found the man in England to marry her – he would have to make three visits to Russia – that the telephone calls from Leicestershire to Leningrad brought no response at all.

We had a fine time however. She took me on the Metro, a 1950s vision of Salyut life, in which one rides for four minutes down the blank white escalator tunnels, to get the depth under the Neva, all in silence, everyone reading as if in a trance. Lena said she no longer noticed how beautiful it was. 'Only foreigners notice.' I said that in the future I hoped she would too. We saw the ballet *Petrushka*, in which the puppets take on independent life and the clown triumphs over the puppet master. The audience watched this subversive political myth with a whey-faced impassiveness.

Then one day to the Hermitage. It was Harrods in a steel town. The best, most sumptuous, most comprehensive shop jungle one could imagine. Golden melons and silver nectarines hung from every branch. One of the greatest collections of twentieth-century painting in the world is pushed into a low-ceilinged attic which almost nobody visits, baffled by the swags and spandrels, the ormolu and mar-quetry, the sheer gross volume of opulence in the floors below. It is an exercise in exhaustion, a monstrous display of the inaccessibly rich. It is also a sort of history zoo, where strange creatures from other worlds are gathered and displayed away from the network of relations that produced and sustained them. And there is more care, more thought for beauty in a chest of drawers and a lampstand than in your whole flat, your whole block, your whole street. The faces above the eighteenth-century silks look as uncomprehending and as genuinely foreign to their own painted surroundings as do we who now regard them in our worn-out masses. I asked Lena what she thought. 'It has nothing to do with me,' she said. 'It's a shop in which you cannot buy, but where they have put everything good from the city.'

I had begun to think the same, how all the rhetoric about 'people's palace' and accessibility was another tease like the placards on the General Staff building to be seen through the windows. Until suddenly we arrived at an English corner with Kneller portraits of Grinling Gibbons, John Locke, Cecily Croft and himself. There was something truthful in this warty brown corner. Lena thought it as boring as the rest. Perhaps all over the Hermitage small groups of Italians, Germans and Frenchmen were finding sudden ecstasies at their own little patches of nationality too, like a Watney's 'pub' in Madrid, while the Russians sifted past the lot, theirs and not theirs at the same time.

The evening before I caught my night train to Tallinn we had dinner in a restaurant near the Finland Station. The coat check inside the door was full of naval uniforms. You can never forget that Leningrad is a naval city. Old men wear their sailor's caps into their eighties. Sailors crowd the pavement five abreast like true Soviet cartoon heroes among the furred Mrs Tiggywinkles of the citizenry. But here it became marvellously concentrated. The black Baltic greatcoats hung in ranks on the hooks and had flat caps above them at a tilt. It was a dead chorus line. The names of the ships in gold letters were printed on the cap-ribbons and the footlong tails hung half-way down the coatbacks ending in two golden embossed anchors, puma eyes on the cloth. All the romance of a military state was there in the cloakroom.

Inside the restaurant, with sequin ash-dust on the black ridged floor, was the other side of it, the state with its coat off. The air thickened towards the back of the room where a jazz band played. In a stately alternation the parties of sailors and their women would stand up and dance for three minutes, holding themselves a few inches apart, and then sit down to little conversations. A spiv in the corner made up to a pory young woman who was fingering his polka-dot tie. Courtesy mixed with a borrowed smartness, with the sort of bulbous black noses in men and creased exhaustion in women familiar to me only from films. Lena and I eventually danced too, but awkwardly. I had asked to come here. It was the restaurant behind the window I had passed on my first night walk through the city where a saxophone was playing. I wanted to have a better time than the situation allowed. Lena was anxious that I had understood the full and complicated details of coming and going by which her marriage could be arranged. There would be three trips to Leningrad for the chosen Englishman. On the first he would simply meet her; on the second register their desire to get married; on the third, if the papers came through, get married. He would then leave alone for England. She would follow some months later. I knew all this. It wasn't so difficult.

Our dancing was gauche and unjazzy. I began to feel clumsy on the drink, more like the men who came in at the side door now and then into the hot room and drank one joyless tumbler of vodka straight down before leaving than the forgetful, growing-intimate people at the tables. They were separating into self-absorbed couples. I wanted to leave like the vodka-straitened men. Lena stayed sober. She sometimes wished she lived in Stalin's Russia, where it was all closed, where there was no dangling of foreign bait in front of one's eyes. At least then you could turn your attention away from the border and that too would be some sort of release. But I should watch out for the Estonians. 'Their noses are pushed up in the air,' she said and flicked the end of her own with the varnished point of a mid-apricot fingernail. Perhaps they would all be like Lena.

I bought her a bunch of white chrysanthemums from the stall at the mouth of the Metro and left her there. She waved goodbye to me with them like an illuminated wand as I slid out of sight down the escalator to take the Metro under the Neva and across the city.

4

Ghost Frontiers

The Tallinn train left from the Warsaw Station. Half a regiment was waiting there, packed hotly in the waiting-hall, pushed up against sleeping women on the benches, string bags like children squashed between them.

I was leaving Russia itself for the three Baltic Republics of Estonia, Latvia and Lithuania, or at least for their three capitals, Tallinn, Riga and Vilnius. Between 1920 and 1940 these tiny countries were independent. Each is big enough to claim a real political identity, each small enough to be politically impotent. But in the unique circumstances between the wars, when their neighbours on either side were so radically weakened by defeat, revolution and civil war, a vacuum opened in which President Wilson's nationalist ideals of self-determination were able to flourish and bring all three to full statehood. The western diplomacy of the 1920s and 1930s – principally French – aimed to protect them with a network of agreements, non-aggression pacts and mutual assistance treaties, so that in those twenty years the three Baltic states signed over 750 international treaties, protocols and conventions. But the whole elaborate filigree was made useless by one overarching agreement on 23 August 1939. It is a famous black day. Ribbentrop the Nazi (Hitler: 'the best Foreign Minister that Europe has seen since Bismarck') and Molotov the Soviet signed a secret protocol in Moscow by which Estonia, Latvia and Finland would fall within the Soviet sphere, most of Poland and Lithuania within the German. The Nazis were in a great hurry, as the military build-up for the invasion of Poland was already under way. Hitler had originally wanted the southern half of Latvia too. Ribbentrop telephoned him at Berchtesgaden in the middle of the night. The Führer called for an atlas and looked at it while they talked. He decided there and then that the Soviets could have southern Latvia if they wanted it. One of Hitler's aides, Groscurth, wrote in his diary for 24 August 1939: 'One is crushed. Everything is lying and deception. Not a word of truth. There is absolutely no ethical foundation for this.'

Lithuania was transferred to the Soviet sphere after the German conquest of Poland, on 28 September. Between the middle of 1941 and 1944 the Germans occupied all three countries, collectively naming them and the Ukraine Ostland. Since 1944 they have been constituent Republics of the Soviet Union.

These then are conquerable and conquered countries, their frontiers ghost frontiers, momentarily transubstantiated between the wars. A Hobbesian would see that short period of independence as a bug in the system, as a rare moment when the great vice of eastern Europe was unable to operate and when bogus dreams could be lived out between its jaws. He could adapt Stalin: the birth of a country may be a cause for celebration; its death is the working of statistics.

The fiction in the Soviet Union maintains that it is a union of separate soviet socialist republics, fourteen of them, each with its separate government, parliament and ministries, including a foreign office. It is explicitly written into the constitution that any of them may withdraw of its own free will from the union. In the waiting-hall of the Warsaw Station, sitting on my suitcase in the hot air, I read a pamphlet about Estonia by someone called Nikolai Khitailenko. It said: 'The fact that throughout the USSR's existence not a single Union Republic has availed itself of the right to secede shows that the Soviet Socialist State meets the interests of all its people.' He doesn't mention the 350,000 Estonians – a third of the nation – who were exiled in Siberia in the two waves of Sovietization before and after the German occupation, 70% of whom never returned to Estonia. One brief sentence dismisses the 'former factory owners, merchants, rich peasants, bourgeois functionaries and other riffraff', who were the necessary casualties of the socialist transformation.

It is difficult to know how to react to this sort of dissembling. It strands the mind. Can Khitailenko be unaware that such self-imploding vacuity destroys its own ends before achieving them? One of the alarming aspects of the pamphlet is that it is designed for export to the English-speaking world. It aims to convince the West that the USSR is a free union of peoples by saying so. It fails to imagine western attitudes or to put itself in the place of its reader, to understand that this emptiness destroys understanding. It cannot be generous enough to allow that people in the West also know the difficult relationships of freedom, strategy, justice and power. And their mutual contradictions. Nor that national self-determination was not a possibility for the Baltic states in the 1940s – only Nazification or Sovietization.

If most conversation and most contact between people and peoples is in the nature of a borderland, of a mixture of meanings in half-fumbled articulations, then propaganda is the language of the frontier, the barbed, hermetically tight product of nationalist mental constipation. Propaganda must assume a void in its recipient and be contemptuous of all intelligences but its own. Propagandists like Khitailenko may eventually not be talking to those whom they claim as their audience but to themselves, in a complete and self-convincing circle of delusion. Propagandists shout into the wrong end of the megaphone, the trumpet mouth covering their faces while squeaks of half-thought emerge from the microphone end.

I pressed my face to the corridor window for the first half hour on the train. The fifteen blue carriages curved through the night. The telegraph wires tautened and sagged in front of the blue moonlit snowfields, where the fronds of the pine trees absorbed the light from our passing windows. The apartment blocks of Leningrad gave way to an older Russia, where small wooden houses stand inside their rimed and bent fences, part buried in snow. It all jolted past inaccessibly – not Intourist country – revealed because of the moon and the clear sky. I had asked for a day train to Tallinn, but that was not possible. If it had not been for the moon, I would have seen only occasional lights.

Back in the compartment there was an Intourist guide: Mrs Khitailenko. She was five feet tall, wore grey woollen flares, a grey woollen jersey, grey boots with zips (woolly inside) and a spring blue knitted hat. She projected a sort of professional sweetness which I think she had forgotten was artificial. Professionally sweet was what she now was, whether with her aged mother in Moscow or with tourists like me.

'My name is Masha,' she stated.

'I'm Adam.'

'Oh, really, how very interesting,' she said, recognizing a Jew when she hadn't met one. 'And which part of Israel do you live in?'

'England.'

'Aah . . . how very charming.' Her mother must have hated her.

Masha Khitailenko was used to dealing with the imbecilities of foreign tourists and with encroaching parental dementia. They had become one in her mind, to be cancelled with a kilogram or four of processed sugar, and the soothing repeated words 'of course' like a balm. The pale moonlit Russia went past us outside and the compartment was filled with her bright lying chatter. She went on about the Supreme Soviet, its two chambers. In the Soviet of Nationalities each Republic had equal representation, even though Estonia had only 1.5 million and the Russian Federation 140 million people. 'Estonia is like any other country in Europe,' she said. 'But with the help of its friends it is not dominated.' Of course. Of *course*. She then set off on a quick-firing metaphor about a bundle of sticks. One nation, one stick. A bundle is better. 'Where would your Israel be without the United States?' One could detect the vestiges of an old and admirable principle in what she said. Masha quoted Lenin at me and it sounded generous and humane, but I had an inkling that the words had stayed put and the meaning had moved out from under them in a sort of verbal Leningrad, a polished show-lobster on the fishmonger's slab. I asked her about the 350,000 Estonians exiled to Siberia, and she said I had the wrong numbers. I asked her about the Russification of the Baltic States, by which less than half the inhabitants of Estonia are now Estonian by birth. She said this was a move towards the development of people, whatever that meant.

'Like the abolition of slavery?' I suggested.

'Of course, why not?'

I asked her why so many people went into exile when, according to Khitailenko, 92.8% of the electors in 1940 had voted for Estonia to become a Soviet Socialist Republic. German propaganda during the occupation had changed their minds. Of course.

She told me that the Baltic States had guaranteed their freedom and their sovereignty by uniting with Russia. The Germans had wanted to make them a colony. Now they still fly their own flag.

'What sort of flag?' I asked her. She couldn't exactly remember. I read her the description from Khitailenko: ' "A rectangle of red cloth with a hammer and sickle in gold in the upper corner next to the staff, with a five-pointed red star above them." '

'Go on, go on.'

' "The lower part of the flag is intersected with a wavy blue stripe." '

'There you are,' she said triumphantly. 'Wavy blue stripe! That is the flag of Estonia!' But what else could she have said, poor woman? I suggested they might have a flag, a very thin one, consisting only of the wavy blue stripe – no bourgeois revanchist associations. She thought that wasn't a good idea: you couldn't see a thin flag very well.

Masha went on to the offensive. 'London is filthy dirty,' she told me smiling, 'and there is acid in the rain.' I gave her a long speech about Clean Air Acts, the smogless metropolis, how a salmon was caught off Battersea Bridge the other day, how new towns plant wild flowers between the blocks of flats, before I realized that I was sounding like her. There is something natural in propaganda, like a blush.

'Very nice,' Masha said, meaning she didn't believe it. 'And the air is clean because your factories don't work?'

'Probably.'

'Very nice. Will you go to Israel?'

We were saved from trading national disasters by a large woman who looked like a poster. She told me through Masha that I didn't eat enough and gave me four Ukrainian nougat cakes in a paper napkin. We passed the place where she had fought in the trenches during the siege of Leningrad and she held up both arms in the Popeye flexed bicep position. It wasn't difficult to imagine this broad-faced Slav woman, now with dyed yellow hair and a great amethyst on her finger, carrying and working a heavy machine-gun in those trenches. Salmon in the Thames seemed silly in comparison. There can be no forgetting. A million Russians – three times the number of Britons who died in the whole war – died in Leningrad during the siege. It lasted from September 1941 until January 1944. About half the dead died of scurvy or starvation. The shadow of the Great Patriotic War will last until the next, whose name it will share. *'Shchastlivogo puti!'* she said, 'and a good time may you have!'

Tallinn – it means the Danish town in Estonian; the Danes called it Reval, the Germans Revel – is quite distinct. It reeks of bourgeois cosiness. Tallinn was a Hansa town, the port through which the Novgorod trade was channelled. Colonies of Scandinavian, German and Russian merchants had quarters here. Its great days came to an end in the early sixteenth century, when the Hanseatic merchants closed the office in Novgorod and the Dutch and British began to open up the White Sea trade through Murmansk and Archangel. By then Tallinn had already grown rich under its tight mercantile oligarchy. Only a merchant, a wholesaler or a shipowner could become an alderman, and then only if he possessed his own house in the town and had a wife. There was no bar on nationality.

The pantiled medieval houses in the centre – restored in time for the Olympic regatta held here in 1980 – culminate in large triangular attics like flattened spires with jerry hoists outside their doors into space. That is the image of Tallinn: the ceilings in the first-floor living-rooms sagging under the weight of the accumulated bales in the lofts above them. In the creaking of the boards is a reminder of the source of well-being and of the primacy of material things.

I walked around the cobbled streets and passageways, feeling relief in the smallness and reliability of this town. None of the obvious dissociation of Leningrad: this was Europe itself, not Europe recreated in a marsh. The shops were full of more flowers, more different sorts of flowers than in the whole of Leningrad. There were windows full of expensive hand-knitted jerseys – at a hundred roubles or more – and Swedish light-fittings. No wonder Lena thought the Estonians toffee-nosed and no wonder over a million Russians come to Tallinn as tourists each year. It acts as a surrogate West where, more than the cobbles and the unobliterated evidence of a bourgeois history, the constant stream of Finnish television from Helsinki only fifty miles away across the gulf provides a perspective on the world. Only here in the whole of the Soviet Union was the news of the shooting down of the Korean airliner to be heard and seen in full.

I took a tram out to see Peter the Great's palace in Kadriorg. Every word written in the tram was in Russian. Peter arrived here in 1718 with the Italian architect Niccolò Michetti to build himself a pink palace and a geometrical park. The Russians had scorched Estonia in the Great Northern War so that not a dog barked and not a cock crew between Tartu and Narva. Gaetano Chiaveri was the second architect. A plague had crossed Estonia in 1711. Antonio Quadri came to do the stucco. Harvests had failed for years in a row in the 1690s. Salomon Zeltrecht from Sweden did the sculptures. The population of Estonia had dropped to a third of its level before the Great Northern War began. A Rigan German, Heinrich von Bergen, carved the fireplaces. The population of Tallinn itself had fallen from 10,000 under the Swedes to about 2,000 under the Russians. The palace was unfinished when Peter died in 1725. It is now an art gallery full of brown pictures by Jaan Koort with no people and only a rare hut in the Estonian mud; and an extraordinary white ceramic pig.

Across the refrozen snow of the park, scabby plane trees in the crust, was the office of the Novosti Press Agency. A sleek villa in a terracotta wash, with a porch and a place for the cars. The residence of the papal nuncio to independent Estonia. Leonid Obshirnov, the Tallinn correspondent, led me into a room dominated by a wide Goyan mural of naked full-breasted women with jugs treading grapes in Andalucia. 'A little mundane for the priests,' Leonid said, 'but we have never wanted to dress them up.' He giggled. His red hair was slightly coiffed and curled around the ears, which he tugged at. Another man on the sofa in the corner, entrenched in his overcoat, said in heavy consonantal English: 'That was the bourgeois style of pleasure.' He had three silver teeth in his Mongolian face and small square hornrims pushed up against his eyeballs. Ulan worked for the Mongolian *Krokodil* – a sort of Steppeland *Punch* – and I came to realize that his remark about the fresco was an example of Mongolian satire at its most oblique.

Leonid took both of us around Tallinn. We looked at the town walls and in the Lutheran church, at the restored merchants' houses and at the outside of the palace. But the tour was not a success. Ulan didn't like it. I saw a devastating critique of Estonian lifestyle formulating behind the hornrims ... revisionist structures ... pseudo-West ... false history adulation ... manipulative personalism ... hegemonic papality. Fragments of it emerged now and then. He was outraged by our visit to the Lutheran church. Leonid proudly talked about the women pastors. Ulan bumbled up and down the aisles with a slight movement of the shoulders, like a large dustbin on wheels at the back of a restaurant. Papal lasciviousness, delusions of an opiate dream, solidity of atheism. Leonid joked about the 'church' at Greenham Common where we should all go and pray. Ulan picked at a silver tooth. He refused to enter the Orthodox cathedral (1904) and sat in the car writing notes about the Estonian and English journalists kowtowing to an antique idol. He didn't answer my one question: is it true that the Mongolian for love is *amour*?

He was right. There was something bogus about Tallinn, as fake as the flag. None of the boutiques were privately owned. None of the merchants' houses were merchants' houses. The variegated roofs of Toompea, the high part of the town, pitched and angled according to individual choice and the contingencies of site, in different ratios of warmth and shadow, covered a web of government offices. Ulan's eyes lit up at the revelation. It was ingeniously done. Behind the façades discreet concrete passageways and bridges joined the separate buildings to make the administrative network of Estonia. It was the real image of Russia's federalist empire, in which the separate parts were rigidly and secretly bound, each house an Estonia.

In London I had been to the Estonian consulate-general. It was a wet day in autumn when the leaves from the plane-trees had already begun to slick on the pavement. The legation is a tall brick house in Queen's Gate with octagonal panes in the windows and a polite Tuscan loggia for a porch. There was no flag on the staff that day. Its façade is as non-committal, as unnoticeable as any of the smaller embassies in London, but inside it reveals itself to be the saddest and most ridiculous of all.

The British Government recognizes the absorption of Estonia by the USSR *de facto* but not *de jure*. As long as there were diplomats alive who had been accredited at the court of St James before 1940, this house was officially recognized as an embassy. But the minister, Mr

August Torma, died early in 1971 and his head of Chancery three months later. Nothing could replace them. Death simply removed the diplomatic status of the legation. Now, despite the brass plate on the door, its lettering almost polished away, no policeman stands outside.

A still and flowerless vacuum. Gas fires burn on one panel between pink and grey mosaic tiles. There are stopped clocks and broken barometers in cartouches on the panelling, next to brown photographs of old Tallinn. The leather on the armchairs is split, the ticking below them sags to the floor. It is a hoovered, dusted, dead emptiness, with the black, white and blue flag of Estonia standing in miniature on the chimneypieces. The silk Empire furniture in the Ionic reception room is covered in dustsheets, which are removed once a year for the National Day party. The visitor's book was brought here from Rome in 1936. It records a decline: from the festoons of flamboyant autographs before the war – mother-of-pearl cigarette holders, rosebuds in the spreading lapels – to the sparse unimportance of the names after it.

Only Mr and Mrs Taru now live in the legation. Both are growing old and neither was ever a diplomat. They are courteous people, more *déracinés* than émigrés, not here by choice. Mrs Taru came here with her father, a sea-captain, in 1939, and was caught by the war. She has never since returned from this extraordinary limbo, filleted by exile and events. Her husband is more fragile. His jacket and tie hang forward off his chest as he stoops. But she is efficient with files and pamphlets that are sent over from the equivalent office in New York. It is American money that pays for the upkeep of the expensive house, made more expensive since the withdrawal of diplomatic status. She is matronly, with crimped white hair and a sort of purple *gilet*, frogged in places. Unlike other legations, Anna Taru told me, the Estonian must pay rates. She asked me not to publish the figure, as if it were a source of private shame, but it runs into many thousands of pounds.

In the safety of Kensington their etiolated and vestigial nationalism is pathetic. It is as though Mercia or the Hwicce were maintaining an embassy in Paris. Estonia is bigger than Switzerland, the Netherlands, Belgium, Denmark or Albania, but its tiny population and above all its geographical circumstances make any claim to modern statehood hopeless. Most of the bits of paper which Mrs Taru showed me in Queen's Gate were plaintive pieces of propaganda about the virtues of Free Estonia, in which none of the serious flirtation with Nazi Germany was mentioned, nor the regular murders of Estonian Communists between the wars, nor the increasing deprivation of freedoms as the war approached. They also gave out strong signals of racial purism: 'The Estonians . . . have nothing in common with Slavs or Teutons.' The dirty tail-end of President Wilson's ideals seen through the lens of Fascism.

In the bulletins from the Relief Centre for Estonian Prisoners of Conscience, based in Stockholm, one can read of the pitiably slight gestures of modern Estonian nationalists and of their punishments. Three employees of the Vöhma Meat Combine in Central Estonia – Toivo Orula, Sulev Selli and Jaroslav Zirk – spent a lunch break in 1983 shooting at a picture of Brezhnev with an airgun. Orula got three years in a labour camp, Selli and Zirk two each for malicious hooliganism. They are now in forced labour camp number 422/5 near Tallinn. Their address is: Estonian SSR, 200001 Tallinn, Tisleri 31a, Uchrezhdenie, YuM – 422/5. Estonian teenagers have received up to five years' forced labour for hoisting the real flag, for sending 'false information abroad defaming the Soviet system' – some photographs. Estonian pastors have been committed to psychiatric hospitals for 'an insane belief in God'. One of the most extraordinary of these people is Tiit Madisson, a young man from Parmu. He was a signatory on 23 August 1979 – the black day – to the so-called Baltic Charter, demanding the reversal of the Molotov-Ribbentrop Pact. From prison in Siberia he smuggled an open letter in 1983 to the Madrid Conference on Security and Cooperation in Europe, one of the successors to Helsinki. Part of it read: 'Let it be known by all that we may be punished unjustly but that we cannot be broken, not even by years spent behind barbed wire in Soviet slave camps.' Madisson was appealing to the Soviet Union to stand by the humanitarian clauses of the Helsinki agreements. He is now in solitary confinement, allowed no visitors and no letters. He must have known what would happen to him. Can he have believed that the effects of the past could ever be reversed?

The hotel that evening in Tallinn was full of Finns. I rode up in the lift with two of them. Grey leather blousons, clipped hair and slacked-off ties. 'Have you met the girls?' one of them asked me. '*Girls,*' he said, 'what a happy time.' He brought a pair of purple knickers out of his pocket, held them up to his nose and mmmmmed through them, his eyes bright and closed at the same time. The other man was looking at himself in the mirror from three centimetres away. He found a spot on his forehead and squeezed it. Nothing came out. He then said: 'Yo yo yo yo yo yo yo yo yooooo,' with a finger on the lower lip for the last syllable.

I had heard of vodka tourism, but this was the Mardi Gras of the species. On the brown carpets of the hotel bar there was a man asleep in cowboy boots. The people walked around him like a traffic island. I sat down on a sofa and was approached by an enormous man with a shrunken quiff and the bent brow of a neurotic. 'I am Soviet man,' he told me. 'I am Estonian man. I live in Moscow. I play wallaby.'

'Wallaby?'

'Yes, wallaby. I am very big man and have big hands.' He put one on my thigh. 'Vodka is good for my nervous. I am heavy Soviet soldier in the Caspian Ocean.' He played volleyball for the army. 'I have very heavy hands,' he continued. 'You understand me.' His wet white face came up to mine and I understood him. 'You are smiling. You are all smiling. Do not laugh here.' I told him I had a pressing engagement. 'Good boy,' he said sadly. The print of his handsweat stayed on my jeans for a couple of minutes.

Outside the hotel, as ever, there was a young man wanting to change dollars and buy my clothes. Lined at twenty-three. He told me not to be frightened of him, but I wasn't. He had been 'doing the business' for four years and had dropped out of technical college. Most of the business was with Finns, whom he despised as loud-mouthed, violent and lazy people who never learnt any language but their own and expected the Estonians to understand them, because that was what they had learnt in school. Finno-Ugric solidarity! He claimed to be able to make 400 roubles a week, in a good week, but that was difficult to believe. We talked about the things he liked. He would go to bars and listen to the most turgid western pop music, Yes and Artwork. In summer he injected himself with raw opium taken from the poppies in the villages round about. The rest of the year he smoked Russian hash. He had many girlfriends. I asked him if he loved any of them. He snorted at the naïvety of it. Even asking the question showed that I was married with babies. He said he was never satisfied with a day in which nothing happened. But a day in which something – one thing – happened, that was good enough. One deal, one girl a day, that's all he needed. He would never do anything to change his circumstances. Why on earth should he? He never had to kill time; it always died by itself.

A rusted blue Lada drew up with a moll in the passenger seat. The most glamorous man in Russia stepped out. He had fawn kid bootees and a green Italian jacket covered in zips and poppers. Three folded magazines transferred inside the amazing jacket and the Lada pulled away. The fence, a footballer who had been to Yugoslavia. I was lucky to have caught him.

The hustler never thought about Estonia. He had never heard of Tiit Madisson. A story about his mother: she had seen in the paper that some American students had never even heard of Estonia. He asked her if she knew anything about Montana, what kind of place was that? Probably, she said, it was some little country in America, taken over by the United States and no longer able to fly its own flag. He bit off a crabbed laugh.

I queued outside the glass door of a Caucasian restaurant. The bouncer-manager in a black shirt and white bow tie selected customers from the huddle outside it. I was bypassed eight times. I tried pushing in after four and again after seven. At each attempt he simply pushed me out again with the tips of his fingers. Influential women in leather gloves and white ski-hats always went straight in. The rest of us continued to stand under the one working light-bulb and its cracked shade, the soles of our shoes sticking and releasing on the wet tile floor, looking at the greased luxuries beyond the glass. There was a short collective triumph when one of the Unsmart managed to burst in and start slamming the desk in front of the bow-tie. It wasn't long before he was out again. At one point a large woman in a fake astrakhan coat that stopped at her knees was somehow jammed in the doorway. We all pinned her there from behind like removal men with a sofa. The manager started banging the door backwards and forwards against her body. She couldn't move. No one said anything. We listened to the padded banging of door against bosom, chipboard against nylon astrakhan, before the bouncer at last gave way and she popped into the warmed air of the restaurant. After an hour and a half I realized that the longer I waited the more ridiculous it became. I thought it was the siege of Minsk; he knew it was Stalingrad. I went back to eat the remains of the nougat cakes in my hotel room.

The air in the train to Riga was edible. I woke up at two in the morning to find a Russian bottom in white underpants next to my head. Its owner was rearranging his blanket in the thickness of the compartment. The bottom expanded and contracted as he bent and straightened, the cloth catching between the cheeks. I got up to find some air. The windows were sealed and the only fresh air was between the carriages. Past the stewardess's room, past the loo, and the carpet and heating come to an end. A functional grey space, the end of the carriage itself. Past another door and you come to the gap between carriages, where the two humped metal plates jigger on the rails. The only walls two rubber sheaths, overlapping but unconnected. Between the lower edge of the walls and the floors is a small polygonal space on either side, where a wind blows up full of spindrift into the black metal space, where the handrails have been cold since they were made and where the only light is from passing stations, reflected off the track, increasing and decreasing as the stations come and go. I stayed there in between the carriages for hours, smoking and freezing in relief.

Riga is grander than Tallinn. It is twice the size, and the capital of Latvia, a far larger and richer republic than its northern neighbour. Riga is more like a southern Helsinki than a preserved enclave. It too was a member of the Hanseatic League and there is a medieval centre, but its great days were in the nineteenth century, when it became the third industrial city of the empire after Moscow and Leningrad. Victorian swank informs the place: boulevards on the line of the old ramparts, an opera house in the park, autodidactic verse in the large crowded bookshops, a neoclassical church converted, with atheistical wit, into a planetarium, flatly labelled 23 Lenins Street. Another is a recording studio. There is nothing fragile or precious about Riga and nothing provincial. The prestige industries – electronics, cars, radios and televisions – are gathered on the outskirts. It has the first robot-operated factory in the Soviet Union making mopeds. There is actually a shortage in the labour supply, made up by Polish *Gastarbeiter*.

It is a cheering, sophisticated, ambitious place. The trams run well, there is none of the multiple queuing in shops – tickets, goods, collection – which bedevils Russian life. Delicious milkshakes and ice-creams in clean cafés. The air of 1870 is inescapable: a dominant work ethic; great emphasis on sporting achievement (there are four Latvians alive who are Olympic gold medallists at the javelin); the primacy of industrial production – at least in public statements; the trumpeted national ideal and the apparently benevolent imperial vision.

One extraordinary building is well in place. In the middle of the old city there is a red brick Anglican church, the same plain model to be found from Pulborough to Poona, which was built by English merchants in the last century. Not only the bricks, the mortar, the polychrome tiles, the windows, the bells and the roof slates were brought from the old country, but also a shipload of English soil was carried to Riga so that the merchants could worship on verifiably sacred earth. It now supports a youth club.

However, like 1870, there is an underside. Half of all marriages end in divorce and half of the remaining couples are said to apply for divorce and are refused. It is one of the highest rates of failure in the Soviet Union, where the rate is high everywhere. It may be a combination of Latvia's circumstances: there is the Soviet problem of the 'double burden' for women, where the state ethic expects them to work a full day and the traditional family ethic expects them to main-

tain the house and family without help from the husband, exacerbated by the reliably high 'Scandinavian' rate of divorce in an affluent
society, where, for example, the proportion of doctors to population –
one to every 260 people – is the highest in the world.

There are one-gulp drunkards in Riga. There is no public mention of
the Nazi-Soviet Pact and there is the fostered memory of war.

I wanted to visit Salaspils, a memorial on the site of a German
concentration camp. I was only allowed there in the company of an
Intourist guide. Guna was thirty. She would have been an executive, a
reader of *Cosmopolitan*, if things had been different; she was dressed
now in a wool suit, with clean styled hair and mascara. Very executive, very factful. Salaspils was 17.5 kilometres out on the Moscow
highway. It was a blue icy morning. We drove through the pale birch
forest, leafless in the frost. Guna said that 38% of Latvia was covered
in forest.

I asked her about the Germans. She told me the folk story of
Lāčplēsis (it sounds like Large Places). He tore a bear in two, fought a
witch and wrestled the black crusader, whom everybody knows to be
the German foreigner, one of the Livonian order of Teutonic Knights
who conquered the Baltic States in the thirteenth century and dominated them until the Revolution. Lāčplēsis now lives in the River
Daugava near Riga. Every midsummer night he comes out of the river
here – she waved past the buildings of a collective farm like an
architect's model and the crashed body of a truck that had slid off the
road in the ice – and he and the black crusader fight again. Until now
there has been no result, but one day, the story says, Lāčplēsis will
certainly kill him. Who was the bear?

'That is not historically important.' But Latvia didn't feel severed
from the Germans. They were part of the cultural inheritance. 'Part of
us is part of the Germans,' she said, 'but they have treated our people
like draught animals. The Russians are more like us and more with us.
My grandmother twice suffered German invasion. My grandfather
was killed by the Germans. The Germans' – she never said Nazi: the
lesson was historical continuity – 'had a plan to move 39 million
people from Ostland, from here and the Ukraine, to replace them with
10 million German peasants. That was one generation ago.' This was
not propaganda. This was unclouded belief in the repetitive nature of
history. It was Lāčplēsis made real. The world was waiting for the next
midsummer night.

We arrived at Salaspils. A gravel track curved through the forest
towards the wide open meadow where the camp had once been. It
was covered in dry caramel grasses patched in snow. Behind and

around it ran the pale frieze of the forest. It was a morning in midweek and nobody was there. A heavily roughcast concrete wall about sixty yards long lay across the track. There was no gate in it and the wall would have blocked off the meadow if the whole structure was not lifted about five degrees above the horizontal to make a wedge of light between the wall and the earth through which one could pass. This was done in 1967. There was raised iron lettering on the concrete: AIZ ŠIEM VĀRTIEM VAID ZEME – Behind this gate the earth moans.

Between the autumn of 1941 and 1944 53,000 people were killed here, 30,000 of them Jews from Riga, 7,000 of them children. Before the war it had been an army range and when people heard shots in the forest they assumed the Nazis were using it for the same purpose. Only in 1943, when they began to disinter and burn the corpses and the smoke blew the smell towards Riga, did the Latvians realize what had happened. Enormous concrete statues, sixty feet high, now stand around the meadow expressing resistance, humiliation and suffering. There is no flame but in a black marble box to one side there is a knock once a second all the time. An inscribed concrete cube stands on the site of the display gallows, where weekly victims were left to hang for a week.

It's as though the privacy created by the barbed wire allowed its own kind of barbarity. The camp, like the many others, was a closed-off satellite world where civilized values could be suspended and where people, floating in this amoral, pre-moral world, went back to the beginning almost by default.

That enclosure of the place has its implications now. Salaspils remains a capsule massage for a visitor's conscience, to be entered, left and – if one is honest – enjoyed. The sense of enjoyment – *schadenfreude*, self-congratulation, the 'tragic' emotion, whatever name one wants to give it – is a shocking experience. It is horrible to recognize that there is pleasure in indignation and horror, to realize that one is looking at the camp as a theatrical experience, as a slightly more real version of the substance of a thousand thrillers. Its sadism is endlessly reimagined in the warm cathartics of fiction. We can all imagine it and, given the circumstances – that is, the removal of the moral, social obstacles placed in the way of cruelty – we could all have done it. Perhaps that is the real meaning in the myth of Lāčplēsis: the constancy with which cruelty will resurface and reinvade, to be fought off every midsummer night.

On the way back in the car I asked Guna if she hated Germans. 'No,' she replied. 'We distinguish between governors and governed.' She sometimes guided groups of Germans, descended from the Teutonic

Knights, around Riga and other places in Latvia. 'They like to see what used to belong to them,' she said.

I went to the circus later. The ringmaster in blue was a figure out of George Grosz. He wore blue eyeshadow and smiled on the diagonal, prodding the elephants with a metal spike. The Latvian crowd went silent when he did it. I left as a moustachioed Hispanic woman set foot on a high trapeze, only to fall off sideways and dangle twisting from the safety wire.

'Do you think you could meet me downstairs in a minute or two?' Embassy voice on the hotel room phone. 'I'll have a copy of *The Times* with me.' Alexander Yemelyanov was the representative for the Novosti Press Agency. Leonid had phoned from Tallinn. His copy of the paper was headlined: 'First of Cruise Missiles Arrive at Greenham Common'. Grey double-breasted Lieutenant Colonel in the Irish Guards, fifty-eight, hair oil by appointment, polished lace-ups. He patted me on the shoulder with the paper and we drove to his Spartan office. Buttoned green plastic sofas, no Pompeian women on the walls. There was a poster of a cavalry trooper outside Horse Guards Parade eating his chinstrap. Mr Yemelyanov loved England and Scotland and Wales all quite separately. I expected a federalist lecture. His favourite was Scotland.

'Where did you go?'

'Glasgow, Ravenscraig. It was lovely.' He had been to various meetings of the Communist Party of Great Britain on the most recent trip, in Glasgow itself, Cardiff and Llangollen, and was disappointed. There was no real idea of the revolution left in the young people. He stroked his flat hair back over his head. What else could one ask for? A rigidly conservative government, armies of unemployed, a million with no job for over a year and what were they all talking about? Gradualist improvements of one or two side benefits. He knocked his fists together like playroom blocks of beechwood. 'Nothing radical, nothing courageous, nothing Marxist in the meaning of the word.' He was disappointed in the Europeans. Eurocommunism was a contradiction in terms, a sympton of decay. Watery eyes, Cadogan Square image and this Sandinista talk.

Alexander was half Russian and half Latvian, and concerned to preserve the Latvian, mother half. 'I must fight Russification in me too,' he said, as if it were some awful immune disorder. He made some tea from a Jackson's tin and we had biscuits. He frankly disliked the lasting drawbacks of the Stalinist legacy. The Soviet Union was overcentralized, he said. This may have been good for the army and in the war, but it wasn't good for the *sensitivity* of government now. The

Latvian government cannot make any serious economic decisions without referring them to Moscow. Light industry could be supported here, but major industrial or infrastructure projects – that needed central approval. The Five Year Plans are drawn up in Moscow. This of course was at the heart of the fraud about the idea of 'sovereign Union Republics'. With no control of expenditure or taxation there can be no government. Mr Yemelyanov admitted that the balance was not right, but he was quick to insist that the western propagandists were indulging in wishful thinking over the so-called nationalities problem in the Soviet Union. 'It is not a problem,' he said. 'It is a question. Will the empire' – he laughed: 'I use your words – will it disintegrate under what you call the nationalist impulses? Maybe a few intellectuals in Uzbekistan or some Azerbaijanis might feel: "Who are we to give loyalty to the Russians?" – even after they have been given so much by the Russians – and it *is* the Russian peasant who has suffered because all of it has gone to the more distant republics. But those intellectuals are the exceptions. You must understand, my dear friend, that we have gone further on this road. We have left behind this idea of fragmentary nationalism, which made Latvia a little separate client state of the Reich. That idea of one people with its own outfit of frontiers, its own way of thinking, its own expensive foreign embassies, its own miniature foreign policy – all that crumbles the world like a biscuit. You will ask me in a minute about the Russification of Latvia.' He was talking to me like a teacher, almost a guru, generous with his superior knowledge, reaching down from his more advanced phase of social organization. I was stumbling in the conflicts and confusions of bourgeois capitalist nationalism; he had emerged on to the broad upland plain of universal brotherhood. 'And of course it is true,' he went on. 'It is only now about 55% of the people in Latvia who are Latvian. The others are many of them Russian and many other peoples. It is the natural development. You are interested in frontiers. What was the frontier like between Estonia and Latvia?' I thought of the bottom and the dream space between the carriages. '*That* is our ideal for the frontier, not the guns and the wire and the dogs.'

It was all very lulling, if one forgot the shocking double standards, the simple maltreatment of individuals that it represented. He saw Berlin as the heraldic image of everything that was wrong with western divisiveness. (It fringed into Belfast. 'Haven't the soldiers put up a "peace line" there?' he asked in inverted commas.) 'The Berlin Wall separates the people from their natural friends,' he said. This was scarcely believable. 'How can one really still justify the artificial arrangements made at the end of the war?' he asked. 'The old allies should withdraw from both sides and it would become one German city.'

'East German.'

'Yes, but with a neutral Germany that too would change.'

'Don't you think it is only wars that can change frontiers?'

'Not if there is trust.'

'And doesn't propaganda betray trust?'

'No. Propaganda is a national duty. It is not a dirty word for a Communist.' He argued like this: Communists understand that everything that emerges from a society or a class will, whether it likes it or not, be propaganda for that society or class. The bourgeois view of things is a romantic view. It assumes the free working of each mind in a classless universe. Propaganda for the liberal is a distortion of the definable and classless truth. For the Communist it is simply putting things in a good light. Nothing is more ridiculous than (inevitable) propaganda which does no good for the cause from which it springs.

He talked about the idea of Europe. More tea and biscuits and cigarettes called Kosmos. There was something of the original ideal-ism of the Revolution here. He *knew* the tendencies of monopoly capitalism to be bad, with side-effects that may occasionally and for some people have been fortunate; and the tendencies of Marxist-Leninism to be good, with rare and ugly aberrations, of which Stalin was the epitome. To start with, Communism was the right choice for the Baltic Republics. Secondly, even though they had always had a feeling for Europe, the real allegiance was to Russia. The German knights had been oppressors. The Baltic peoples had battened down their languages and their souls, waiting for the moment of release when Russia would adopt them as her window on to the Baltic. (He ignored the fact that the Baltic Germans never did better than between 1710 and the Revolution, precisely the period of Russian control of the Baltic States and precisely at the expense of the indigenous popula-tions.) So in the neutralized, federalized Europe which Mr Yemely-anov envisaged, the Baltic States would remain part of the Soviet Union. That was their destiny. Estonia, Latvia and Lithuania, unlike the aligned nations to the west, had already come to their richest possible historical fulfilment. Only minor adjustments should now be made.

It was a world on the verge of the ideal, but between here and there stood the villain in the shape of America. It was dangerous for us all that power in the United States was now concentrated in the hands of the Californian money-military-politics triangle, against which even

Eisenhower had warned. Yemelyanov saw American policy in quite simple terms. Its aim was to break the Soviet economy with an increasingly expensive arms race which would divert money to the military, force sacrifices on the Soviet peoples and stimulate discontent amongst them. Victory by money and technology alone. By raising the stakes and scaremongering in various parts of the world, by rearming Japan and South Korea, by militarizing space, the Russians will be hurried into sacrifices. The new Nato missiles in Europe were of course part of it, it was the Cuban missile crisis of the 1980s, but Reagan had none of Khrushchev's sensitivity. The Russians had sacrificed before. 'You know our history,' he said. They would do it again.

He drove me back through the cleared and snowed-on streets. I said how delicious Latvian ice-cream was. Alexander agreed. The milk in Moscow was disgusting. 'Now *there* is a national characteristic! We're safe with that. If there wasn't any cottage cheese to be had in Riga,' he laughed, 'then there *would* be a revolution.'

These were capsule days and capsule places, each contained by the night journey from one city to the next. Each was separate and unconnected by a landscape. It was a means of travel in which frontiers seemed unnecessary, where unitary and self-sufficient places existed in a desert of ignorance. One jerked between these states in the vacuum-pack of a night train, between states of mind identified as different languages, histories, religions and ways of building. It was the perfect problemless model of the nation-state system where exactly focused cultures were arranged with each other as neatly and coldly as snooker balls on the baize. There was no fringing at the margins, no ambiguity of character, no need to consider the remains of the Livs in Estonia or of the Latgals in Latvia, nor the complicating Yotvings, the Galinds, the Neuri, the Zhemaitians and Augshtaitians, the Kurs or the Zemgals, nor the bishoprics of Kurzeme, Dorpat or Ösel-Wiek. It had all been sifted and sorted, all the layers of a borderland, into three Soviet Socialist Republics, with three separate capital cities joined by night trains.

'You have a saint's name,' the girl behind the check-in desk said to me as I arrived. 'Things will go well for you.' She was called Maria. Lithuania is different. The Teutonic knights had never been here. Under the Grand Duke Gediminas, between 1316 and 1341, Lithuania spread as an empire almost to the shores of the Black Sea. It held an ill-defined frontier with the Khanate of the Golden Horde in the southern Ukraine. The empire, which filled the vacuum created by the

Tartar destruction of Kievan Russ, was a model of tolerance. The conquered Russian principalities were allowed wide degrees of autonomy. The Orthodox church was given complete freedom. The Lithuanians themselves believed in an ancient Indo-European thunder religion. In 1385 Grand Duke Jogaila became King of Poland as Wladislaw II. Two years later the Lithuanians were baptized into the Roman Catholic Church.

The Grand Duchy fell into the Polish cultural orbit. The aristocracy was Polonized to the roots. Vilnius became a Polish city. The rights of the Lithuanian peasantry were eroded and they descended into a serfdom indistinguishable from the Russian. In the third Partition of Poland in 1795 Lithuania became part of the Russian empire. Intense Russification followed rebellions in the 1830s and 1860s. After the liberation of the serfs in 1861, 100,000 Lithuanians emigrated to the New World.

The Germans occupied most of the country during the First World War and sponsored the creation of a bourgeois republic at the end of it. Events then became complicated. Do not expect to understand them.

THE VILNIUS DISPUTE

Late in 1918 bourgeois Lithuanian government set up in Vilnius.
January 1919. Red Army takes over.
April. Poles invade Lithuania. Capture Vilnius.
Poles demand union of Poland-Lithuania.
Lithuanians refuse.
Western allies demarcate Foch Line through country. Separates Polish and Lithuanian armies. Narrowly prevents war between them.
City of Vilnius (Polish in pop.) plus surrounding area (Lithuanian pop.) on Polish side of Foch Line.
Lithuanians unhappy.
June 1920. Red Army retakes Vilnius. Hands over to Lithuanians.
Poles fight Lithuanians.
League of Nations intervenes, 7 October 1920. Gives Vilnius and district to Lithuania.
Poles unhappy.
9 October 1920. Polish general, born in Vilnius, drives Lithuanians out of city and district. Proclaims Independent Republic of Central Lithuania.
Everyone unhappy except general.
Bogus elections in 'Central Lithuania' February 1922 (fixed by Poles) arrange for its incorporation into Poland.

League of Nations accept, 1923.
Lithuanians unhappy again.
No diplomatic relations Lithuania-Poland until March 1938, when
   Polish ultimatum threatens war unless Lithuania accepts
   ambassador.

Far away countries, full of people of whom we know nothing. But the
Vilnius dispute was the Ulster of north-eastern Europe. Lithuania is
almost the same size and has nearly the same population as Ireland.
The political problem was the same: the interpenetration of one
people with another, divided to some extent by class, conflicting with
the abstract notion of a visibly integrated single state. There is no
civilized and peaceful way of reconciling those opposites. But the
Vilnius dispute had tragic and uncivilized consequences. The
argument between Poland and Lithuania prevented the creation of a
really secure system of alliances between the countries that separated
Germany and the Soviet Union – or at least deeply flawed it. It brought
on the events of 23 August 1939 which made the whole question
hopelessly irrelevant. Lithuania was transferred to the Soviet sphere
on 28 September 1939. The first Soviet bases were established in the
country – still nominally independent – 10 October. On 15 June 1940 –
German Kirkenes Day – it became a Soviet Socialist Republic. The
Nazis invaded in the summer of 1941. They killed the 30,000 Jews who
lived in Vilnius. The Red Army retook the city after a five-day battle in
July 1944. The Vilnius region was restored to Lithuania or, as a piece of
propaganda by Antanas Barkauskas says: 'The Lithuanian nation
fully realized the greatness of the deed performed by the Soviet
people and the armed forces of the USSR. It was due to the victory
achieved in the war that the statehood of Lithuania was re-established
and it was for the first time in the ages-long history of Lithuania that all
its territories with its ancient capital Vilnius were united.'
   I walked about in the ages-old historical beautiful centre of
Lithuania's fabled grand ducal capital city. It was a fat spurt of
southern Europe shot up into the snow on the backs of the Jesuits.
They founded an academy here in 1579; it is now the university. The
city reverberates with a baroque, catholic indifference to the
functional. It sprouts adjectives, coiled and sculpted, elaborate in
tight corners. Recent events have set this spirit only slightly off true.
The Soviets have performed a miracle of restoration on the churches,
in the same way, I guess, as archaeologists preserve Neolithic querns
in Somerset bogs. But they have removed Christs from pediments,
leaving gaps; turned all the pews in the cathedral – an art gallery –

around to face the door; hoisted another new flag – similar enough to Estonia's – over Gediminas's castle tower.

Catholic Vilnius survives in the flamboyant sixteenth-century brick of St Anne's Church, crocketed like a bit of Pugin furniture and laced together with string-thin blind ogees; in the punctured black spires of a Jesuit church, where the letters IHS encircled by a diagrammatic sun are still faintly visible in the plaster; and inside the university church of St John, past the bunched Corinthian jungle in front of it, a marble space in two different pinks sat on by white plaster babies as if at a milk bar, breaking into quiverfuls of golden rays.

I went into another church hoping for more. Written in the dome in swash capitals were the words: HOMO EST CREATOR ATQUE DEUS EST CREATURA ET FACTURA HOMINIS: ERGO NON EST DEUS (Man is the creator and God is the creature and product of Man: therefore there is no God). It was the Museum of Atheism, a shrine to the unforgiving ergo. A museum of cruelty, power and ridiculousness. The first objects one met in the showcases were graphic life-size models of Australopithecus and Neanderthal half-people, the consummation, one realized, of religious man. The exposition that followed was long on superstition, the Crusades, the Inquisition, the connection of the Church with the brutal serfdom of Polish and Tsarist Lithuania and on the *Gott mit uns* belt-buckles of Nazi stormtroopers; short on charity.

Alexander Yemelyanov had said that there was freedom of worship in the Soviet Union. There was only one condition under which the churches were required to work: they should not arrogate any of the functions of the state. The meaning of that condition depends on how many functions the state has arrogated to itself. There is no doubt that the Roman Catholic Church in Lithuania is persecuted. The Polish connection disturbs the authorities. Vatican Radio frequently broadcasts the prayer of Pope John Paul II that the 'Lithuanian nation should be able to express its faith in total religious freedom'. In November 1978 four priests in Vilnius set up the Catholic Committee for the Defence of Believers' Rights. As in the nineteenth century, the church is the focus for nationalism. Hundreds of Lithuanian priests have been imprisoned for 'systematically slandering the Soviet political and social system' in their sermons. The case of Father Sigitas Tamkevicius was described to me in Vilnius. He was one of the founders of the Catholic Committee and Tass alleged 'that foreign special services engaged in subversion against the USSR paid attention to this vain and money-loving man'. In fact, I was told, the KGB tried to recruit him on several occasions with promises of a good parish and the chance to study in Rome. But he refused them all and was in prison awaiting trial. Other priests have died recently in strange circumstances: falling under a lorry on a clear day in a Vilnius street; in the course of 'robberies' in which nothing has been taken. One petition recently sent to Moscow concerning a priest serving time in a strict regime labour camp carried 148,000 signatures.

The alliance of Catholicism and nationalism is not a natural one – the words themselves contradict each other – but the continuing strength of that alliance in Lithuania is a measure, if nothing else, of the inertia of belief. Or perhaps nationalism becomes a form of spirituality only when unfulfilled, to be absorbed and expressed in the available spiritual structures.

There was a picture gallery across the street from the Museum of Atheism. Hazed fragments of sentimentality, disjointed bits of precious landscape, half-imagined dream scenes, flap-eared surrealist flannel. It was a retreat not only from the political, but from the civic, the social and the public. It was incommunicado art, self-abasing and self-coddling at the same time. The baroque architecture outside was a visible reproach, the public monuments of Soviet Realism perhaps the source of its effete non-existence. That official cartoon style had monopolized the public sphere and pushed the souls of Vilnius back into themselves.

Ranemune said it was like people brushing their teeth on stage. She was a dancer. Red dress, yellow lace around the edge. And when not dancing a student of economics, English and computers. She danced because she loved it, studied economics because she had to (no Keynes or Friedman, but Smith and Ricardo because Marx had learnt from them), computers for the economics and English because computers speak it. We had lunch in a café called the Bear and walked along the banks of the Neris afterwards. She said the ice-floes in the river were oil-spots on puddles, cubes in a cocktail, a tie and a leopard one after another. She liked the Lithuanians best – the souls of the Balts grew warmer as you came south – and looked down on the Russians with the same withdrawn snobbishness that some Europeans treat Americans to, a sense of inevitable and generous superiority. She didn't think the baroque was foreign to the snow. 'Less foreign than *that*.' That was a yellow brick Orthodox church under tin onions with a padlock the size of a briefcase on the door. Lithuania was a pea between mattresses, a hope which had no hope, a cause for extremists to whom something would always matter, a closed church itself, a restaurant with the menu in another language, Russia's euphemism. This was no tragedy. 'We are well!', and then a long laugh. Lena was on another continent.

We had a drink in the hotel. It had just been finished, five years late, and was a joke in Vilnius. Russian incompetence. Ranemune would not have been allowed into its chocolate foyers and leatherette bars without me. The uniformed doorman locked and unlocked the door before and after us. It was designed on the international model as an upholstered morgue for executives, with too many barmen wiping clean the wipe-clean surfaces and chairs like diseased toadstools with gilded stalks and various mini-levels for conversation. Everyone was under twenty-five, geysering Marlboro smoke at the loudspeakers. 'This is what I think England is like,' Ranemune said.

In the taxi to the station a fat, curly-headed, thigh-slapping, thigh-holding, fifty-two-year-old ex-sailor with a son of thirty-seven (conception at fourteen) had been to London, Edinburgh and Aberdeen, got spliced (two fingers, whooeep, slice and junction) and was now a taxist never mind.

I was to fly home from Berlin. Thomas was due. There was no train direct from Vilnius and so I went by Minsk. The train was a familiar rigmarole. Green smoking length in the lights of the station, its bogeys exposed, the rolling out of the rolled-up mattresses, the non-intimate intimacy of the compartment, the silhouettes of medieval chateaux and lighthouses on the plastic curtains, windows stained by miles of weather. Tonight to Minsk on the Moscow train a Romanian like a Spaniard in high heels and keys hanging from a belt-loop; a Lithuanian Raymond Williams as though the force of gravity not age had destroyed his features, the hair smeared up and away from them, separating chromosomes, the holes in a violin. A woman in a bobbled wool suit and a black diamanté B on her bosom, its ascender curving round like an ornamental gate's. She unwraps her parcels. A salami is missing. She gives us each a chocolate from a box that falls open. Joint squirt of sweet liqueur. Everything external and compact. The light from the windows is a luminous fur the length of the Moscow train. The restaurant car is a form of escape. The green chief waitress – 'Metrodotelis' somehow attached to her hair – sits me in the one place left. Glamorous Lithuanian writing a doctorate in agronomics. Speaks French. Mitterrand is not a real socialist because French missiles are aimed at the USSR. The Korean airliner was a CIA plane. The Lithuanians are not prime Catholics because there is too much of the north in them, but good Communists because Catholics make good Communists.

His own sense of nationality. He said he was a citizen of 'the great country of the union'. It was more complicated. A Lithuanian like a

Tadzhik, a Lakk, a Kazakh, a Shor, a Mordvin, an Udmurt, a Selkup or a Ket, has a particular (did he mean private?) attachment to a small piece but that wasn't political. It was wrong to confuse it with any political idea. There was an oak tree in his father's garden. It belonged there and only there, but there wasn't anything nationalist about it. He laughed. That was the nature of local attachment. It could be nourished and looked after whatever the political circumstances. 'You must understand,' he said, 'the difference between the culture in the place and the national idea. There is no connection between them. Each has its frontiers. Sometimes they coincide and sometimes they are different.' There was nothing wrong in that. People shouldn't sacrifice themselves on some abstract altar where the national and the cultural frontiers intersected. That was a waste and a failure in understanding.

We smoked a Kosmos each in the space between the carriages. The apartment blocks and lights of Minsk surfaced outside and I left him in the train.

Minsk was dusty even in midwinter, an old lazy place after the Baltic Republics. I arrived at the hotel soon after midnight. A plant was dying on the reception desk. For once Intourist had made a mistake in the arrangements. My appointed train to Warsaw and Berlin left at four the same morning. I had three night hours. The hotel was sour and peeling. I walked out of it into the frozen avenues and spaces of the Hero City. Minsk was twice fought over, on the way there and the way back. The consuming, mobile death strip of the front line, with two passes, left so little of Minsk that the Russians considered moving it to another site – a city of over half a million people.

Now in the dark, minimalized by winter, it was slack with the expansions of post-war planning. Acres of indifferent grout filled the spaces between the unlit and self-sufficient monuments. Rare taxis slide-turned on the boulevards. The traffic lights flushed red and green to no applause. The Palace of Sport and the Obelisk Pobedy, the Aquatic Complex and the Partisan Cinema, the monument to Yakub Kolas and the Academy of Sciences, scattered in space like orbital rubbish. Hero City with an organized memory. In one stretch of the vacuum I found the National Exhibition of Economic Achievements of the Byelorussian Soviet Socialist Republic. Glass. For a moment I did not understand which particular Achievement was confronting me. It was a pair of plastic inflated lips six feet wide and two thick. A balloon in the shape of Yuri Andropov was staring back out at two in the morning with dead MacGregor eyes and scrotal jowls. A pneumatic figure on the carpets of power. Another piece of Mongolian satire. From behind him a larger balloon in the dark, the pure Shakespearean pate of Lenin himself, effortlessly dominating the tractors and earthmovers achieved in Byelorussia. Lenin was an inflated sphere of pure mental capacity. His eyes were bagged out with clever tailoring of the fabric, made percipient from great depths. Andropov was blubber next to it. Had he sanctioned this grotesque image? Perhaps it was simple democratic modesty that made him do it? Subversion by hideousness. He died a week later. Imagine the puckering deflation. Man of plastic folded up in a warehouse.

On the Russian train in Poland, stripped and striped and incomprehensible to me. 'A naturally mobile nation encouraged by history to excessive displacement.' Bolting for the comfort of West Berlin. The interval between Churchill's after-dinner matches slid across mahogany for Stalin's consent. Half-asleep at Brest. I called it Brest-Litovsk. The guard clipped back, 'Brest, Brest, Brest,' at me without looking. 'Brest-*Litovsk*!' he said with a raised eyebrow to the customs man. The carriage jacked in the half light. Winch screws on either side edging it up. The materials in the carriage creak under the strain, each material a different creak. Different bogeys for a different gauge.

In the compartment a Polish technical engineer returning from Moscow. He eats his dry Polish cake on which he has survived the whole trip to Moscow and back. The technique is to fill the mouth cavity with cake, as far as possible, and then fill any of the spaces that remain with tea. This is difficult but he manages it and waits for about a minute while the tea percolates through the cake, when mastication can begin. Once every eight seconds. The sound he emits is sticking-plaster repeatedly torn off and replaced on the same piece of skin. He does not enjoy it much. His eyes water like Yemelyanov's. He leaves at Poznań.

A Ukrainian woman and Anya her daughter. A brown monkey with red lips and a yellow face the same size as Anya's. The Polish border guard asks the monkey for its passport. The mother is ill and wipes sweat from her white face. A private quick retreat. No contact with Poland. 'Bourgeois subjective isolationism.' The stain of propaganda. Made intense by the Germans, jolly at 4 a.m. Anya is promised a 'Capitaine' at the DDR border. She asks for him every ten minutes until we reach it. A steam engine, black and lit and steaming, a brush of steam from its chimney and skirts of it among the lights down the side. All in our little boxes, the mind becomes diseased with this one idea. The mother sleeps curled around the child, singing her a

Ukrainian song. Now in the Russian carriage in the DDR. Not one thing searched on any border yet. Soft exits in the borderlands of Europe. Privacy is an agreed blindness. Frankfurt-an-der-Oder. Geography another neon light in the tracks of armies. Geography only its latest distortion.

Berlin Ostbahnhof. Anya runs down the platform with the monkey to her father. Her mother has trouble with a tied-up box in the door of the carriage. S-Bahn to Friedrichstrasse. Greasy mods on the wood seats and hippies with headbands more foreign than I could have guessed. To the *Ausreise* section. Hostility its fabric, the plasticated border underground. Fluorescent tubes in clusters make no deception possible. The materials of a vet's parlour. The stencilled signs for *'Bürger der anderer Staaten'* to sift away from the Germans and West Berliners. The foreigners young, the Germans old. Boxes for greyhounds. This land, cut off, will not communicate. (Remember the frozen border on the Bug, the girders of the iron bridge, the woods and fields.) *Konzept* city. Face up to the border guard in his little box, only the glass between us, the desk up to his chest, the mirror at an angle above me for him to see my luggage. The straight look, the grease in the thin hair, the red scurf around the nostrils, the four thick hairs he missed shaving on his upper lip, close and disgusting. He must see us in this way too. '1957 or 1951?' 57. The click in the door where pushing has worn away the brown pine formica. Another lit hall with too much space, no comfort, the clustered light tubes, blue railings, standing-around guards. In the U-Bahn past the dead stations to Tegel. It seems I have forgotten to read the way in which people dress here: the real significance of tight or loose trousers.

5
The Louvred Blind

Berlin is separate. I flew to Hanover, where I waited for the captain, a friend of mine now in the British Army, defending Europe from the Russians. He was exercising in his barracks and could not meet me off the plane. I waited for hours. Plum pie and coffee krem in the Cockpit Bar like Olav in Neiden. Apologetic English salesmen submitted to their tweeded German clients. I fell asleep on the marble floor. Miniature spaniels pranced on the width of the concourse. From the lemon yellow notice about terrorists at every exit, those who were caught had been cut out with a Stanley knife to leave square holes with their names below them. Half of the remainder were women.

The captain arrived. 'Hallo to Berlin!' he shouted across the marble and then pinned me from behind in a move he had learnt at Hereford. We swung out on to the autobahn. He told me that he felt (a) serious; (b) marvellous; and (c) that travelling up the Corridor to Berlin was the nearest a mature human being would ever come to the sensation experienced by a sperm *en route* to impregnation.

The heating in his ancient but polished MGB was jammed on. Warmth for an office block emerged at one's feet. He recommended that I should, as he had already done, remove both shoes and socks and roll up my trousers to the knee. I did so, he opened the windows and we progressed towards the Intra-German Border at Helmstedt, established in Lancaster House by the Allies on 12 September 1944 according to the London Protocol, adequately dressed for a paddle on the sands at Cromer. Germany expanded and flattened into pastures and the night around us. We passed a stream of green-grey Hungarian trucks on the way to the border and soon afterwards pulled off and down a slip-road, following signs to the Naafi Roadhouse, an army café. It is here that the Autobahn Control Detachment of the 247 (Berlin) Provost Company of the British Royal Military Police has its headquarters. The captain – Captain Valentine Ashplant as he had better be known – got dressed and we went into the HQ.

'Evening sa,' the corporal said.

'Evening corporal,' said the captain.

The corporal's neck continued for about three inches above his ears. He was standing behind a desk on a dais. The revolver on his hip was level with our noses. Ashplant handed over a piece of paper and his passport.

'Oh dear. Oh dear. Oh dear. Oh dear, sir,' the corporal said. The captain in his yellow v-neck and curling hush puppies hung his head. 'This is not, I am afraid, sir, in anything like any sort of an order, sir.' The slight flush of a blush began below Valentine's ears in the side of his neck. 'Your passport, sir,' the corporal said down to me, the last word drained of its meaning. 'The Sovs aren't going to like this, sir,' he said, flicking through the passport like a flip-up book. 'Not a bit of it.' I explained that a Pyrenean snowdrift had soaked it once. 'All very heroic, I'm sure, sir, but they're sticklers and you can't read a word of it.' This was almost true, but again I tried to explain that the Sovs in Sovland itself had thought it all right. 'I'm sorry, sir, I don't know about the situation in the Bloc. All I know is about our lot and they won't like it. Not one little bit of it.'

The corporal sanded the ends of his fingers with the back of his head. He turned again to the captain, whose chances of generalhood were quietly sliding under a Béarnaise snowdrift. 'You haven't got the BTD, the Authority, the Sponsorship, the Directive, the Agreement or the S29, sir.' These things, it turned out, were pieces of paper.

We were sent over to the sergeant-major. He was half sitting on a bar-stool with a crown embroidered on his lower arm and a cigarillo in one hand on his thigh. The huge power invested in the man was almost audibly ticking over but even he deferred to the captain's theoretical superiority. 'Not very impressive on the background, sir,' he said, and the captain looked thinner by the minute, like a dog that has shat on the carpet. 'You should have done the background on this one. You must have known it was Black at the moment, Keen Wind with the minister's movement. We might be going Rocking Horse in a day or two. You can try unit adoption by Commcen if you like.' He sipped lager. As he must have known, the captain didn't have the security vetting to use the Commcen. Nor had he even heard of the minister who was making the movement.

So we left the mess and smoked cigarettes next to a petrol pump. The corporal screamed and we put them out. We tried to drive out of the gate, but we didn't have our seatbelts on. We put them on. The headlights faded unexpectedly. The corporal was unimpressed. Eventually we managed to leave, back to barracks aged seven and a half. The captain says it happens all the time and scrapes the wax out of his ears with the blunt stub of a biro, travelling west at ninety miles an hour on the autobahn. 'It's the only lesson from the Somme,' he said. 'Corporals know best.'

The barracks were two buffer hours back from the border. 'I warn you, Ash,' a man in a monocle said to the captain, 'I'm immaculately tip-arsed.... I don't think I could really prosecute much of a conversation.' Strafer Gott looked like a Bishop on the wall. One small section of the British Army of the Rhine was coming to the tail-end of a party. About eight hiphooley junior officers of the regiment were disposed at various degrees around the club fender and leather armchairs. There was something of very experimental German ballet about it. Valentine explained his trouble with the fuzz monkeys. 'They're immaculate,' the monocle said, slipping five degrees. Captain St Crispian was heir to half of County Wexford. When the regiment was in Belfast three men in his platoon were killed in a Land Rover, as the Provisionals fired a machine-gun down the street into the back of it. He had gone to the hospital to identify them, one of them without a head. Valentine said he was a damn good officer. The men loved him. He always wore the monocle patrolling on the Falls Road.

A thruster made the mistake of referring to 'perfume'. He was about to become ADC to a Field Marshal. The others sat upright and he was lectured on the use and abuse of English. He couldn't have cared less; he knew he was the only general among them. There was a lot of sex talk and car talk. One rifleman had been to a fancy-dress party in his pants. He won the prize as 'The Anxious Teenager' because he had come in his knickers. The chaplain had a reliable Austin. A man on the floor, with his hands in his pockets and his eyes closed, told a tale, familiar to the rest and unlistened to, of a rifleman in Belfast who had kept a girl in a sangar for three weeks, running it as a one-man brothel, charging a packet of cigarettes a go. 'How extraordinary!' I said. The others had gone off to watch a video. 'But why didn't she leave?'

'She didn't have any legs, did she?'

In the morning, while the captain rearranged the documentation for the Corridor, I wandered around the barracks. It was like a marvellous country club or an eighteenth-century estate, where hundreds of men and servants arranged entertainments for the small privileged party at the centre. There was a horse ring and tennis courts, rugby pitches, stands of ash and poplar, everything efficiently and exactly mown and maintained, in a style absent from Europe now, outside the great wealth of institutions and the ancient aristocracies. Personnel carriers in the garages were lined up like golf-carts. It was an island as deeply old-fashioned as the class distinctions it enshrined. An upside-down place of dominant froth.

Armed with the sheaf of Authorities, we arrived back in Helmstedt. The best of the papers was the Berlin Travel Document. It was a movement order, a *laissez-passer*, a ПУТЕВКА. The three languages of the wartime alliance. 'Under the authority of the Commander-in-Chief, British Army of the Rhine,' it said,

| Ashplant, Valentine James Henry Mandeville | Capt. | British |
| Nicolson, Adam | Mr | British |

will proceed to and from Berlin in connection with the occupation of Berlin.' This disarmingly dramatic document – the guarantee of a weekend outing – with its preservation of forgotten motive and its juxtaposition of languages once aligned and now divided, above all in the slipped meaning of that one word *occupation* – for which both the English and the Russian have borrowed the French – was the first signal of the odd, time-suspended status of Berlin.

The sergeant-major at the roadhouse marched past us in the car park with a pace-stick in his armpit and a jersey round his belly, saying 'Have a sooper time', without deviating an inch from his course towards Schleswig-Holstein.

The gate through the Iron Curtain is up the road. It is called Checkpoint Alpha by the armies. Bravo is at the far end of the autobahn into West Berlin and Charlie, of course, on Friedrichstrasse through the Wall. We follow the signs saying 'Allies' and pull up at a low building like a drive-in bank. The flags of the three western allies are lined up outside: a long high counter divided in three. The captain has to tell another British corporal that his speedometer is broken. The freckly corporal looks at the ceiling; the captain hangs his head like a vulture. The two US MPs are talking about a Magnum revolver. A Bulgarian lorry accelerates westwards outside. 'Two rounds in the block of that and the fuckin' thing would stop right there, no question AT ALL.' One of them began talking about Gooks. 'A round in the chest and a round in the neck,' the self-darkening glasses said to the thin-rimmed eyes. 'I put about fifty in the guy and I knew after the first ten he was dead.' A grin on the killer, an affected wisdom in his pupil. They wear short-sleeved Elvis shirts. A beautiful colonel in the French paratroops smokes a white cigarette in the corner. The captain describes his MGB to the Scottish corporal. No contact between the nationalities.

We were ushered into a room where slides – secretly taken – are shown of the route to Berlin. No business must be conducted with any East German official. Only Soviet officers are competent to deal with members of the 'other allied forces'. Instructions are given by the pedantic corporal on what and what not to do, exactly, complicatedly conveyed, always stopping to refer to his notes – which particular lane to follow, which particular exit to take. No one could understand this stream of similar instructions. The captain asks: 'Do we keep in the right-hand lane when the Soviet asks us to stop at the second (closed) barrier or should one then transfer to the Allied Military Convoy (single and unaccompanied vehicles) lane after the red flag?' No one has ever asked a question before. 'I'll go through the whole procedure again for you,' the corporal says. The captain is trained to stay calm and intelligent when faced with a regiment of tanks advancing on his company scratched into foxholes and with his Milan anti-tank system defunct. He accepts the slur of stupidity from the expert corporal without pain. The rest of the audience – an RAF sergeant – sits on his hands. I look out of the window through the louvred blinds into some leafless birches. A man is looking back at me through fieldglasses, his arms up to make an arrowhead of his body. Between him and me a placard on a post says:

Halt!

Hier!

Zonengrenze

He is one of the incompetent East German officials with whom we are to have nothing to do. I stop myself from waving. He has no features, only the fly-eyes of the binoculars like a uniform.

Helmstedt was the conduit for Germans from the east, from the Soviet Zone of Germany, and those parts of the Reich east of the Oder-Neisse line which became part of Poland and Russia. Between 1945 and 1947 five million people came across the zonal boundary here, five out of the thirteen million Germans shunted west after Potsdam. Helmstedt was a wild place in the chaotic backwash of the war. Fish and cigarettes were smuggled across the border. Extortion, manipulation and killings. Seventeen murders at Helmstedt between 1945 and 1947. But most figures in the desperate anonymity of the times are vague. Perhaps a million Germans died in the forced move westwards. Applications for lost relatives at Hanover post office were at one point running at over 50,000 a week.

The pity of that era is forgotten and the flow has stopped. The crossing-point is tended and dressed. The western side is modelled on a giant freeway tollbooth. Until the recognition treaties between the two Germanies, signed in the early 1970s, the frontier authorities had to make do with temporary wooden buildings, advertising the insignificance of the frontier they supervised. *Ostpolitik* had made life more comfortable here.

The speedometerless MGB follows an RAF Austin Maestro as a speed restrictor. We move in tandem into the traffic stream, sliding off into the lane marked 'Military'. Linenfolds in the pine-woods on the frontier of Lower Saxony and Saxony-Anhalt, tailored back to make a field of fire. A pincushion of watchtowers around the crossing. Concrete walls sidle up and along the autobahn itself. Frosted glass walls divide the military from the civilian lanes. Red and white striped barriers open and close behind us. The captain stops at the stop sign below the red flag and gets out. He march-walks in the held-body way of soldiers up to the Russian with eastern features and red splashes on his buttoned uniform. The captain draws himself up in his hush-puppies and buttons his wrinkled tweed to salute the enemy. 'No enemy of mine,' he says later in the car. They look eye to eye without a smile, so near you would think they might yet kiss. Into the net-curtained, prefab cabin, where there is no meeting of any official, only a slipping of documents into a slit tray and their return, noticed but unmarked, a few minutes later. Through the frosted glass beside us distorted civilian beetles queue for admission.

Out with relief. The border itself is the foreign country, the country beyond it at home. Sperms in the corridor, tailing the broad-bottomed Austin Maestro from Godalming.

The captain described to me the difference between the game and the real thing. In the Falklands on Mount Kent one of the soldiers was shot by a sniper. His lieutenant was told that it was a 'no-duff' wound. A regular part of military exercises is practising the treatment of the 'wounded' but, if someone genuinely hurts himself by accident, the game is suspended and the 'no-duff' wound is attended to. The lieutenant for a moment imagined that he was on exercise and stood up to go over and look at the genuinely wounded man. As he stood up he was shot dead by the same sniper.

Too much training blunted the innate responses to danger. The captain had a scheme to remedy it. The British Army was too professional. It had come to rely on rational pre-planning when its real strength was pragmatic intuition. The captain wanted an Incompetent Battalion. It would be a crack guerrilla force which would spend no time on military preparations. Instead, its members would produce a scholarly edition of the letters of Alcuin; design kites; establish the links between Persian and Chinese porcelain in the sixth and seventh centuries; investigate the shopping habits of Danish widows; retranslate the works of Sir Thomas Urquhart into sixteenth-century French;

play Ouija on as many of the intersections of longitude and latitude as could be reached in the space of one year; botanize under Spaghetti Junction and design a collection of beachwear for both the spring and autumn seasons. They would have no cap badge and the motto would be: Hope for the Hopeless, followed by three dots gules. To these men and women, their wellsprings of invention richly watered, the defence of the realm would be finally entrusted.

Magdeburg came up smelling like a laboratory. The flat tank country around it was lined with willows and poplars, emptier, poorer and prettier than the same on the other side. It was south of here, across the Elbe, on 25 April 1945, the day on which Berlin was encircled by the Russians, that the western and eastern fronts of the Second World War joined hands. There was a popular assumption in Germany that the occupation zones would be formed by the armies remaining where they had met. But over fifteen months previously, at the first session of the European Advisory Commission in Lancaster House in January 1944, Sir William Strang had circulated a plan which set the western border of the Soviet Zone almost exactly where it is today. The Russian delegation accepted it almost unchanged. The Americans were disorganized, half suggested a much smaller Russian zone, but eventually had no effect on the Strang line. When the western armies withdrew early in July 1945 to that line, it caused consternation among the Germans. Many of them had simply stopped their migration westwards when they found the western armies. Now they were forced to move again.

Why should the British and Americans have offered so much of Germany to the Soviets? Sir William in his memoirs justified the choice of line by recalling that the opening sessions of the European Advisory Commission occurred six months before the Normandy landings in June 1944. Nobody could have foreseen how far into Germany the western allies would penetrate. It was generally assumed that the Russians would end up on the Rhine. The division he suggested would, in that case, have involved a large-scale *Russian* withdrawal from the territory they had conquered. He felt, in addition, that there should be broad equality between the three zones. (The French were brought in later.) The Soviets were designated 40% of the area, 36% of the people and 33% of the productive resources. This was more than fair, but the figures did not take into account the vast slices of German territory east of the Oder-Neisse line which were to be annexed by Poland.

Strang was also under pressure from the British military authorities not to stretch the western zones, for fear of shortage of manpower with which to police them. But above all, he wrote, ten years after the events,

> If we had tried to thrust the limits of the Soviet zone very far eastwards, there would then almost certainly have been no agreement. Had there been no agreement by the time the western forces met the Soviet forces at Torgau on the Elbe in 1945, we and the Americans might then have negotiated a settlement fixing the eastern boundary of our zones on the Elbe, over 100 miles to the east of the line actually agreed upon; but Berlin, of which the Russians were then in occupation, would then assuredly have remained a part of the Soviet zone and would not have come under joint administration . . . the free world would have lost the asset, uneasy and precarious though it may be, of having a foot in Berlin and of establishing an oasis of freedom in the middle of the desert of the Soviet zone.

This was published in 1956. It is infected by the Cold War (Heikki Kirkinen's axiom). None the less, it preserves intact the prize-sharing attitudes of victors. Strang says that: 'The moral effect in Germany of the undivided control of their capital by the Soviet forces is not easily measured, but would have been far-reaching.' Can this really have been in his mind early in 1944? What about the 'moral effect in Germany' of the Dresden raids? Or of the Morgenthau plan which considered turning Germany into a pastoral state after the war, full of shepherds? Concern for the well-being of German national consciousness after the war was far from the mind of western planners up to the day on which the war was won. Surely Strang is transferring an emotion? Isn't he really talking about the moral effect on the western allies who were fighting to *destroy* Germany at the time? Berlin was the atavistic prize. To have fought and won the war and to have got none of it – what sort of victory would that have been? It would simply have been unfair – the implication is – for the Russians to have got the whole of the capital city, and Strang was ready to concede lots of cake for even a segment of cherry. To renounce Berlin would have been to core the target and remove the bullseye. It was also, perhaps, a means of concealing the uncomfortable fact that the real beneficiaries of the war were the Russians, who had made good their frontiers by the Curzon formula, capturing not only the passes but the entrance to those passes in the Reichstag. The 'oasis of freedom' idea belongs to a different phase. The division of the German capital was a form of vengeance, of owning and containing an important piece of the defeated enemy.

It was surely a mistake. It pushed the border of the Soviet bloc many miles westwards, at one point within a hundred miles of the Rhine. In plain mathematical terms there would have been more Germans living in a democratic, capitalist society if the line had been drawn along the Elbe. The economic problems in supporting the two million or so West Berliners would not have arisen in the large stretch of Saxony-Anhalt and Thuringia contiguous to and continuous with the rest of the Federal Republic. There would have been no blockade or airlift crisis. The dangerously symbolic issue of the freedom of the West Berliners – never raised in the negative for the people of Erfurt or Leipzig – would simply not have existed. And a city would not now be divided.

I read to the captain in the car part of the speech made by Colonel-General Bersarin, the Soviet Commandant of Berlin, in May 1945, eleven days after the war in Europe had ended:

> We have come here to wipe out the Hitler gang once and for all. From here, Hitler's German army launched its surprise attack on the peaceable Soviet people. At no time and under no circumstances did it even occur to the Soviet people to take up arms against the Germans. . . . In my whole life I have never seen anything like the bestial actions German officers and soldiers took against this peaceable population. All the destruction you have in Germany is next to nothing compared with the devastation we have suffered.

'No love in that,' the captain said.

Even the names are divided. Official West German documents refer to Berlin (West) and Berlin (East), one city with two categories. On the East German road signs and maps there are two distinct places: Berlin and Westberlin, the capital hidden in the lower-case b.

Pension Imperator on Meinekestrasse. High knobbled white buildings opening at the bottom in a series of toad gapes. Marbled hall and tortoise-shelled staircase, goats' heads on the keystones, mineral veins in the dirty plaster. Creaking caramel light and the stale of cigarettes. Frau Anne-Marie Seibt wore black and smiled ironically with the left-hand side of her mouth. A cigarette always smoked on the ashtray on her table, trailing up into the light. The empty cigarette boxes were arranged in an angular loop like toy railway carriages across the leather. She was eighty and creaked up and down her wooden corridors in the light from faded linen shades. There was a pearl on each ear and a golden rod an inch long below it. I had to stop the captain from saluting her.

We went to a party in Kreuzberg. In the car along by the raised girders of the S-Bahn the captain sang to himself the same sentence again and again: 'The sea lost nothing of the swallowing identity of its great outer mass of waters in the emphatic individual character of each particular wave.' Kreuzberg was the other side of the coin from Meinekestrasse. Between 1871 and 1910 Berlin grew from 900,000 to 3.7 million, or one new Berliner every seven and a half minutes for forty years, three village-worths a week. The middle classes painted goats' heads in Wilmersdorf, the working classes were cramped into vast rental barracks in areas like Wedding, Neukölln and Kreuzberg. Wilmersdorf is now hotels, the others are lived in by students and Turks. Kreuzberg was the scene of squatting battles a few years ago. They were interpreted as a sign of Youth's Indifference to Hard Won Liberties.

The party was in one of the workshops of a disused factory on the banks of the Spree, which happened here to be the border itself. The walls in the long-empty workshop were white and the floorboards bare and unvarnished. At the far end a big uncurtained window looked out over the river and the Wall towards the giant mace of the TV tower in the east, the red top light flashing as it revolved. The only piece of furniture was a violent orange and green painting of a man on a horse. The English words: THIS MAN WAS ONCE ON A HORSE were stencilled diagonally across it in black. There was also a long fluorescent lighting tube in its own casing which the host – a relation of an acquaintance of the captain's – carried about with him from one conversation cluster to the next like an admiral with his pennant between ships. On this nearly pristine canvas the party was arranged. Its guests divided neatly in two between leather and cotton. Leather wore leather and had arranged hair, some of it oiled, tight clothes, black or dark brown, mildly militaristic, the men shaven, the women with cosmetics. Cotton was in pastels, some with beards, hair that flopped and was pulled back behind the ear, the health look, clothes loose on them, brothel creepers, no conscious glamour, post-materialist, green and convinced of the worth of human virtues. But they were not arranged in two camps. It was all mixed in together, mobile, loud and at home on the *tabula rasa*. They shared one thing: an ability to make themselves look as they wanted to appear. The captain swam off into the pool. I later heard him discussing baby clothes with a (leather) historian.

The whole party had spent the day at a seminar on *zusammenleben und neue architektur* (no capitals) in which Le Corbusier was the villain cast as *Baukünstler*-cum-*Führer-Architekt* (many capitals) and a tentative vision of life between nostalgia and concrete *Imperialismus* had been hinted at without anyone daring a Formulation. When someone had moved towards Definition she had been pulled up short with all the laden reminders of the city and its history around them. Here they now were, at the end of this hesitant and interrupted day, apparently pleased with all the inconclusiveness of their discussions, lacking all conviction, as neatly tucked in with each other as any yin with her tadpole yang, drinking kir from mugs and glasses.

'The disposable nappy,' the captain was saying to a man whose face was hidden by pipe-smoke, 'has always seemed to me the most instant of betrayals.' *Another Kind of Blues* was put on to a record player, but nobody even tapped their feet to it. The Wall outside the window was neglected. Only I went over to look at it on the far side of the river. The bare tube-topped concrete, in the confusion of half-objects and sheared-off buildings through which it passed, was as neat and as total as the white party room. There was a connection between them which I could not quite establish, in their purity and obviousness. One of these people said to me later in the week: 'The Wall is not everything. That is a mistake which strangers make. But it affects everything here.' In the room there was a veering away from the Wall, and that was an effect of the wall itself.

I found myself next to a beautiful girl from Darmstadt with a round brown face and a jersey with a zip up the front.

'Do you have a *Konzept* for your book?' she asked me.

'No,' I said, rather desperately. 'I just want to see what the frontiers are like.'

'Yes,' she said, 'but in the *book*, what is the *Konzept* in the book?'

'Just going from place to place.'

'Is that an idea?'

'Sort of.' I thought of the captain in the car. 'I suppose it might be about the swallowing identity of the great outer mass of waters losing nothing in the emphatic individual character of each particular wave.'

'That is extraordinarily interesting,' Darmstadt said. 'Whom do you quote it from?' I pointed at the captain, who was showing the elasticated waistband of his boxer shorts to the historian. Darmstadt rushed over to talk to him, taking a yellow woollen scarf from her head and wrapping it around her bottom as she got there.

I went out. Notice-boards on the riverside in German and Turkish advised against entering the water, since the frontier runs along the near bank and the river itself beyond the sloping cobbles is part of the *Ostsektor*. Red and white lifebelts were hung up on the bank under the sparse urban willows. On the far side was the Wall, lit sodium yellow, and of a piece with the appearance of the city, no more divisive from down here than a wall around a factory plant yard. In the dark waters of the Spree an unlit patrol boat – a bronchial undergurgle – went past in midstream against the lights on the far side. The voices of the crew were snatched at and guttered in the wind. I waited until the wash clapped up against the bank and looked at some terns playing on the underside of the closed-off Oberbaumbrücke before going back into the party.

The captain was gurgling like a diesel into Darmstadt's ear: he looked like a pensioned-off janitor. It was time to go. He wanted to go anyway. He knew of a little night spot which I had to visit to get any idea of Berlin *as it was*.

Club Madame was back in Wilmersdorf. Valentine was now behaving like Long John Silver, whispering 'What a wild time we had of it!' at the parking meters, and then roaring out his high-pitched deep-down enriched belly of a laugh.

Twenty-five marks to get into Club Madame. Red carpet on the walls. The first sight of a mostly naked hostess figure and the giggling captain declared himself at ease with the world, pulled his chin into his neck, folded his arms across his chest in a sort of Double Boston and shut up. The naked women had tiny white boy-like bodies. We sat down within a foot of a little carpeted stage with whisky. A foot or two along the same padded buttoned sofa a thirty-eight-year-old sociology graduate held his chin. It was scrimmed in beard. A man of good liberal conscience, he had his wife along with him in a yellow hair-do and an up-to-the-neck dress. She leant back as he leant forward like the two stopped levers of a pump. On the other side a large settled Canadian officer, shaved around the head, had two small naked women next to his legs. They spoke to each other around the equator of his chest. He looked straight ahead as if sitting for a portrait, resting a hand on each naked thigh to the left and right of his trousers. The captain said with his eyes shut that the road of deprivation leads to the palace of wisdom.

A series of strippers on the podium. Automated Audi production line followed by Upstairs Downstairs (Ruby). And then a cynic with a flick of greasy hair and a leer. The sociologist remained intent and forward, the Canadian colonel monumental. She wriggled out of a red spangled dress to reveal a five-point star on one buttock, a tiny anarchist A high up on the other. A tape machine began to play a dismal piece of violin music and she mimed to it with a bow, at first on a flat nipple and then between her legs. She invited the colonel to saw the bow between her legs, which he did without interest, and then drew it herself along the nostrils of the anxious sociologist, who turned halfway through the experience to smile up at his wife, so that the bow slid away along his cheek and ear. She smiled back at him reassuringly. The captain was now asleep. The colonel took his women through a curtained doorway and it was time to leave. As I pushed Valentine towards the exit, a drunken child of about forty-five in a suit was allowing himself to be undressed by another girl in lace, while the watchers who remained were cheering. The sociologist twisted his brow. For all the captain's assurances this was not Berlin. 'Nyars,' he agreed, and withdrew into the night.

Seven hours later we went down to Kladow to visit some Fusiliers. The barracks are among the suburban villas, entry phones and quarry-tiled drivelets of Berlin at its most sedate. Large bits of leather furniture through the sliding smoked windows. The ex-lanes come to an end in notices:

End of British Sector
Do not pass this line

———————

or

Achtung!
Sie verlassen jetzt
West-Berlin

or

Ende
des demokratischen Sektors
von Gross-Berlin
(this one fading)

or in other parts

Achtung!
Hier
beginnt die
Sowjetzone

all in a chaos of typography and varied hidden attitudes. Some of the older notices are only in English, French and Russian, with no message for the policed Germans.

Beyond the notices in Kladow there was nothing but scrubwood, the wet smell of half-woodland mulch. The fence was deep in out-of-bounds. A squirrel ran away from me towards it and then along the mesh. The fence was made of sheet metal punctured with a harrow and then stretched on an industrial rack to open out sharp-edged lozenge holes too small to push a finger in. It was about forty metres into East German territory. The captain remained the far safe side of the woodland belt, by now invisible to me. There was another fence across the sanded strip, about another forty metres away, with the line of tank traps called Spanish horsemen like collapsed gravestones in a rank between the two. Across to the right in the concrete golf-tee tower, with railings around the roof like on a ship's side and a searchlight on a turntable, a man picked up a telephone in silhouette. Two others hooked their rifles over their shoulders. A domestic bell rang among the houses in East Germany, among their concrete mansard roofs. A door at the bottom of the watchtower opened. I waited a second – they would have taken twenty to reach me – before scrabbling through the hazels and wet mast to where the captain was singing to a Bach cantata in his car.

The border around Berlin was established on 27 April 1920 by the Law on the Formation of a New Municipality Berlin. It merged the city with seven surrounding towns and fifty-nine villages to make Gross-Berlin. This was the entity that was divided at the conferences in London in 1944. The Fusiliers lived in some Luftwaffe barracks – renamed Montgomery – built in the 1930s for units operating out of Gatow airfield a mile away to the north-east. The Luftwaffe paid no attention to the municipal boundary and their barracks straddled it.

A friend of the captain's showed us around with a party of old Luftwaffe hands in sheepskins and tartan capts. There was cheery reminiscence about one night in 1943 when the Royal Air Force did very well with 'your fire-bomb damage' as we walked about between the playing-fields and the poplars, and the grassed-over sites of living quarters. Lieutenant Phelps led us down to the border. There was nothing official to mark it save the familiar notice board announcing the end of the British sector, with the line below the words.

The world changed beyond this line. A range of garages ran across it, on this side pert and repainted, on the other turned dusty, gone loose. The pantiles were browned and partly missing, the windows unwashed since the war and the timbers blanched between the fragments of Nazi paint. Sheened fire-engines stood in the openings on this side, lined up by their hoses and buckets. On the other, stale grasses had sprouted in the concrete. Ash trees had colonized the guttering and their roots had levered the bricks out of true.

'Some start-line,' the captain said.

A man from the Luftwaffe said, 'And I thought it was over there, *drüben*, that the German style was really preserved.'

The Wall was virtually invisible, about two hundred metres away through the trees. A detachment of the GKN border troops lived in the rump of the barracks beyond it. They were a new lot at the moment and they were having trouble with their goon towers. They kept collapsing. There had been an incident in the night with flares and some firing, but it was trigger happiness, the lieutenant said. 'Probably rabbits who knew which side their bread was buttered.' He thought it a routine duty, little better than where Valentine was holed up on the Central Front (this in a John Wayne voice). 'There's never any development, never any chance of development. They're not the IRA. It's really a question of waiting for them to admit they've been building a ring road for twenty years. We offered to lend them the tarmac.' The Fusiliers use the ruined garages as a playground for urban warfare training. It is the only place in the world where Nato troops practice on the territory of the Warsaw Pact. It will be a service station when the ring road comes into use.

The captain and I had a cup of coffee in one of the Kladow villas. It was the married quarters of a major and his wife. They padded round their shag-piled ornamented home, up and down the riserless staircase, in and out of the oak veneer panel breakfast area cum kitchen holding mugs of coffee with the names of their cats on. She hated the Americans, the Germans and Berlin. He had just returned from guarding Hess up the road in Spandau, but wouldn't say anything about it. (I heard later that the British had plans to turn the prison into a giant Naafi when Hess died. The Russians refuse to release him because to do so would be to renounce the main regular presence of Soviet troops in West Berlin.) Both of them hated journalists. The captain wasn't even faintly embarrassed. The major was a severe case of clipped balls. He was an apparatchik who would probably end up as deputy governor of the Tower of London, when Mummy Knows Best could meet the Queen. It was another version of the border guard, safe in the structures and so anxious not to spill his coffee on the carpets that he put his mug down on the nest of tables half-way through a story in case he found his own punchline 'amusing' and laughed. Mummy said that she had to go into Berlin in the afternoon. Her own house wasn't in Berlin. It was on the outskirts, a spreading Surrey vision of her circumstance, or perhaps even a Berlin in Berlin, an oasis of shag in the desert of urban degradation.

The captain took me to the Olympic stadium. He loved it. 'The best war memorial you could think of,' he said. The whole construction excludes fragility in a muscled 1936 Roman/Dark Age conglomerate. The rhetoric of brutality demanded an unnecessary glacis at the foot of the monumental walls, and a deep net of rustication cast over the whole building. It is a conscious reversionist shrine, both pure and primitive. From the top of the clock tower, which we climbed on foot on the metal staircase, ignoring the lift to absorb the ethos – the captain's idea – one could get a picture of the stadium as a whole. Its vast rationality has been taken to the point of a disturbing and irrational belief, soaking its sterility in a sort of decadent lusciousness. And something of Berlin beyond it. But distance lent vagueness to the view and there was no idea from the top of the clock tower that this was a pie-chart city. It was damp and wooded, bobbled like the suit in the Minsk train, utterly different from the schema of the stadium and its surroundings, with no division or separation apparent in the drizzle and encroaching dark.

Almost level with the viewing platform, a mile away to the south in the northern edges of the Grunewald, is the Trümmerberg, the Rubble Hill, where the ruins of Berlin were dumped after the war, piled up to 120 metres above sea-level, the highest point of the city in either half. It is now capped with the white ears and buildings of an American listening post.

Those two high points, Hitler's clock tower and the rubble-built Nato listening hill, are the two feet of the arch under which modern Berlin was born. It is – at least in the West – a city still under military government. The commanding officers of the three western garrisons form *de jure* three quarters of the government of the whole city and *de facto* the whole government of half of it. The Kommandatura, as the four-power committee is called, from which the Soviet representative withdrew on 16 June 1948, still leaves an empty chair and a short pause at the beginning of each meeting, during which the commandants of the British, French and American garrisons wait for the Russian to arrive. Their meetings are not an empty formality. There is a full municipal framework for Berlin (West), but the Kommandatura reserves the all-important power of veto. In October 1950 the three-power Kommandatura suspended the Berlin Constitution drafted by the Berlin municipal assembly which stipulated that Berlin was one of the constituent Länder – or States – of the Federal Republic of Germany. The law is annulled in Berlin, but remains in force in the FRG. For the commandants to have accepted it, whatever the increasingly absorbed status of *East* Berlin in the GDR, would have undermined the Potsdam agreements by which the allies occupied the city in the first place.

The military veto remains. The three commandants have prevented the twenty-two Berlin delegates who sit in the Bonn Parliament from voting in plenary sessions; suspended the jurisdiction of the Federal Constitutional Court in Karlsruhe over the city and rejected a Bonn proposal that the World Bank and the IMF should hold their meetings in West Berlin. When Reagan came here the Kommandatura stopped the police removing anti-Reagan stickers from cars.

None the less this state of affairs turns the arguments about freedom and self-determination strangely upside-down. On the one hand President Kennedy could say in a television address to the American nation in July 1961: 'We are [in Berlin] as a result of our victory over Nazi Germany and our basic rights to be there, deriving from that victory, include both our presence in West Berlin and the enjoyment of access across East Germany. These rights have been repeatedly confirmed and recognized in special agreements with the Soviet Union. Berlin is not a part of East Germany, but a separate territory under the control of the allied powers. Thus our rights are clear and deep-rooted.'

Against these victor's rights, arranged over the head of a defeated nation, Khrushchev could pose as a champion of nationalist freedoms. 'Apparently the time has come', he said in a speech in Moscow, 'for the signatory powers of the Potsdam Agreement to relinquish the occupation regime in Berlin in order to normalize the situation in the capital of the German Democratic Republic. The Soviet Union, on its part, will transfer to the sovereign GDR those functions in Berlin which are still performed by the Soviet authorities.' What could be more reasonable, generous or humane? Gromyko suggested in 1962 that 'normalization' meant 'abolishing the occupation regime and replacing the occupation troops by troops of the neutral states or the UN for a definite period. . . . West Berlin would be converted from Nato's military outpost into a free city of peace and tranquillity.'

The East Germans had fenced off the frontier between East and West Germany in 1952, but the border through Berlin had stayed open. The creative manpower of East Germany geysered through the gap. Nearly three million East Germans crossed the zonal boundary between 1949 and 1961, an average of a quarter of a million a year, a village a day. Three quarters of the refugees were under forty-five, half of them under twenty-five. By August 1961 2,000 a day were arriving at the Marienfelde reception centre in West Berlin. It was this haemorrhage the Wall was designed to stanch.

It did its job and international tension moved elsewhere. If nothing else, the Wall made the political landscape more obvious. By genuinely isolating West Berlin it had simplified the realities with which the statesmen had to deal. In a sense, the building of the Wall was the first step towards the *Ostpolitik* of the late 1960s and early 1970s. This is only a shallow paradox. Delineating differences in the most concrete way imaginable is itself a confidence-building measure, a valuable clarity, Torhag thought.

Ostpolitik linked the status of Berlin to the promise of a Conference on European Security and Stabilization which would legitimate the borders of the Soviet sphere in Europe established in the 1940s. For Berlin the culminating moment was the Quadripartite Agreement between the foreign ministers of France, the United Kingdom, the United States and the Soviet Union which came into effect in June 1972. It recognized for the first time that 'the ties between the Western Sectors of Berlin and the FRG will be maintained and developed' although 'these Sectors continue not to be a constituent part of the FRG and not to be governed by it'. In exchange for the recognition of these ties the western powers agreed to limit the activities of the Government of the FRG in West.Berlin, so that the Federal President may no longer be elected there and full sessions of the Federal Parliament may no longer take place in the Reichstag.

More immediately significant for West Berliners was the re-establishment of telephone lines between the two halves of the city, suspended in 1952, the agreements on accidents in the Spree and the canals, on the disposal of rubbish and sewage (the flow is entirely from West to East), the sorting out of some anomalies in the borderline itself, traffic agreements for the Corridor and on the s-Bahn and u-Bahn and on new access for West Berliners to the GDR, closed to them since 1952, and to East Berlin, closed since the Wall was built on 13 August 1961.

Most of this has worked well ever since. Only the GDR's manipulation of the amount of money that has to be exchanged at the crossing points by visitors to East Berlin has spoilt the overall effect. Politicians in the West talk about a 'financial Wall'. It now stands at twenty-five marks a day for everyone, including pensioners.

For the foreseeable future West Berlin remains no part of either Germany, ultimately governed by allied ex-victors.

The captain took me to the British Officers' Club, where on prints of eighteenth-century shoots spaniels waited for the collapsed dead upside-down ducks, still travelling through mid air, to land.

At night we walked along the Wall. In the pavement booths there were post-cards of the frontier glamorized through star-filters and a colour wash. But there is none of that distance, that gloss-coat to the Wall itself. The shock is in the tangible, concrete actuality of what should – in a moral, a straightforwardly moral world – have remained an idea. It represents all the failures of a grand political system to be good and generous at the level of the individual human life. It represents bad means for good ends. It swallows up in one obvious physical demonstration anything that has ever been said about governors and governed and the gap between them.

This makes it a Sight, to be visited by tourists. Nineteenth-century ramblers, if they wanted some delicious terror, some unclothed confrontation with the unassimilated Other, would go to Gordale Scar or Karnak, where the sheer scale of unhuman power in Nature or Time would titivate the jaded cosmic sense. Now we come here and, like them, write our names up.

The original wall, quickly built in the last two weeks of August 1961, at least had barbed wire along the top, something *echt* in the violence of its finishing and something incompetent in the bulging mortar between the blocks, but the modern frontier, like the slick agreements of *Ostpolitik*, has moved beyond all that. There is a stabilizing flange on the western side and an unholdable concrete tube along the top. Discreet doors that come flush to the concrete panels are used by guards before the visits of American presidents and Prince Philip to come out into the yard or two of East Berlin to the west of it, where they whitewash the remarks that have been painted on the giant's bottom. Here too, like in Leningrad, is a vertical excavation for a future archaeologist, peeling away the layers of attitudes and their whitewashings. For now it says:

MADE IN GERMANY
Dessous les pavés et le mur C'est la plage . . .
Die Verbrecher
I huffed and I puffed but, you know? I think I just smoke too many a day?
Wo die Freiheit endet beginnt der Mensch.
One lung is better than none.

An American, with name, address and phone number in Des Moines supplied, had written: If socialism needs this, who needs socialism? And next to it a Frenchman had taken up several square metres of East German property with:

Seulement l'amour,
L'amour douce
et féroce,
peut
remuer tout ce qui est là.

Il faut
attendre. Il faut
dire «nous».
Tout ce qu'on fait
qui impose,
qui impose les différences,
les haïres, perpetuera
tout ce qui est là. Il faut
attendre. Il faut
espoir.
IL FAUT TRAVAILLER!
Nous.
Ensemble.

He may have tried to get this published elsewhere.

Yankee we want to kill you.
Germany for the Germans.
Hey Jude – IRA
Is this a dead phallus?
John Wayne was a Nazi.

I began to write down another, which began

Un mur, ça coupe,
il y a toujours un mur
qui coupe

before I recognized the style from two kilometres away to the north.

The Pretty Wall
1 butt – 2 buttocks
To be or NATO be.
Unsere Freiheit ist Ihr TOD!

Have you ever been a wallflower too?

LOOK AT THE
BRIGHT SIDE
OF LIFE

Happiness is just a shot away!

A simple six-foot

> Eugene, your name is on the Berlin Wall, like I
> said it would be *and* I did it – Max.

and endless 'Wot no Watneys' figures, crawling over, nose and fingers first, and simple crosses where people have been shot trying to escape. Over seventy have died since 1961.

One cross can stand for them all: a large brown wooden crucifix, wrapped in barbed wire and with photographs attached to it of the dirty shot body of the eighteen-year-old Peter Fechter who bled to death at the foot of the Wall on 17 August 1962, after lying there wounded for fifty minutes and shouting 'Help me!' over and over again. A US sergeant refused to climb down into the space between the walls to give him first aid before he died and was carried away.

Beyond that first western written-on wall is the blank space between the walls known as the death strip. The West has provided scaffolds from which one can look over into this strange space, the middle of a landscape of which the one law is the Law of the Excluded Middle. There are no mines in the strip, but fences that ring bells and illuminate the area when touched, dogs on runs, Spanish horsemen, an anti-vehicle trench and the towers with outward-leaning windows, the ultimate monuments to traffic control. But, for all these objects, the real character of the strip is emptiness. The Wall itself hides this gap in urbanity. It is easy, perhaps, to accept the Wall as part of the urban division of things, the allocation of space for function and property, but this blank passage, electric with threat, does not belong in any landscape outside the fictional. It is a hovering non-space, a negative made apparent only by the positives it separates, a hiccough in the continuity of the real world. It is the place on earth where the state of nature actually exists, the landscape of distrust.

The death strip has no connections or dependences. It induces a sort of vertigo, perhaps a nostalgia, an irrational desire for its vacuum glamour, inviting one to try it out for the hell of it. Occasionally people attempt to cross the strip from west to east: lunatics, criminals, the sublimely ignorant like the American hitchhiker a few years ago who was trying to get to Sweden and thought it a disused railway track, blocking his way across the city. More often than not, these people are wounded and returned.

The captain peed from the scaffold and it steamed like a night-thought on the concrete flange. We had come to the back of the Brandenburg Gate. Schadow's quadriga faced away into the East. The captain said: 'Never be frightened at the back of things. They're either yours or they're running away.' Another corporal had told him this.

The next day we squeezed through the jubilee clip at Checkpoint Charlie. 'City with a screw loose,' the captain said. The most famous border crossing in the world. In uniform by law, he slipped through the military channel uninspected, preceded and followed by two square busloads of cleaned up GIS. With the other civilians, a Pole and a young American in loafers, I waited an hour in the various netted and plastic booths. The barriers on the allied side came down to a definite stop. The East German barrier bounced in its rowlock cup. Metal rods hung vertically from the bar to the ground. Two escapes had been made in the 1960s in an Austin Healey that was low enough to go under it. The rods were putty in the mousehole. We were asked if we carried any 'guns, ammunition, newspapers, magazines or books' – in the one category – and to declare every penny we had.

It's a broken and interrupted transit. Action is slowed down to one zigzag frame at a time, where it can be examined sprocket hole by sprocket hole. Only one of them need be faulty, a little tear, a roundness at the edges, for the film to tangle in the gate. The result is an elaborate flow diagram, as complicated a dance step as at the entrance to Maiden Castle, replacing the chalk and turf with concrete blocks and weld-link netting.

Valentine had only a few hours in East Berlin before he had to leave again for duties in West Germany. We walked about together in the Mitte, the Schinkel monumental centre of the city, and drove out to the all-Russian war memorial in Treptow Park, where the 5,000 Soviet soldiers who died in the battle for Berlin are buried between willows and under stone. The captain thought it would make a good stadium. 'This is what we're up against,' he said, and was moved by the image of Mother Russia.

He was in two minds about appearing competent in the streets of the other city. Hope for the Hopeless soldiers would, perhaps, deliberately look silly in these circumstances. We met a cardinal outside the cathedral in layers of puce clothes, with strings and ribbons holding them together, and Valentine appeared competent. We met some West German students in flecked mauve Kathrin scarves outside the Pergamum Museum and he appeared incompetent. One of them spat on to the pavement next to his shiny feet. There, the gob said, is a wall-builder, a military mason and an alien to our desires. The city *is* desire, the Wall a suspect will, of which you are the uniformed agency. Germany for the Germans, the spreading gob said, leaking into the dimples in the granite. You are the creator of these Newtonian circumstances where one block makes equal and opposite reactions to the movements of the other. Your motives are suspect. We identify capitalism with imperialism. There is no liberal middle here. Germany for the Germans now, despite the wall of which you have shared in the building, divider, Versailles-minded anti-Germanist and alien. *Die Mauer muss weg* – the Wall must go.

Was he uncomfortable, was he indifferent? Had he somehow lost his squadron of high horses on the far side of the Brandenburger Tor? He picked his ears again with the keys to his car. He began musing on the wet sand and the dry sand on Weymouth Sands. On Unter den Linden he recited 'This limetree bower my prison' and then went on about 'the fire and the fire'.

I said goodbye to Valentine at Checkpoint Charlie in the darkest, zero hour half-streets of East Berlin, where everything appears half what it should be or was. I watched the tail lights of the MGB slide away into the coils of the checkpoint with something like regret. A small queue of cars formed at the barrier. A silver vw Golf with British number plates drew up to wait its turn. In the back an Englishwoman of mournful appearance – she had not enjoyed her first sight of Communism – watched me looking across to the American Sector. She thought me an East Berliner pining for freedom. Even more sadly I gazed after the disappearing captain and then turned this hopeless face towards the silver car. She smiled at me unsteadily through the glass. I, Buster Keaton, smiled back and then looked westwards again. An East German guard began to walk towards me and I turned away as if in disgust without giving her another look. Perhaps she was a reporter from the *Mail on Sunday*. I hope it rounded off her weekend in Berlin.

West Berlin is the frontier town *par excellence*, but East Berlin is no frontier town at all. It does have a blank lobotomized hemisphere appended to it, which on the GDR maps contains no streets, but in the East that other separated half can be forgotten in the uninflected atmosphere of a true capital. Walter Ulbricht once referred to it as 'the western suburbs of the capital of the GDR'. All the invented, exacerbated, out-on-the-edge air of the western sectors evaporates beyond the Wall. This has a strange effect: the individual and ignorant experience of the Wall is what it is said to be in the eastern propaganda. Its apparent effect now is not to prevent East Berliners from going into the West, but to isolate all the subversive and dangerous 'anti-social' influences that breed over there. It is a city wall turned inside-out like a pelt.

In the West the Wall cannot be ignored. If you travel in a straight line you will eventually meet it. But in the East, for which of course it was intended, it seems like no more than a boulder in the stream, to be steered around and left to itself, or like a neglected rotten molar that aches only when you are worried. Inside the Wall, in the West, the Wall itself is positive, oppressive, highly visible, inviting graffiti. From the East, where not so much care has been taken in cleaning it up, it is oddly withdrawn and recessive, not an imposition but a blank, a negative on which graffiti – were they possible – would somehow not be *seen*. It was the Leningrad effect: with the sense of frontier everywhere, the real frontier ceases to matter.

Part of the reason is historical. Until 1800 what is now West Berlin was at best aristocratic villas and parks, at worst forest and fields. The city ended at the Brandenburg Gate. In the 1945 zoning of the city the Soviets, as its conquerors, were awarded the middle, the medieval city and its Hohenzollern extensions. West Berlin *is* an old suburb. Its centre around the Kurfürstendamm – the London match is Kensington High Street – is unmetropolitan, almost provincial, shifted sideways. East Berlin may have lost a limb, but West Berlin is the limb itself. If these organisms lived, the East could survive on crutches, the West in nothing save an iron lung.

I exchanged the western Imperator for the eastern Metropole, which is nearly a Holiday Inn, so that if you didn't know the difference, you wouldn't know the difference. But the truth is in the nuance, where the switch in the lamp feels unimportant, where the lampshade is nylon, where the lock on the drawer in the desk is stiff, where the reading-matter on the low hall table is not the *New Yorker* and *Vogue*, but *Pravda*, *Moscow News*, *Morning Star*, *L'Unità*, the joint declaration for peace by the Communist parties of East and West Germany, earnest and serious political discussion scattered on the rosewood as if it were travel writing.

The minibar was the same and the room was big. I solemnly measured it out: 264 square feet or, according to some propaganda I had, half the size of an average family flat in the GDR. It was also eight times the price of Frau Seibt's room in the Pension Imperator. Nothing creaked here in the isolated and meaningless luxury, in the pastiche nowhere, the foreign exchange Utopia about which I had no choice.

I went to a concert. Oleg Kagan, the swept-back soloist in the Schnittke, was cheered like a cosmonaut. No reluctance over the great man theory of creativity. And no reluctance either about generating some emotion with cocktails. The woman next to me in the annular crush bar was quite content in 1953. She wore a yellow transparent blouse through which you could see the delphiniums on her bra as if under street lighting. She held the Martini cocktail about two feet away from the yellow, looked at it as though in a fog and began to bring it towards her lip. Fully one foot six inches before it arrived there she opened her mouth to accept it in the round O of an aquarium fish. After a minute the lipsticked ridges printed on to the rim and the whole Martini slipped away. She was one of the few people to enjoy the Brahms. Her husband, a camera technician, watched the process standing to attention about three inches below her mouth. He alternated sipping his own drink with running a hand through hair that had once been *en brosse* but now looked like part of the Potsdamer Platz. He did this seven times before the Martini sank into the aquarium.

Gromyko was in town. Everyone was stopped by ropes while a black convoy went past with flags. We craned and saw nothing. I looked in the windows of the western embassies. Idea shops. Embassies *for* the GDR, not *in* the GDR. People played in Cumbernauld and Milton Keynes as if in Sverdlovsk. The Americans displayed German Americans: Hannah Arendt, Gertrude Stein, the Rockefeller and Steinway Bros, Kurt Vonnegut and Henry Kissinger.

I looked at cars. A Trabant is a shrivelled Austin Cambridge with a snub-nosed spaniel eagerness in the wide arrowed spaces; a Wartburg, more solid, runged up; and the culminating beautiful Czech Tatra, of which there were few and all black, as long as a Mercedes with an enriched American roundness and a single curve down and back from the top of the windscreen to the rear bumper, taking the back window in its stride – a Brylcreem car, shark among pilchards.

I walked north and west from the famous middle into the city of unspecifics. In East Berlin the Don't Walk signs at pedestrian crossings show a red man holding his arms out sideways, barring the passage. In West Berlin the Don't Walk signs at pedestrian crossings show a red man holding his arms down by his side, waiting for himself to turn green.

East Berlin was like most of London, more like London than like West Berlin. There is nothing flash or chosen in the eastern half, nothing exacerbated. There is a casualness and self-effacement about the place, a workaday ordinariness which is impossible in West Berlin. Over there everything is either odd because it is odd or odd because it isn't. Here in the East there are bullet-pocked streets and unrepaired apartment blocks. Many of these (200,000 flats in all) are still privately owned but with rents centrally frozen at 1945 levels landlords cannot afford repairs. Around Karl-Marx (ex-Stalin, ex-Frankfurter)-Allee the people's palace arrangement of slab apartment blocks built since the war embodies a grand idea, but it is one with which the world is familiar. Each is a tower hamlet.

I walked up to find the Wall from the eastern side. It had seemed important in the West; no more than a morbid curiosity here. I found it in a graveyard where Baron von Richthofen was once buried. He has now been removed westwards with the permission of his family. The Wall was on the far side of Roman portals and red granite sphinxes, past black-trunked limes, broken angels and the clotted urban earth between them. Mounds of ivy testified neglect. The stones with dates after 1945 were small.

A neat tarmac strip hemmed the cemetery and kept the concrete wall distinct. There is no tubing along the top of the inner wall. For sheer information, I suppose. The authorities would like would-be escapers to get into the death strip. Only the border zone notice distinguished it from other walls. I sat down next to it on the curving wet root-stock of elm tree and made notes. A pair of sagging black boots appeared in front of me. They disappeared under the hem of a green nylon raincoat which didn't hang properly and looked like the uppermost of several. The full flush neck of a policeman came out of it higher up, buckled into a collar and a same-colour tie. He wanted my passport. It was back in the Metropole. Where was I going? I chose at random. 'That church over there.'

'The church?'

'Yes,' I said.

'You cannot go to the church. The state ends here. The church is on the other side of the state border.' He looked at me. We laughed and he rustled in his raincoats. About 550 members of the border guard have escaped over the wall since 1961.

'But you cannot write here,' he said.

'I'm only writing about' – I looked for the word – 'death', and waved my arm past the fluted bits and pieces, the ragstone ziggurats.

'Ah, the dead are OK. It is the border you must not. The dead are very good.' And he left me to it, like Chatterton in the attic.

I made one appointment in East Berlin, to see Karl-Heinz Gummisch. He was an official in the six-storey Information Centre on Alexanderplatz, the Corbusian skating rink gouged out of the middle of old Berlin. I wanted an official view. There was a time when visiting journalists were taken to an office in the Brandenburg Gate where the techniques and justification of the *Antifaschistischer Schutzwall* (Antifascist Protective Rampart) were described, but no longer.

Herr Gummisch was relaxed. In a masterly piece of semiotics he wore a thick black corduroy suit *quite* like the overalls worn by building workers I had seen in the morning and rather more like the uniform of a television executive. He was forty-seven and wore a big pair of glasses. I told him I was writing a book on European frontiers. 'Yes,' he smiled and put his hands together on his stomach, looking out at the gulls over Alex-Platz. 'And I wanted to hear something from this side. One gets so much from the other.' He picked at the midnight-blue hessian on his parabolic chair. 'And I wanted to know what kind of effect the Wall had on this side of Berlin. Economic difficulties, general cultural questions . . .' He looked at me over the top of the dark blue frames.

'Well,' he said, 'I have these tourist magazines for you and some information on the hotel booking system we have introduced. Here is a deliberate brochure. Will you go to Dresden? We have a new hotel in Dresden.'

I thanked him. What he said was very interesting, but it wasn't the particular area I had in mind. He spread his arms and stretched, pushing his body into the desk. He said, 'I only hope this information will help you to write a good book. I have a plastic for you to put everything in it.'

In its way, this was an accurate description of the Wall: an efficient shut-out. Perhaps Herr Gummisch was being more than obstructive. Perhaps he was saying: the wall has no effect on this side. There is nothing to say about it. It is where the country ends, nothing more. Not a hole in the heart, nor a hole in the head, only the kind of hole you make if you put your finger and thumb together.

The temptation is to expect the mirror image of attitudes in West Berlin to appear in the East, to fold over the bumps and hollows of one half into the hollows and bumps of the other. But it does not work. Berlin is no longer a divided city. After nearly a quarter of a century it has become two places which happen to be next to each other. Even the German spoken on either side of the Wall is said to be moving apart. East German German has a strange collection of English words that have arrived through Russian: 'pioneer', 'dispatcher', 'combine' and 'meeting', none of which are to be heard in the 'fun OK' Gerglish of the western sectors.

Back in the West, in the aquarium, *ein Stück Natur* as the ads said, with the gratuitously gaudy fish. 'LSD *Fisch*,' a furred woman said to her furred-up companion as the jaggerlipped instruments snooker-kissed her on the glass. Emptily exotic creatures in beautiful oxygenated worlds of rising bubbles and concealing sustaining plants, only there because they didn't belong there. One-message neons in their lemon slice existence, cohabiting with their permanent and jokeless clones, either drop-jawed in discontent or mouthingly and lippily sucking particles from the rocks, each fish an oasis in its silent and organized tank.

Picasso on show near the Wall in the National Gallery, Mies van der Rohe's last glass raid on the articulate, finished a year before he died in 1968. The mauve students crowded around one object, *The Warrior* (1933, bronze), about four feet high. He has a fat silly round face with a simple round smile on a simple chin and an engorged bull-walrus nose. His spherical eyes have popped away from their sockets with the self-important optimism of a cockatoo. Stemming from the back of his head, where the cranium does not really exist – it comes out of the back of his face – a great Achilles crest as big as the head itself. No helmet, straight out of the deformed bronze bone. This head-assemblage is balanced on a chicken-scrag of a body. It would collapse but for the plain metal rod at the back. You had to laugh.

Near the National Gallery two sorts of urban wilderness approach the Wall. Both are intentional. The Tiergarten was a deer and wild boar reserve for the Brandenburg princes. Frederick the Great cut avenues through it and imposed a French geometry on the park. In the early nineteenth century it was changed again into a less formal *jardin anglais*, which was destroyed by English and American bombing in the war. Everything growing there today has been planted since the 1950s, a large part of it with trees from English towns.

At the south-eastern corner of the Tiergarten, beyond the zonal boundary but still west of the Wall itself, is the triangular piece of land once filled with the salons and cafés of Königsgrätzer Strasse, Lenné-strasse and Bellevuestrasse, the Bond Streets of pre-war Berlin. It is now a wilderness of man-high weeds and wild rabbits, a trial-ground for the scrubby return to nature: un-Tiergartenized chaos.

The Wall cut off this triangle of the Soviet zone. Beyond it is the Potsdamer Platz, once surrounded by the Imperial Chancellery, the Gestapo cells on Prinz-Albrecht-Strasse, and the headquarters of the Wehrmacht, by the Wertheim department store, the famous all-German drinking and dancing Haus Vaterland and the Potsdamer Bahnhof. After the war this whole bombed and ruined piece of land which lay across the border became the pitch for black market dealings between the sectors, for crime, prostitution and daily police raids, all against a backdrop of burnt-out and shelled buildings with collapsing shacks between them.

It has been planed away. The Potsdamer Platz is an empty concrete expanse, where the buildings have been demolished, the tram tracks torn up and turned into Spanish horsemen and where a pristine field of fire is maintained.

The four elements are curiously symmetrical:

– the artificial naturalness of a replanted English park where iron roses and iron serpents are tendrilled through the Art Nouveau bridges;
– a collection of galleries, libraries and concert halls where the Heritage of Europe is treasured and paid for by the FRG's Foundation for Prussian Cultural Possessions;
– a scrubland of urban wall-blight, owned by one state, effectively in another and visited by no one except the more exotic and ironical Berliners who picnic there on summer days; and
– the plastered-over core of a city from which its history was determined for nearly a century.

Each is a version of memory and oblivion.

I went to see a photographer called Hans Mende who had published a collection of photographs called *'Grenzbegehung – 161 Kilometer in West-Berlin'*. The whole perimeter of West Berlin is 161 kilometres long and *Grenzbegehung* means something like Border Journey. His walk had never crossed to the other side. It was about the claustrophobe fingering the edge, bumping up against it like one of those self-reversing toys, at the edge where, as he said to me, everything stops like a photograph. There are no journalistic pictures in the book of the 'Inhuman Divide'. There are virtually no human figures in it at all. There is no dramatic lighting. Most of the photographs are shot in dead white cloud light. It is full of a casual emptiness and acceptance of the Wall, like scuffed paint and shabby skirting-boards in one's own house. It transfers the East Berlin attitude to the West. Mende carries an emotionless camera, taking in all the distracting elements with which the Wall is surrounded, never isolating it as a form of portable tourist shock. There is no outrage in the book, only an honest grey reproduction of what is there, with no textural romance and only rarely any sort of projected meaning. But this exclusion of the easy inferences is so rigorous that the pictures become disturbing for their formless and uncertain relationship to the historical fragments. Like a man who never offers an opinion, they make you feel stupid for all your enthusiasms and fears.

Everything about Hans was moderation. His flat on Siemensstrasse near the docks on the Berlin Canal was not white and empty as the purist fad dictates. There was furniture in it, the floorboards were painted *blue*! The tall porcelain stove in the corner was given pride of place. His girl-friend Ulrike was there and we had *milky* coffee out of *thick* earthenware cups with spoons *and* saucers. Current Berlin style is about reduction, about not making a claim on the world for fear of it being an imposition, and an agent of domestic imperialism, but this was different. Ulrike wrote journalism to survive, philosophical essays to live and novels to breathe. Only the first of these had been published so far.

Hans was adamant that his photographs were not about the Wall. They were about West Berlin. He happened to have used the Wall as a tool with which to look at the place, but I should look at the product, not at the tool that produced it. 'The book is not a few pages out of *Stern*, some article about *"Leute an der Mauer"*, with all that power-blocs-with-their-fists-together gunk. "Innocent victims crucified on Power",' he said. No. It was an old German habit to change between the love for authority-structures (he had spent time in LA) and a Young Werther lyric freedom in the forest frame of mind. The Wall had provided a cliché picture of these two German loves up against each other. The Wall was both at once, a sort of authority-forest, by which people were both entranced and frightened. 'There is something appealing in that,' he said. 'But no book needs say it again. I have tried to escape from it. My photographs are documents, they must have no emotion.'

He described the other walls, the historical barriers, the class distinctions which had always been divided Berlin. There was some continuity between those divisions and the Wall. It was not an aberration; it was the consequence of a series of what he called Universal Nationalisms, a straight domino line between Napoleon, Hitler and Stalin, by which a vision of universal empire had resulted in a series of divided continents.

Hans described the continuity across the city. The above-ground S-Bahn is operated by the East in both halves and employs many West Berliners; the underground U-Bahn was divided in 1961 and two western lines, Nos 6 and 8, cross under the eastern salient of Berlin Mitte, with dead stations blocked off at street level. They look grey and unwashed from the closed carriages that slow past the platforms. There is the extraordinary infolding of the multilayer S- and U-Bahn station at Friedrichstrasse, with the frontier curled round inside it, where the two systems are wrapped around each other in weird placental intimacy. 'A city is not a block of cheese,' Hans said. 'It's more like cutting through a lung with all the stringy pipes still in there.' He mentioned the sewage, 100 million cubic metres of it a year, drained off from West to East. But they had no friends on the other side. The financial wall and the sheer clumsiness of paying a visit there had destroyed any efforts at friendship they had made.

Hans was not a Berliner by birth – but then, as Ulrike said, no real Berliner is – and had all the expatriate's affection for the place. Not for its vaunted impulse to the pulse, not for the 'night-circuses, *Negertanz* palaces, *nakt-balleten*, *flagellation bars*, and sad wells of super-masculine loneliness, shining dives for the sleek stock-jobbing sleuth relaxing' (Wyndham Lewis in 1931) which had now aged into Club Madame (*Intim★Elegant★Diskret*). All that was associated in Hans's mind with a dirty past, an extremist habit of mind of which the implications had been disastrous and inhuman. He distrusted excite-ment, above all that specious version of it, and was in love with the ordinary, with the safe unsifted banality of things. It was only a superficial paradox that he should have chosen to live in Berlin and to have taken his photographs of the Wall in order to express this. It was, after all, in Berlin, along the frontier, in the *Konzept* landscape which quite literally surrounded him, that his theoretical choice – plumping for the actual – could most openly be made. In the isolated city, in the creature of history, he could find, oddly enough, exactly what he wanted: Germany without a past.

Which was his favourite photograph? He opened the book at a page of grey caravans with Touring Club pennants in the back windows. They were herded between ash trees and blanked out for the winter. To take the picture he had to stand on the roof of a caravan from which he could look over the Wall and into the East. But, rather than that, he had turned around and photographed the other caravans instead.

I took a bus out to Steinstücken. Hans recommended it. It was far out beyond the Grunewald and the Wannsee, twenty-five kilometres from Siemensstrasse in the American Sector. It bordered the Potsdam suburb of Babelsberg, where the conference had been held in 1945. In 1920 the small village elected to be part of Gross-Berlin, separated from the main body of the city by about a mile of woods and fields that remained part of the Landkreis Potsdam. In 1945 this casual and insignificant distinction between the village and its surroundings, with some slight advantages perhaps in schooling or rubbish disposal on either side, became more concrete. Steinstücken turned into an island of the West in the East. In 1951 the East German police occupied the village and announced its incorporation into the county of Pots-dam, but it was returned to the West a few days later. Between then and 1976 access to and from Berlin itself was strictly controlled by the GDR. The Americans performed their own small helicopter airlift into the village whenever the superpower barometer fell. A monument –

two black helicopter rotors with orange tips set vertically – now marks the old landing site, with a plaque. The US Forces 'served to protect the freedom of the former exclave of Steinstuecken'.

A minor clause of the 1971 Quadripartite Agreement provided a stalk for Steinstücken. The approach is now along this modern umbilical, the road nicely fringed on either side with young fruit trees and rowans. A walkway beneath them and then on either side the plain tube-topped walls, a double death strip beyond that in cleared woodland, with watchtowers and Alsatians on runs from green kennels, all folding out exactly from the long dotted lines down the centre of the road. I walked along the lines themselves to preserve the symmetry in the sandwich.

At the far end the corridor flowers into the polyp head of Steinstücken. The village was like Haus Vaterland: a few Bavarian big-eaved chalets; a couple of Baltic townhouses with Gorgon heads; some Bauhaus purisms; and an import from Beverly Hills, all sliding glass and aluminium rails. Around them a pretty little arrangement of baby gardens where fibreglass dolphins hung in mid air arc-aiming into kidney-curve pools, where storks stuck and the weightless sails of foot-high windmills span. Gnomes peopled it, order in *petit-point* swamped it.

The Wall made no concession to the sweetness it bordered. The gardens did not abut the concrete itself and I walked the circuit of Steinstücken on the strip of East Germany between the garden fences and the Wall, a muddy path that writhed over roots and slunk under branches. I rubbed along next to the concrete and under the top-tubing until I came to the railway track which cuts through the village from the south and then on into Berlin. A dirty locomotive tanked and banged through above me like a building, pulling leaves in swirls in its wake. The Wall simply stopped at the edge of the track ballast. Dirty brambles weevilled into the stones. I put my fingers on the blunt end of the stopped wall. It was about four inches thick and had chipped away into tiny climber's fingerholes. I kept my hand on the end of the wall and turned around it inwards, towards the gap. There were no sidewalls lining the railway. The death strip – about thirty yards wide here – was open to me, suddenly naked. I could have walked straight into it, into a space I had so far depended on for being shut off to me. It was like a sudden sexual invitation from a teacher. I stood looking at the sand and the black leaves tucked into the grooves made by the rake. There was a rabbit eating its fingers next to the touch-sensitive fence. There was no chance of my stepping in there. A man was looking at me through binoculars from fifteen yards away in the watchtower. He made me feel safe. I knew then that I shouldn't and I couldn't. Back to the windmills and dolphins with impunity.

I met one man in Steinstücken. He was gardening next to his trellis fence, raking up dead leaves. A few lank hairs flopped into his glasses. Had the new road made much of a difference to his life? It had. It had brought in a flood of horrible *Touristen* like me. Steinstücken used to be such a nice neighbourhood. Now it was a tourist sight. Didn't I realize I was trespassing on East German State Property?

My last evening in Berlin I spent at a dinner party. It was given by Stefan, whom I'd met at the first architects' gathering in Kreuzberg. His own large white flat had the floorboards and the furniture painted white, the curtains white wool, the ceilings high and white, the plates white and the food yellow and creamy. It was a model of an amnesic brain.

Ten people sat around the table. Nobody was at the head and nobody was in charge. Stefan himself, who had a long aristocratic name which he had shortened but from which he had not dropped the *von*, moved about from seat to seat and the party itself moved between kitchen, floor, sofa, telephone and table. It was a half-conscious, slow-jazz-backed exercise in freedom and mobility. A man doodled on a clarinet between mouthfuls of spaghetti. Stefan was twenty-six, a history student and to be admired. He voted Green, was thinking of declaring himself a conscientious objector and thought Hans Mende's photographs 'a humble archaeology'. He had registered his flat with Amnesty International as an asylum and an Afghani had been staying there recently. It was an accumulated, bit by bit authenticity. West Berlin was full of Afghanis and Ethiopians. The East had been shoving them over.

I asked Stefan about the cleaned-up, deodorized air of Berlin youth. 'The city barometers isms,' he said. 'The current fashion is anti-ismism. It is a phase that recurs.' It was not true that Berliners, at least the people at this party, rejected history. All that they rejected was that careless fragment of the past which rejected the past itself. History was unavoidable in Berlin. You didn't have to think about it; it was a tangible experience. 'But these people', Stefan said, 'are looking for untainted tradition, without narcissism, without a fault in the casting. We are all Green now. It is a kind of soft anarchism, a retreat into micro-thought, an anarchism which in ten, twenty years will have degenerated into petty bourgeois behaviour. That is what Marx says. I can't tell you if we're radical or conservative.'

I talked to a woman called Brigitte with hennaed hair and grey eyes. She was flying to Rio the next morning. 'I like life,' she said.

And then to a man in a tight T-shirt, rucked at the armpit, and shorn black hair, who was always opening his eyes further than they would naturally go. His teeth were visibly rotten, the rot seen through a gauze of intact enamel, and his grin was amphetamine, planed-down hysterical. He told me, expanding his bicep eyes:

I That he was planning to make a series of garden gnomes, a *fantaisie*, out of gypsum in the shape of Greek Gods but with the features of Chancellor Kohl and his cabinet. The Chancellor would have his hands on his hips. The rest would be fishing.

II That playing a wind instrument destroys the lungs/windpipe and many millions of brain-cells because of (i) the pressure in the mouth cavity, and (ii) the increased absorption of oxygen in the blood. This explained the failure of jazz to be intelligent.

III That I must cross every border illegally. The *Grenzübergangstelle* was no part of a border.

IV That no, he had never been to Steinstücken.

A Björn Borg figure in a transparent beard and ECT pupils sat down next to me. He used to live in Leipzig, but had been expelled for taking part in a clandestine peace movement. Since 1978 the East had been ejecting subversive youths 'to purify the society'. Expulsion is cheaper than imprisonment. Most of his friends had taken part in order to be expelled, not through any belief. He had no beliefs. A weary confessional.

He had been terrified by the West on arrival. In the two years it had taken for his application to be processed in the East, he had been repeatedly interrogated, ostracized ('you say *put in Coventry*?') by his own parents and their friends, had doubted the rightness of what he was doing, had feared the inability to return and had sanctified the West as a pleasure zone. On arrival there – here – he had been interrogated again to ensure that he wasn't coming over 'just because the dresses are prettier' and had then been shoved out into a cold climate.

After a life in which everything had been on tap, including the stability of opposition to his surroundings (he had refused national service and even to be a non-arms-bearing member of the military, a 'construction soldier' as they are called), he had suddenly found himself unemployed, without a flat, without a bed, shifting for himself in a world whose freedom expressed itself by isolating him. He hadn't been able to imagine that. It was all made worse by the final cut-off from friends and family.

He left Germany to purge the system. He drifted to Harlow,

Norwich, Valencia and Santa Barbara. He didn't like Harlow. And now, back in Berlin, he existed on the fringes of an expatriate Leipziger community – there may have been a thousand of them – quite unhappily. He told me a joke. A young man from Leipzig was seen on the Küdamm one morning, with his hands in his pockets wandering round and round one of those pavement columns on which advertisements are pasted, saying to himself over and over again: 'Do you know, I can't seem to find a way out of here.'

6

The Smiling State Blush

Two larks dubbed over the border fences in stuck morse until a red kite coasted them away and hung there instead. Its forked tail equivocated in the wind like a hand. This was the border between the Germanies, the Iron Curtain, at one of its 1,393 rural kilometres, between the villages of Niedergandern and Kirchgandern in the south-east corner of Lower Saxony near Göttingen. It was a warm morning early in May, the spring barley had chitted in the unhedged fields and a small orchard in blossom next to the frontier itself had a metal notice about privacy nailed to one of the trees.

I had come eastwards across the breadth of western Europe, past armchaired border guards at the edge of Holland, army engineers making practice bridges in the meadows, one green beech tree in a wood of old oaks near Reinhardshagen in a soaking mist; overtaken by helmetless village boys on motorbikes twice the size of my own, tilting their heads sideways, listening to the change of note in the gears, past barn-houses with quotations from the Psalms the length of the building in golden blackletter, continuous saxifrages on the floor of a wood and – and at the end of a lane, next to the orchard, at the buffered terminus, had come to this.

Three fat women leant over a striped pole barring the lane. It was a notional barrier. One could simply walk around the ends of it and on to the part-grassed eastern cinders of the old track to Kirchgandern. It is one aspect of the propaganda battle that nothing should enforce the division of Germany from the western side. Some Nato strategists recently – in the debate over enhanced conventional warfare – have seen the so-called Deep Strike offensive strategy, by which Soviet forces are destroyed deep inside Warsaw Pact territory, as unnecessarily and dangerously provocative and have suggested instead large Maginot-style fixed defences lined up along the Intra-German Border. Whatever their military virtues, such defence systems will have to overcome a deep West German reluctance to have anything more permanent or fixed than those fragile striped poles to mark the border.

One rather eccentric but serious idea is a forest belt twenty to thirty kilometres thick the entire length of the border. Tanks like nothing worse than trees and the forest would foul up any conventional attack for days. As current Nato strategy is to go nuclear within four days at most, the forest bears thinking about. It has the added virtues of being neither overtly military nor very expensive, with the chance, even, in due course, of an economic return. And Germans love forests. At a time when one such national addiction is being destroyed by the exhausts from another – the limitlessly fast cars on the autobahn – the anti-Soviet green belt has a regenerative appeal which could dress all sorts of political wounds.

But at the moment there is nothing. Everything imbalances at the border. I joined the three doughnut bottoms lined up at the bar, watching nothing happen on the other side. We looked at the dark outline of the steeple in Kirchgandern and at the interleaving of deciduous and conifer beyond it. A baby screamed. The border was a layered naval braid, as thick on the ground as marked on a small-scale map, not a line but a border. At the boundary itself there is a clutter of western notices, as apparently ad hoc as roadwork diversion signs. Some of them warn, if the fences are close, that there is a danger of flying fragments from accidentally exploded mines.

Along the boundary there is a line of white marker posts and at five-hundred-metre intervals the border monuments, as they are called, of the GDR. These are concrete posts about six feet high painted in state livery like Switzers, red, gold and black in chevrons, coming to an obelisk point with the badge of state, a hammer and compass (advance on the sickle) enclosed in sheaves of corn, on an aluminium plate near the top. They mark the first empty line. Occasionally in the scrub growth you can find the mossed-over stones marking the original provincial boundaries that were chosen in London in 1944 and which the officers of the allied armies searched for and cleared in the nettles and brambles of the following summer.

East of the line the ground is cleared, full of stubbings in the forest, sprayed with defoliant and paler than the natural earth. The line of double fences, the real border monument, that encloses the mine strip, runs through this cleared space. The fences themselves are about three metres high, made of a dark mesh. They are transparent when looked at from right angles, but darken as you look along them. The mesh is supported by concrete posts but nothing caps it. The sharp net stops in diamond points. The fences may be twenty metres apart but the mine strip itself, in three invisible zigzag rows, may be anywhere inside that space. The would-be refugee has to treat the whole area between the fences as mined. Self-firing guns called SM-70s are attached to the fences and triggered by wires run along them. They are a development of a weapon conceived by the Nazis for use in concentration camps.

On the inner side of the inner fence there is a ploughed strip which guards can search for footprints, and inside this an anti-vehicle ditch alongside a concrete roadway for patrolling vehicles.

The border is overlooked by about 500 observation towers and is floodlit from tall curving arc lamps. Bunkers, tripwires and dogs on running leads complete the fortifications.

Over the whole length of the border about 11,500 hectares or nearly 29,000 acres are devoted to containing the population of East Germany within its frontiers. Make no mistake. These defences are militarily feeble. They are intended to trap and kill unarmed individuals.

The annual cost of maintaining the border, including the waste of land, was calculated in the late 1960s, at a time when barbed wire and rotten box mines were being replaced with mesh fencing and new Russian plastic mines, at about one billion Deutschmarks (then £104 million). Three quarters of it paid for the 50,000-strong Border Command of the People's Army. Cumulatively, since 1952, when it was first closed, the border has probably cost East Germany something like 12 billion Deutschmarks – at today's rate about £3,500 million.

We saw all this on our beautiful Saxon morning, leaning on our western bar. And it looked lovely. It was not horrifying . It had all the topographical confidence of Hadrian's Wall on Windshield's Crag or of the Wansdyke above the Kennetts. There was no decay in it. The border was half sensitive to the contours, half imposed on them, alert to the shape of the land but not dictated by it. The Germans have made something beautiful in their anti-people frontier, something large in conception and exact in execution. It's quite as good as Christo's Running Fence. There *is* a beauty in borders. To detail the layers of which they are made up is to miss the point. The great aesthetic virtue of the East German frontier is its run across country, its loping completeness. Here what Sir Cyril Fox called 'the intellectual quality' of Offa's Dyke becomes clear too. The intra-German border is beautiful for the strange reason that it crosses two horizons in strength. Beautiful along one axis, fatal on the other.

I had imagined that the three mackintoshed women leaning on the barrier with me were tourists from somewhere in the west, bumped up, as I was, against the eastern edge. But two of them were from

Leipzig in the GDR, two aunts visiting a western niece, allowed out because they were pensioners and inevitably drawn back to the frontier which enclosed and separated them. The niece, whose full corporeal substance was in the same league, if not quite in the same division of that league, as her aunts', told me how this interrupted lane had enjoyed its one famous moment in the summer of 1959. The people of Niedergandern had come with a brass band to this gate and serenaded their neighbours across the wire in Kirchgandern. A small concert was given through the strip, shouts and applause coming back the other way, until the People's Police, the Vopos, drove the villagers of Kirchgandern back indoors.

'You have something like this in Ireland, don't you?' the niece asked. Perhaps it was an accusation after I had told her that all we had in the way of a frontier was the coast. It was not like Ireland. There are interrupted roads in Ireland, blown-up bridges, concrete-blocked farmtracks, palings in the stream, as they have been called, but none of this continuity, this overriding obviousness of division. In Ireland the frontier shrinks like hot fat on water into separate and intimate globules around the police stations, the prisons, the half-armoured landrovers trailing grey-mesh skirts, around the chests, the bullet-proof vests, of the soldiers and policemen themselves. In Ireland the frontier has been atomized for political advantage, for the look of the thing. Except for the restrictions on the movements of the police forces and armies, it has effectively been deprived of a geography. The incidents that pepper the British news are really frontier incidents, but they occur anywhere in Ulster. The geography of discontent in the six counties has become impossibly confused – at least in the average English mind – so that the names of Creggan and Bogside, Springfield and Falls, Andersontown and the Short Strand, Ballymena, Ballymurphy and Ballymoney, Strabane, Dungannon, Forkhill and Crossmaglen – all these separate streets, housing estates, villages, slums and ex-slums in industrial cities – have muddled together in the one generalized landscape of semi-domestic violence and daubed skull-faced houses by which Northern Ireland is known throughout the world. A frontier like this between Niedergandern and Kirchgandern effectively distils that violence, filters it out and localizes it. But it demonstrates – it confesses – the failure of the state to represent the nation. That is a shocking political price, of which the Communists are of course aware. It is said that Moscow prevented the East German regime from erecting the Berlin Wall for two years before 1961, because of the disastrous propaganda effect it would have. But eventually the economic well-being of the country made it necessary. If the

East German frontiers had not been closed, and emigration had continued at its rate in the 1950s, another ten million people would have come over to the West. The present population of East Germany is seventeen million. Each year 40,000 are allowed out: they are pensioners.

But if the frontier between the two Germanies and the frontier between the two Irelands are as different as they can conceivably be, there is one way in which they come to resemble each other: in the forbidden zone which stretches five kilometres back into East Germany from the fences. This enormous area – along the length of the border it adds up to more square kilometres than are contained in the state of Delaware or in Counties Armagh, Derry and Tyrone – is accessible only to those with special registration passes. The unreliable have been moved further east and those who have reported strangers in the area have been encouraged to stay.

How can this purified, imposed-on landscape, with its assumptions of general criminality in the population, resemble Northern Ireland, of which the dominant character, after all, is an interfolded complicatedness? It is the *invisibility* of the frontier in both places that connects them. Looking over the borderline and its fences at the church in Kirchgandern and at the hazed pastures beyond it, there is nothing readable in the country that says 'frontier', nothing beyond the physical and botanical details that repeat the western side. All the definite ferocity of the border fortifications, their summary of everything in the Auden-romantic notions of the frontier, throws the plainness of the countryside beyond them into relief. And that – apart from the few television-famous places – is also the character of the Ulster landscape, its hidden loyalties and divisions and its rare invisible dangers, made paradoxically apparent by the defended oddities in its midst, the jungle camouflage uniforms on the Armagh pavement between the cake shop and the library.

I moved off south on the motorbike, aiming eventually for the Czech border at the far end of Bavaria. From there I would pursue a course averaging south-east towards the Aegean, tracing the frontiers towards Turkey, as a thread in the labyrinth. I had no experience of riding a motorbike. I had bought it a few days before leaving England in a Corby bike shop, feigning the knowledge I had read up in a magazine a few minutes previously. I mentioned the word 'twin' to start with, but was soon forced back on to 'easy to drive' and 'comfy'. The salesman had seen it all before – the attempts at preserving dignity when all one had was money; the pretended *au fait* with facile technicalities; the generous 'quite tricky' at the first total stall start; and at the second; the bawl of the jammed-on throttle; the jerked horse-refusal as the brake was first gripped; and the terror of the machine one had bought for £385.

But I survived and in a full suit of black oiled Belstaff jacket and trousers, quilted in places, black helmet and black wool-lined gloves, I practised Balkan gear changes on Leicestershire lanes. The bike was a marvel. A Honda 'Benly' CD 125 Twin with Electric Start. It once went at 69 down the side of a Carpathian and uphill struggled for 30, but never failed to start first time in all the erratic 4,000 miles to the Aegean.

As one small part of the visa jungle of eastern Europe, an International Driving Certificate is required. I had not, of course, passed any motorcycle test and there was no time before I left. Perhaps the AA office in Leicester would be a soft touch. It was a little plastic shop in Charles Street. I wore the black oiled jacket, flipped the leather gauntlets on the edge of a desk selling insurance, expertly played with the spanners in the Roadmaster Tool System and was apparently about to leave the office before I remembered the small detail of the AA stamp in the certificate. The uniformed guard behind the desk was due to have her hair dyed again later in the week. She was all buttoned up in brown despite the early spring warmth. I explained how I had bought the certificate in the London office. The girl there had forgotten to stamp the motorcycle section. It was the strangest of oversights. My own hot border guard was all helpfulness. She pushed back the parti-coloured hair and opened the certificate. 'British driving licence, please.' Unaccountably, I had left it behind. This after searching. Her lipstick buckled at the corners. She couldn't stamp it without the UK licence. I had brought my wallet out on to the desk. I fingered past a couple of fivers and, at the critical moment, looked up at her with my hands still on the notes. I had seen someone do it in a film. She looked straight back at me. I smiled and widened my eyes. It was the first time in history that anyone had tried to bribe an AA clerk. She sat back and the ruckled uniform tightened around her breasts. The brass buttons popped outwards. The hair looked a mess. 'I must say, I am not quite sure what you are getting at, sir, but I think you might have run away with yourself a little. You're not in eastern Europe yet, you know.'

'It's only one small rubber stamp,' I said.

'Not without the UK licence it's not.'

The scene had begun to degenerate. In the film she would have said: 'Given the circumstances, we can certainly make an exception on this one,' and the fee would have been twenty pounds. But this was Leicester. Not even the promise of hairdos for life would have brought the stamp down on to the certificate. 'We do have our rules,' she said. 'I don't know.'

I forged the stamp with some india-rubbers and a razor blade. After two duds I produced a good one. Slowly lowered on to the certificate and pressed there, the mark was virtually indistinguishable from its official neighbours allowing me to drive lawnmowers and steamrollers on Bulgarian motorways. Any close examination would show that it was about a millimetre wider than the real thing. A professional would have known that a stamp spreads a little as it is pressed on to the paper.

I rode south across the *Land* boundary into Hesse and from the British sector of the front into the American. The Eleventh Armored Cavalry Regiment was on exercise. APCs at the corners of woods and jeeps parked in the laybys as if waiting for a war. The Americans were entrancingly sexy. They were unshaven, smoking, lounging on the huge metal technology of the business, swinging the machine-gun to and fro, guitarists between sets. The chinstraps hung from one side in the lasting image of the American soldier, whether from Iwo Jima, Hollywood or Vietnam. The Eleventh Armored Cav had served a few tours in Nam, but none of these young men. It was a commemorative signal now.

The Time Frame came to a Movement Junction and the big olive-green personnel carriers were snort-choked into starting, farting black and then white smoke in separately exhausted combustion clouds. The machines pulled away up into the forest, chucking earth-clod confetti out from the tracks in handfuls, jerking round the corners into the trees like poorly manipulated radio toys. Their ship engines bellowed with too many revs in the wet forest.

On top of a hill near Meinhard Grebendorf, which overlooked a good swathe of border – it was another tailed-off end-lane on the map – I found a picture of German family life. It was a Saturday and the afternoon had turned cold. A horizon-blue van stood off the lane side with its engine running. A curved line of muddied flat wheat sprouts marked the track of the van where it had been run off into the edge of the field. A woman and her daughter sat blankly in the turned-round vehicle looking westwards away from the border. On the lane itself, blocking it, was the kind of machine by which film cameramen are moved effortlessly in any dimension, slewing over the ballroom or swung up and away from the kiss to frame the sunset. Its cogs and levers are so well counterbalanced that a small pair of wheeled handles is all that is required to move the padded cameraman's seat yards through the sky.

Father was pushed out about ten feet diagonally towards East Germany. He was cramped over a pair of fixed fieldglasses that had been rubberized in khaki, with eye-flanges to exclude distracting light. He was also dressed in a one-piece khaki boiler suit. A silk Paisley cravat nested his neck and an old chamois leather skull-cap covered his hair. Another American APC burnt its engine out on a hill half a mile behind us. 'Panzer,' the man said without taking his eyes off the frontier, and then gave a short instruction to his son at the foot of the machine. The little boy in a toy replica of his father's outfit turned the handles and Herr Ritter swung two degrees southwards and one foot up. The boy blew on the ends of his fingers and then wrung his hands. '*Ja, ja, ja,*' the father said with satisfaction. He was looking at one of the new-style observation towers, as square as a milk carton and with copper-coloured glass panes in the platform, through which, from the outside, one can see nothing.

We waited. Herr Ritter pressed his head further into the eye-cups. He flitched his head away like a buzzard and fixed me with his extraordinary double-red-rimmed eyes. One around the eyeball, from exhaustion, and one half an inch out, from the pressed-on eye-cups. It was a sort of wing-marking for Iranian jets. He had himself lowered to the ground and sat me in the seat, dimpled and warmed like on a bus. Vertiginous lurch to the same position marked on the calibrated wheel-scales. 'Look,' he said, 'look.' I looked through the eye-cups and saw the familiar dead-eyed observation tower about half as large again in the haze. 'Pretty good?' he shouted up from the ground. I looked again. No movement, nothing special, no people, just the building, the frontier and the interrupted forest of the Hessisches Bergland. But Herr Ritter was full of limitological enthusiasms. 'So beautifully fabricated, don't you think?' It looked OK. 'But have you noticed the new aluminium trimmings on the windowsill bracket?' I had not. His wife came round from the front of the van in a sort of perforated cardigan, wrapping her bosoms in her arms and curling her shoulders against the cold. She said it was time to get a cup of coffee in the *Gasthaus* down the road. Herr Ritter had moved his head away. The request had guaranteed another ten minutes of the Border Watch.

A grey Zoll VW bus pulled up next to the picnic and the two grey customs men walked past us towards the border, pulling lambswool v-necks down over bellies, anti-militarism itself. Herr Ritter looked at me knowingly. He knew I was on his side. I too, in my buckled black oilskins, was in the stormtrooper look. We watched the Zoll men in their flat-soled lace-ups saunter down towards the border. 'They try nicely,' Ritter said. 'But they know nothing. They're pigeon-food.'

'Chick-feed.'

'Yes, chicken-food. The others, *drüben*, they train the dogs to keep it clean. Look at our side. It is not something to stand up for.' Our side was a swamped brushwood garden next to the mine strip. 'You know the speech *Deutschland nicht hier zu Ende*! [Germany does not finish here]? My family, we like that speech.' Frau Ritter continued to look westwards at the Café Krem. 'We have lost something on this side. Over there, in Kella, they have it.' Ex-Major Ritter asked me if I knew ex-Major Bailey of Wootton Bassett. I didn't. Some strange millennarian connections were hinted at. He took my address and, as a honey-buzzard swung down over the border fences, I started up and left the one German family divided by its visions and revisions.

Imagine the length of the German border on a Saturday afternoon, Lübeck to Hof: the landscape of the protocol; the most symmetrical division in the world; the negation of the Wilsonian ethos; denied in the West for what it is and labelled *Zonengrenze* or in Bavaria *Landesgrenze*; denied in the East for what it is – an anti-civilian frontier – and claimed for what it is patently not, a military protection of the state and nation. It is in fact a protection of the state against the nation, a supra-national, anti-national modern frontier, lined with Herr Ritter and all his mutations, staring into their field glasses at a magnified fragment of the other, a rank of vacuously obsessed men ranged up in the booths of a political peepshow. A percipient German would have invested heavily in optical instruments at the end of the war.

I moved between these worm's-head places, finding eyeglass addicts at random vantage points in the easygoing folds of Hesse. Most of them were not local men. They had raced east on the early weekend autobahn to find their peg on the first drive. One of them near Herleshausen told me that a good day would be the simple mistless revelation of the border fortifications themselves. Better would be some movement among the border guards. Outstandingly good would be a small party reconstructing the fences or laying new mines. Not more than dreamt of was the blue vision of witnessing an IBC – he used the American term, Illegal Border Crosser – actually *en route*. That is the stuff on which *Stern* is made. For anybody except the person daring the crossing – it averages something over a hundred a year, a very high proportion of them border guards or ex-border guards who know the ins and outs of the line – it represents the grand vicarious thrill of statehood denied, or for the Germans, the supremacy of nation over State. Statistically the number of escapers is insignificant: 0.25% of all the East Germans who come over to live in the West each year. But crossing the frontier substitutes the romantic union of the one nation for all the pragmatic and ugly realities of the Iron Curtain. The escaper is the ultimate émigré, deserting a place that is foreign to him and arriving in the homeland, a free Germany, from which he has always been barred. The escape suspends politics and the interfering divisions of the world. It becomes the Grand Utopian Act. The difficulties of adjusting afterwards are nothing next to the political chic, the courageous sense of right in the crossing itself.

High above the village, on the sandy edge of the forest, there is a small Soviet cemetery. Nearly 1,600 Russian soldiers are buried there under copper plates in the grass, with oxslips growing between them and a sort of blue anemone under the leggy thorn hedges. They died of tuberculosis as prisoners of war in a camp, now disappeared, on the edge of the forest.

> Hier ruhen 1593 sowjetische Kriegsgefangene
> die in der schweren Zeit 1942–1945
> fern von ihrer Heimat starben

a plaque says, which is also in Russian. 'In the bad time, far from their homeland'. It is a scarcely disturbed place, ragged at the edges, and dropping away downhill into a stand of beeches where more elaborately, ivy on the greened Stars of David, the dead of the Jewish community in Herleshausen had been buried before the war. No deaths recorded here since 1940. I was disturbed by a woman in black. She was the schoolmistress from the village and had come up as she often did in the afternoon for the view. We sat on the yellow grass side by side and she hugged her knees. The hill looked across the deep trug of a valley at a mirror bluff on the other side. The border ran along the River Werra at the bottom and the fences were on the far bank. A large ruined castle over there called Brandenburg, as big as Caernarvon with double wards and towers, guarding the Thüringia frontier, had been encroached on by the forest. The leaves of the spring beech trees were visible inside and out. It looked as though the walls would soon rot away under the leaf canopy.

The teacher was in her thirties and had red straight hair. She told me that before the war the castle had been the great picnic outing from Herleshausen. Nowadays she came up here with old people sometimes. At least they could *look* at the castle. One of the outings had coincided with a visit to the cemetery by relatives of the Russian soldiers buried there. The Russians had been old too. None of them could speak German. You might have thought that the two parties would have smiled at one another and been friendly. Not at all. They had kept quite apart – it was a lovely summer day – and had actually moved further apart when there was a danger of mingling. The castle was now in the forbidden zone and unvisited. But perhaps that was no great sadness, she said. Castles always look best from far away.

Further west, where the river loops northwards, a spoon of farm-land was contained in the East. In a concertina of cause, effect and guilt, Utte called the wide braided border 'the Hitler stripe'. Families had been divided by it and there was still no direct connection. People in the East had been fined 50 marks for waving across to the other side. You could never telephone there or pay a visit. If people in Her-leshausen wanted to see people in Lauchröden or Sallmannshausen, they could only do it by arrangement on neutral ground, outside the forbidden zone in Eisenach or somewhere else further east. And of course young people never bothered. In ten years, fifteen years there would be no blood ties across the border. The two countries – 'dreamed up', she called them – would *become* two countries, hitched like barges to ocean-going tugs pulling to east and west.

I asked her about the Jews in Herleshausen. They had all been removed, all except one family, and that family still lived in the village.

'Why was it singled out?'

'The woman was a German, her husband a Jew,' she said.

'And what nationality was the man?' I asked unfairly. She held her hand over her mouth.

'They were both German. I mean she was Aryan.'

I packed up the wet nylon of my tent in the campsite at Heringen Leimbach the next morning. A Frankfurt couple asked me over for cakes and sweet coffee in their weekend caravan. Their burgundy running-suits said *Jogging*. It was Hans Mende heartland. Meccan ordinary. The rain-streaked Alps of the potash waste through the half-turned louvred blinds. Where was the best place to see the bor-der? Frau Kundt pushed the cakes half an inch across the formica to the left. Herr Kundt began speaking in the third person absolute. I had released a power struggle between them and we had entered a familiar tract of the sexual battlefield. 'In order to understand the true nature of the *Grenze* that now divides Germany into two opposed and separated camps,' he said from somewhere in his neck, 'one must achieve a considerable metrage of elevation.'

'A hill?'

'One must find a significant junction wherein the complete structural *ensemble* can be observed.'

Frau Kundt offered me another bit of layer cake in silence. Her eyebrows pointed out a fat-tined cake fork. I took the cake in my fingers. Frau Kundt was appalled. Herr Kundt referred to Potsdam. The frothed-up cream squeezed out sideways in four symmetrical sausages on to my cheeks. We had somehow arrived at Adenauer's love of orchids. Herr Kundt glanced down from the horizon.

'Yormph,' I said through sponge, seriously.

'Now one might hear of some people who are over these affairs quite ill-informed remarking that Phillipsthal is a most interesting site . . .' His wife made a little movement and he saw it out of the corner of his eye. 'But they would be quite mistaken,' he shouted. Kundt turned from the view – it ended ten yards in front of him in the rain fog – and addressed the empty cake-plate. 'They would be endlessly mistaken. It is not effective to push the nose on the frontier. There is no contact with the concept in Phillipsthal.'

A fleck of potash slag spiked my eye as I came in at fifty through the dirty outskirts of Phillipsthal. Chemical hoppers stood on the mid-street sidings. Phillipsthal is famous for its divided house, the only one the length of the border. Hans Hossfeld returned from his prisoner-of-war camp in Siberia to find his house in the Soviet zone. He moved in with his father and twenty other relations. But the line had been misdrawn. An old border monument marking the Hessian-Thuringian frontier – a small stone – stood in front of the door. The American garrison commander in Bad Hersfeld persuaded the Soviets to withdraw to the real boundary, in the process transferring several houses to the West. But still the Russians maintained that the Hoss-feld house and the printing works to which it was attached belonged in the Soviet Zone. The front door was just to the east of the re-established line. The Hossfelds would have none of this. Throughout 1951 Hans and his brother-in-law secretly assembled bricks and mortar in the house, bringing them in through a window, bag by bag, at night. On the last day of the year, as Phillipsthal had its parties, they built a wall across the inside of the house along the international frontier which now divided the sitting- from the dining-room. It was finished by daybreak. The Berlin technique.

The isolated rooms are now grey and untended; the windows have frosted in a peculiar way; some of the tiles on the mansard have slipped; a pane or two is missing in the dormer; the rendering on the walls is blotched with damp; the guttering is strangely intact. It is the kind of decay you could see anywhere, like these border towns, where the markets have shrunk. Most of the Hossfeld printing used to be done for clients in Vacha just across the Werra. That is now impossible and the business is sustained by western government printing contracts, the fate, near enough, which the walling-up was intended to avoid.

A small museum displays escape equipment and propaganda shot over in mortar canisters or kicked over in footballs. Sometimes they contain vouchers for free trips to Leningrad. Western soldiers have been known to throw them back filled with porn.

I sat on a blue plastic bench, municipally supplied, by the frontier. Rain-wet Dutch magazines in the litter baskets had one woman fading against her overleaf counterpart, the same woman repeated a little more exposed and the gloss gone off in the wet. *Betti war da* in permanent marker was written on the plastic bench. *Ruf dochmal an 06 617 2106 Kati.*

The Werra was disgusting, scummy with salt waste from the East German potash works, dumped in, it was said, at a thousand tons a day. I sat there under the binoculars, exposed in public, next to the poisoned river. A complete dead tree had washed up on the under-bridge fences. A white twig or two stuck through the mesh. The white trunk was dirtied in the saline mud. I hoped they thought my overalls a uniform. I considered showing them the Dutch magazine, but the womened pages had become lank and fibrous. Held up one at a time they were muddled by translucence, Phillipsthal half-visible through the dampened flesh; held up *en bloc* they confused themselves. And then a family arrived for a look. I shoved the pictures back in with the empty cartons. We were never left unwatched. It must have been one of the better posts.

I felt as sterile as the Werra. Somehow a few mallards and buntings were surviving on the fever-flesh banks of the brown stream. After all, what was more absurd than this, buzz-bumping up against the border like a wasp on a window? Bumping up against the continuous smiling state blush. But perhaps I could make no more obvious discovery than this: the border repeats itself. It is designed to repeat itself. Its purpose is repetition. The more similar the kilometres the more effective they are. It is an exercise in the obvious, where anomaly is weakness and ellipsis failure.

At Jüterbog, about fifty kilometres south of Berlin, in the body of East Germany, the National People's Army runs a testing ground, a mocked-up section of frontier, on which trainee border guards are sent to practise. Ingenious athletes play the hare. Lessons learnt in Jüterbog are applied from the Baltic to Bohemia, so that the border landscape clones over fourteen hundred kilometres, smearing one identity on the multiple natures of the continent.

On another frontier, on the Roman Wall in Northumberland, it had always seemed hopelessly bureaucratic that milecastles, whatever their position, were provided with gates north. Where the line of the Wall is run along the dolerite crags of the Whin Sill, between Twice Brewed and Beggar Bogg, these elaborate double-leaved gates open straight out, in places, over drops of 150 feet or more. But there is no better example of the frontier builder's capital maxim: Continuity is Strength. Herr Ritter would have liked it. It is that maxim which stimulates the attraction of the oddity here, of the escaper, of the soldier who deserts his charge, of the divided house. They are sparkling points of fallibility in the linear desert.

I pulled south and east into Bavaria. The farmers had ploughed and planted into every yard-wide notch of the state and the Honda breezed east. The towns were suffering from a sort of border blight, resembling reservoirs of which half the feed-streams were dry. The swallows swung in and out of my own track in gearless acceleration and gnat-catching ogees of delight. My jacket was speckled with hundreds of midges crushed on arrival. The morning rain had gone and left some woolly clouds. The garage attendant under an Alpine meadow had been captured at Alamein and spent the rest of the war in Emporia, Kansas. His chin had never recovered. I had pictures of Carmen Jones and button-downs. His neck expanded groundwards in a sporting trophy plinth. He had no truck with this one-Germany business. Or at least there was one Germany and it ended three kilometres away to the north. He called the GDR 'Russia'. There was only one thing worse than Russians: Frenchmen. Both had small standards for life. You wouldn't want to get yourself captured by a Frenchman. He rubbed his fist across his face as if scooping up sand and then looked into it for the little brown *würstchen* of grease.

On to the forecourt. Two more Cav units went past at 70 kph and he lifted his *loden* hat to them. Hair kinked at the brim in a trefoil curve. They waved past like conquerors. He said something rude about Strasbourg.

A motorbike separates places by its wind-roar. You turn it off and stand next to its metallic cool-down ticking as the place changes.

Lieutenant Kelvin Mohamet was a Law Enforcement Major from Arizona State. He was, as he said, five feet even and he was digging his platoon into the young wheat field. It was getting cold in the evening. Mushrooms of white breath stood out from our faces. The tanks had already messed up the field like a Moulinex. I read the names of the men on their fatigues: Bosco, Gault, Coffey, Van Horne, Nelms, Krenk, Pollard, Dulles, Agar, Ekirch, Bagby, Matusow, Donavan, Premis, Penistone and Littwack.

'Will you look at that preemier blockhead?' Gault asked the others.

'Is that a preemier physical mismatch or is that a preemier physical mismatch?' Krenk said. They leant on the pointed spades. The farmer was coming across to them filling his clothes as Kelvin scarcely occupied his and about fifteen inches taller. '*That*', Coffey said, 'is a preemier physical mismatch.'

'And *that*', Krenk said again, 'is one hell of a middle-line backer.'

They surrounded their lieutenant. The farmer, right up on his Cranach nose, said, '*Schlaum*', loudly several times. The tanks had come across earlier in the day and ploughed straight through his barbed wire fences.

'Yep,' said Lieutenant Mohamet at an angle of about 45° above the horizontal. The tanks had dragged a skein of wire and wood right through the farmyard before debouching on to the road, which was now a foot thick in mud. The farmer held one hand on top of his head and one on top of Kelvin's forage cap to demonstrate the thickness of mud now on the road. *Schlaum*, neither mud nor slime but incorporating them, flesh-and-blooding them both. Fur and faeces, dung and death. Cars and buses had slammed all over the road – there was an Audi still in the ditch – in the wake of the American havoc. Kelvin had been nodding at the farmer's distorted fly. He began to mention compensation, but the tweeded Bavarian interrupted. He didn't care too much about anything, but he had fought the Russians and he hated them. He pointed a dirty and gristled finger towards the east. His arm had been inside a cow earlier in the day. You could see the big M 60s lined up across the valley behind the thin string of beechwood – the German word is Buchenwald – ready for the next attack.

'We went for them last time because we knew they would come for us if we didn't.' A shadow of Arizona State Law Enforcement scepticism passed over Lt Mahomet's face. Agrarian anger in an old tweed suit, the air in front of him fogging at the outrage.

'Just take a look at the RPMs on that jaw,' Nelms said.

'He may not like them much,' Krenk said to the others, who had started digging again, 'but he sure don't like us at all.'

I was back on the road myself when the tanks came through the position, well before the platoon was ready for them. Nine large, fast machines, nearly black, trailing black wakes through the crop as if harvesting it, dragging a few more of the fences with them, right through his farmyard again and out on to the road. Of course it is not the compensation that counts: the violence of existence has no remedy. I had to walk the Honda for about three hundred yards because the road was unsafe with the mud. The last thing I saw was Krenk and Co. slapping each other's hands. Something must have gone right.

The enormous room was in Hof at the far end of Bavaria. Ernst Tscherne sat behind an Anglepoise at a long black table. A cat sat at his feet. Its fur spread up on one of the bulges in the turned legs. Herr Tscherne's shoes rested neatly on the stretcher that ran the length of the table along the floor and the reflected light off his papers whitened the lenses in his plain round glasses. He looked like Jung, as clean as that, always straightening the papers with the ends of his fingers to keep them in a rectangle. As he finished with each sheet, he pushed it face up under the pile so that when the business was over the pile would look the same as when he had begun. There was only one other light in the room, a standard lamp behind my chair, shaded in a soft yellow material – it looked like wool – and the rest of the enormous room was coated in a warm, absorbent dark. There were dark Persian rugs on the boards and a tapestry behind him. The light was scarcely enough to make it out. It looked like a man with a spear. There was a border of trumpets and laurels. But it was only a fragment, cut out of something much larger. One corner had been patched in wools that had yet to fade to the brownness of the rest, and the border only ran along the top and down the left-hand side.

I had been to the Information Office in Hof. The town is twinned with Joensuu in Finland. There were plans to exchange beauty queens. Only six breweries of the famous ten are left. Hof used to be on the centre line of the Reich; it is now out on the far uneconomic edge of the Federal Republic. The railway has shrunk to one track. The textile mills are in decline. The population is dropping by a thousand a year. The young woman had a tiny badge on her jersey which said '*Jesus lebt!*' in millimetre-high letters behind the perspex, as if nothing else did. She told me to visit Herr Tscherne. He knew everything about the Sudeten Germans.

'Not everything,' Herr Tscherne said.

It was raining on the Honda outside. He and I sat in our separate ponds of light for many hours. He read from his notes like an old teacher who had collected the history of the village from the court leets and manor rolls. He didn't welcome questions, but would pause when he saw I was writing and would repeat the significant words. We were about fifteen feet apart.

He had been my age at the time of Munich and was now seventy-three. After a while he came to call me 'my dear *Grenzgänger'* with a short look over the gold rims. His family had lived in Eger – the place is now called Cheb – on the western edge of Czechoslovakia or, as he called it, Böhmen, Bohemia. Sudetendeutsch. But that too was the wrong word. It was invented by a German journalist in Prague called Franz Jesser in 1902, applying one name to many groups of people. Properly, the Germans in Eger were East Franconian. Double, tucked-away names.

The first Germans came over the mountains that ringed Bohemia and up the valley of the Elbe in the twelfth century. The immigration peaked in the thirteenth and again after 1526 under the Habsburgs. There had always been ethnic antagonism, focused on to the conflict between the Czech Hussites and the Germans loyal to the Roman church. Something of Ireland in the religious mirror. By the middle of the eighteenth century, after large-scale confiscations of Czech landholdings and the exclusion of Czechs from power, German had become the one official, imperial, language.

He turned the leaf, pushed it under, and jumped. 'By the Treaty of St Germain, 10 September 1919,' he announced, as if it were the Second Lesson, 'the Republic of Czechoslovakia came into existence.' I expected some kind of slur. The Sudetendeutsche Landmannschaft, which claims to represent Sudeten Germans now in the Federal Republic, makes regular calls for territorial revisions in Central Europe by which Czechoslovakia would be removed from the map. The reunification of the two Germanies is for the more extreme elements only the first stage in the rehabilitation of a greater Reich. But Herr Tscherne was no Fourth Reichist. He read from his notes: 'The Czechoslovak Republic was a unique, shining experiment in multinational democracy that was sacrificed seventeen years later in the name of a spurious peace.'

'Shining?'

'*Shining.*'

Out of the 14.73 million people in the new state, 3.26 million were German. They were concentrated in the border areas, but Czech and German were utterly interdependent. No line on the ground could be drawn between the two populations. They were truly citizens of one country despite the language difference. One only had to look at the shape of the country. Herr Tscherne held to a belief in natural frontiers. He looked up. 'That is what I believe now. When I was young I believed differently.'

There were riots among the Sudeten Germans in 1919. The Czech army shot fifty-four of them dead. The riots were a symptom of loss, both of status in their own country and of national identity. They had been part of the Habsburg empire, 'an empire which spoke German'. Of all the German populations to have fought in the First World War, the highest proportion of dead was among the Sudeten Germans. Now the army, the banknotes and government announcements were all made in Czech and Slovak. Every town and village was required to have a Czech name even if it was all-German. Dr Lodgman von Auen said in 1920: 'Czechoslovakia has been developed at the expense of historical truth.' Czech language tests for civil servants were made deliberately difficult. Germans were ousted from public service, including the army, local government, the railways and the post office. Herr Tscherne's father lost his job in a sewage works in 1927. He didn't know the Czech words for the materials in which he dealt. There *were* local councils, schools and libraries all in German and German representatives in the national assembly – a permanent and impotent minority – but set against the situation before the war, it was all the difference in the world, exacerbated by the trauma of defeat after such a war. There were many suicides.

When his father was sacked, young Tscherne came to believe in the *grossdeutsche Herrenvolk*. He joined a group of young men called the Wandering Birds who sat around camp fires in the forest, swearing loyalty to the national community. It wasn't political. It was somehow more to do with woods, war stories from the older men and their guilt in defeat.

In 1932 Hitler said: 'The Czechs we shall transplant to Siberia or the Volhynian regions.' Volhynia is part of the Ukraine. He could never talk about the Czechs without shouting. This is said to be due to his Austrian background.

In 1933 Konrad Henlein, a professional gym teacher who looked neat, founded the Sudetendeutsche Heimatfront. Two years later it became the Sudeten German Party (sdp) and Henlein a rather small beneficiary of the *Führerprinzip*. Ernst Tscherne joined it. The sdp concealed Pan-German *Raumpolitik* behind the principles of self-determination, always claiming that the Sudeten Germans wanted to remain within the Czechoslovak state. The wishful thinking of a peace-hungry Europe swallowed the strategy. President Beneš made faint brave speeches about 'the footsteps of Herder, Lessing, Goethe and Schiller ... the genuine ideals of humanity and a sensible

Europeanism', folding paper boats en route to Niagara.

In June 1937 the Nazis drafted plans for the military attack on Czechoslovakia. In November Hitler told his generals that Austria and 'Czechia' would be annexed by force. Two million Czechs and one million Austrians would be transferred to provide more food for Germany.

'Where to?'

'I don't know.'

Beneš, early 1938, to a *Sunday Times* journalist: 'Europe has the moral right to protect the peace at the expense of Czech sovereignty.' Munichism, but he 'was satisfied that Great Britain was sufficiently realistic to know that if Germany dominated Central Europe, Great Britain itself would in due course be seriously and fundamentally menaced'.

In the local elections in May–June 1938 the Henlein Party received the votes of more than 85% of the Sudeten Germans. 'It was ecstatic,' Herr Tscherne said without emotion. The crisis deepened. Britain and France put pressure on Beneš to set up an autonomous region for the Germans inside the borders of Czechoslovakia.

On 12 and 13 September there was a popular insurrection in the Sudetenland which failed. Herr Tscherne saw a man with a banner shot in the street in Eger. It so happened that the banner fell over him on the ground and covered his body. On the 16th the sdp was dissolved. The next day the government in Prague declared an emergency. Henlein directed terrorist raids into Czechoslovakia from the Reich. On the 22nd they occupied the little salient of Asch – Aš – just to the east of Hof. Only the Soviet Union stood by the Czechs. Five German armies with thirty-seven divisions were waiting on the frontiers.

On 23 September Czech Radio broadcast the Decree of General Mobilization. By the 28th, one million Czechs were armed and 9,000 fortified posts, from machine gun nests to fortresses, were manned along the 1,539 kilometres of frontier with the Reich. Some of the equipment inside the fortifications was not complete. There were four Czech armies. The armaments consisted of:

> 1,582 aeroplanes
> 501 anti-aircraft guns
> 2,175 pieces of artillery
> 469 tanks and armoured cars
> 43,876 machine-guns
> 1,090,000 rifles
> 114,000 pistols

The Nazis later seized the equipment. General Heinz Guderian said: 'It was useful during the invasions of France and Poland. We replaced it with German equipment for the Russian campaign.'

Chamberlain described Czechoslovakia on the radio as 'a far-away country' full of people 'of whom we know nothing'.

The Sudetenland was surrendered to the Germans on 29 September at Munich.

President Roosevelt sent a cable to Chamberlain. It said: 'Good man'.

The German troops under Colonel-General Wilhelm von Leeb crossed the frontiers at two in the afternoon on 1 October 1938. Herr Tscherne saw Hitler as he toured the annexed territories on the 3rd.

'What did he look like?'

'He looked as if he had just got married.'

It was now after one in the morning. The little stack of papers was as neat as ever on Herr Tscherne's table. He said it was time to sleep and I lay down in my sleeping bag on the Persian-rugged floor.

He was older in the daylight. In 1938 he had pasted up

Tschechisches Geschäft
and
Jüdisches Geschäft

on a few of the shop windows in Eger. Beneš said 'Freedom is being guillotined' in Prague. After breakfast – the sound of eaten muesli, no talk – he settled me back in my armchair and pulled himself up behind the table again. Light filled the room from windows down one side. The rest of the house indulged the Storskog pine chalet health effect, but this one room was consciously enriched. Mahogany book clamps at one end of it held large illustrated editions of Goethe's *Italian Journey* and two volumes on Tischbein, the complete letters of Horace Walpole and the gilt-laden Waverley novels. A large painting of a black eighteenth-century page in Florentine silks and last night's tapestry, now obviously part of a battle scene.

'We will not talk about the war,' Herr Tscherne said and polished his glasses. 'We will talk about the transfer of Germans out of Czechoslovakia.' He resumed his bitty if precise account of things. His loyalties were no more than partly discernible in the flow of information. And his own participation in the events surfaced only in tiny bits of observation and part anecdote. It was as if he had tried to purify this account and set himself away from it, but with slight success. It was nothing like a personal story but still too quirky to be history.

He coughed into a folded handkerchief and then wiped the corners of his mouth with a point of it. We started again.

Beneš was convinced of the need for a transfer of the Germans out of Czechoslovakia by the middle of 1941. The right of self-determination of the Sudeten Germans would not be recognized after the war because 'such a concept . . . is a priori a denial of the right of self-determination of ten million Czechoslovaks and precludes the very existence of an independent Czechoslovak state'.

Eden accepted this by July 1942 and Stalin was more than positive. In December 1943 he stood with Beneš at his side in front of a map of Europe on the wall of his office in Moscow. The Marshal, who had a red crayon in his hand, asked Beneš what he wanted. The President said he was not one of those who wanted to grab as much foreign territory as possible. Stalin waited with the crayon. Beneš said perhaps it might be a good idea to straighten the frontier with the Reich a little. Stalin was impatient for examples. Beneš pointed at the Glatz region, which bulged south into Czechoslovakia from Germany. Stalin was amazed at Beneš's moderation and grandly stroked the crayon across the neck of the region. But the boundaries of Czechoslovakia did not change after the war and Glatz became Kłodzko as Poland shifted westwards into Silesia following the Teheran matches.

'It is easier to move people than to move frontiers,' Tscherne said. There was large-scale looting of German property after May 1945. About three thousand Germans were murdered and many thousands beaten up. They were given smaller rations (Tscherne called them 'Jew rations') and forced to wear white armbands. Everything they owned was confiscated. They were forced to labour on the clearance of rubble and the resurfacing of streets. Restrictions were imposed on their shopping and they were not allowed to visit places of public amusement. Herr Tscherne said: 'The Czech people wanted to make good everything that had happened in Bohemia since 1620.'

The Germans were put in camps and one and a half million Czechs moved into the Sudetenland before the end of 1947. Herr Tscherne's camp near Eger was put in a train in September 1946. All 1,200 people in forty heated carriages. They were allowed 100 kilograms of luggage each up to the value of 1,000 Reichsmarks. The belongings were weighed next to the train and there was a small pile next to the scales – some people had taken too much. Everyone was allowed to keep their watches, wedding rings and alarm clocks. The Czech government gave each expellee 500 RM and food enough for the journey and for three days after. Families stayed together.

'Your family?' I asked. He went on with statistics.

Two and a quarter million people were expelled, most to the American zone, some 700,000 to the Soviet sector. It was only an eighth of the people expelled and transferred in Europe after Potsdam, 20 million in all.

'You must not be upset by these events, my dear *Grenzgänger*,' Herr Tscherne said. 'There was no choice. It was Munich or expulsion. Some people have said that 200,000 Sudeten Germans died in the transfer. That is a statistical error. They failed to take into account the previous deaths of the Jews in the area.

'There was revenge at first, but after Potsdam, Article Thirteen, the Americans guaranteed some humanity in it . . . the tradition of Lessing, Goethe and Schiller . . .,' he laughed. 'It may be unfortunate that things should have come to this, but having come to it, it was right that the transfer took place. We paid the price for the years in which Hitler was appeased and it was not a high price. Besides, it was forty years ago. The Czechs are still paying. The Russians would not be in Central Europe if not for those thoughts about the *grossdeutsche Herrenvolk*.

'But . . . if not for Henlein, if not for Hitler, if not for Clemenceau, if not for Bismarck, if not for Fichte, if not for Napoleon, if not for Rousseau, if not for the people who painted bison on the walls in Lascaux . . . that is not a game worth playing. I have lived in the past. I am living now. Once, in the Sudetenland, I was sure – in that Böhmer Wald – what was wrong with the world. Now I am sure again, the other side of your *Grenze!*'

He stopped and pulled the chair tighter into the table. 'I would like to give you a short note on the Transfer of Populations.' In his formal oddity he read from a yellower sheaf about the Turko-Bulgarian agreement of November 1913, the Greco-Bulgarian Convention of Neuilly (November 1920), and the Greco-Turkish Convention of Lausanne (January 1923) – all these winter dates. He mentioned Churchill's statement to the House of Commons on 15 December 1944 – 'I am not alarmed by the prospect of the disentanglement of populations . . . more possible in modern conditions than ever before' – about the expulsion of Germans from Silesia and East Prussia.

Tscherne's drift was: people are mobile; ethnic enclaves are dangerous – they are fifth columns; trauma is forgettable; loyalty to place is dangerous and sentimental; the awkwardness of the emotional detail must not be allowed to interfere with the overall rational idea. The great virtue of the Second World War: it made Europe neat. Instead of the disastrous and incompetent Balkanization of Versailles, it imposed two supranational empires on the continent, both with their dissident members – France *was* Romania – and by expulsion and transfers cleaned up local anomalies. It was purgation therapy, good *because* it hurt, because it burnt the old habits out of the place. One of those habits had been his own life in Eger (Cheb).

The rain was continuous as I made my way south to the border crossing at Schirnding. The woods were sodden and the fields black. In a church an air-brushed Luther regarded an elongated Christ. The loincloth was gilded. The toes curled in as they do and the fingers were hooked around the nails. In one church an angel held a bowl of fresh asters and freesias and the wings had been slotted into his adzed back, the tenons grooved and haunched in 1703.

Ten yards west of the German border post outside Schirnding a Turk ran a shop. It was full of rubbish and smelled like a wet dog. A Bulgarian lorry was parked up outside pointing east. The driver and his mate were fingering the goods. The Turk hung over them. Racks of Taiwanese sweat-shirts, their seams pinched, and Brazilian stereos, on which the plastic had somehow been chromed, were clammy under the half-on lighting. The driver was hesitating between a purple bra and pantie set – shot through with the kind of metal ribbon you find in pound notes – and an Indian cushion with mirrors caught in the embroidery. He didn't know if he loved his wife or girlfriend more. The other man was all for infidelity. He already had some little thing tucked up in a paper bag.

7

The Political Activity of Motorcycles

Up and down for a quarter of a mile through willowy scrubland and the road comes to the border. The fences stretch north and south. Czechoslovakia is ploughed for ten yards in from the edge. The fences cobwebbed around the crossing. Red and white barriers shunt the traffic into marshalled slots. But the border post itself was a village wedding. Red flags and Czech flags in circular displays. Messages about peace looped between the lamp-posts. The eye of the dove is a sharp red star. The unity of Slav peoples is eternal. Men stand around in brown nylon anoraks, the ushers. Cheap machine-guns are strapped across their backs, the wood effect on the plastic handles rubbed and yellowed. Everyone is easy, a sort of holiday. Border guards in overalls are plunging the tanks of a dirty bulk carrier, shouting across to each other, prodding for contraband or for a stagnant dissident cowering there in an out-of-date aqualung.

I wanted to join in. I wanted to reveal far more than they asked for, to show them the fabricated driving licence stamp, to confess the unlocalized guilt and make spy-hints. But I didn't. I was the last-minute adolescent guest at another family's party. They discussed the motorbike as if I wasn't there. A familiar, conning look. It didn't impress them. Enough Laverda-borne tyros had come through *en route* to the Aegean for 125 cc to look silly.

They examined my books. This was a success. I had a cold war diatribe with me called *The Triumph of Tyranny*. One photograph in it showed Stalin's head five feet long, lying sideways and broken on some Budapest tram tracks. Young men were standing around it with their legs at an angle. The guard showed it to his sergeant, who was delighted. A crowd of four or five of them gathered around the book. A busful of Belgian teenagers aiming for a beer festival in Prague looked out through their condensed panes, wiping wider circles in the mist. The military anoraks scratched against each other and the plasticated stocks of the machine pistols tocked up against other barrels. The straps hung badly and now and then each guard would straighten his gun with a shrug. The sergeant suddenly stood upright from the pages and with a priestly movement of both hands motioned his men back. I expected a judgement but he nosed into the book again, brailling out the words with a finger on which the cuticle encroached on to the nail: 'Trotskyist, Titoite, Zionist, bourgeois, nationalist traitors' one by one.

'What is traitors?' he asked me in thick English.

'A traitor is a man who lies to his wife.'

'Who lies on his wife?'

'*To* his wife.'

'Distantly, with the ... the thoughts?'

'I suppose so.'

'Oh,' he said, and moved his head sideways in mild confusion. He missed his wife in Hradec-Králové. 'What is your occupation?'

'Geographer.'

'And what is this book?'

'It's about different places.'

'What is Tyranny?'

'It means political activity.'

'And what is Triumph?'

'A sort of motorcycle.' Lorries had formed up in queues on either side while the sergeant thought: *The Political Activity of Motorcycles*.

'There is sex in the book?' he asked.

'Very little. None at all virtually.'

'It is about virtue?'

'You could say so.'

'A *roman*?'

'That's right, complete fabrication.'

'In factories?' he asked. A new element.

'Factories come into it now and then.'

'There you are.' He slapped the book shut. 'Off you go. Enjoy your books. Enjoy your Czechoslovakia.' (A blend of industrial, political and personal motifs, he remembered with pleasure.) 'Eat tripe soup!' he shouted as I began to move away. 'Sink your prejudice! It is food Number One in Czechoslovakia! You love the soft tripe strips!'

What a welcome to a country! Uniforms meant nothing. What were fences? I was Egon Bahr on holiday. The rain stopped. I passed a squad of conscripts marching west. The man at point carried a red flag as if leading a car in 1905. They shouted Honda, Honda, Honda as I went past and the man waved the flag. I tore up Cheb (Eger) in this wild new demythology, exchanging petrol coupons like a millionaire, stripped of everything Teuton and smiled at again by a girl in the back of a car. It was May the 8th. Czechoslovakia was between holidays – May Day and Liberation Day on May the 9th. There were flags on every building, on every floor of every block of flats. There were maypoles eighty feet high in the villages, stripped pine trees, the top ten feet with branches and needles intact, ribbons of every colour twined in among them.

Thirty-nine years before, the Russians had at last entered Prague after the three murderous days of the uprising in the city. There had been many Nazi reprisals against partisans and innocents. General Patton with the US Third Army (by now about 400,000 men) had been stopped by Eisenhower on a line running through Pilsen (Plzen) about fifty miles short of the capital. Eisenhower had consulted Marshal Antonov. They had confirmed the Yalta decision that Czechoslovakia was naturally in the Soviet orbit and agreed the Americans should penetrate no further into Bohemia. Patton was indignant. He wanted Prague. 'If the Russians don't like it, let them go to hell,' he said. Patton might have reached the city on the 6th, the Russians not until the 9th. Thousands of Czechs died in the three-day gap. The imminent arrival of the Americans, as they thought, had precipitated the uprising.

But Patton had to be restrained. He was spoiling for another war and told a member of his staff that he could get to Moscow in thirty days. This was not the required attitude. Meanwhile, he made sure to wear his second-best pistol. It is the habit of meeting conquerors to swop personal arms. He also liberated the Lipizzaners. Patton thought it odd, as he said in his memoir, that a body of fine young men should have spent the war 'teaching a group of horses to wiggle their butts'.

After Cheb I turned south to riffle down the inside of the Curtain. Polonius on a 125. The churches were decayed and the agriculture collective. The rain began again. In Planá I drank an orange jug of Pilsener lager with my soft tripe soup. It was an empty sorted-out country from which two and a quarter million Germans had been removed and the old farming patterns obliterated. Less than one and a half million Czechs had come to replace them and there was an emptiness between the centralized, hangar-like farms. It was, like parts of the Jura, a country of large estates in which all that was left were the rational farm buildings. The great houses that were the source of the idea were not to be seen.

From Cheb (Eger) as far south as Poběžovice (Ronsperg) 80–100% of the population had been German in the 1930 census. At least four out of every five of the Czech families here were newcomers to the place. Some villages were utterly repopulated in the human and actual equivalent of the cartographic switch in names. But of course that is invisible now. I saw one German advertisement for beer fading back into the stone barn on which it had been painted. Too much rectangular rebuilding has occurred for any sense of incongruity or borrowed clothes. The Sudetenland no longer exists. There is no borderland here. Three generations of Czechs could have been born in these villages since the transfer. The nation-state slides up to the edge unimpeded.

The rain closed the country off. It would be a disaster for the May the 9th celebrations. Not that they were actually relevant here. The real liberation day had already passed. But that was pedantic, forgettable. One nation, after all, meant one day. I had to crouch over the handlebars to stop the rain from stinging me under the goggles. South of Planá, I turned south and west on the brown dirty roads, aiming for the border in the forest hills of the Česky Les south of Tachov. I was frozen in the central European rain. I couldn't get over the cold. The muscles across my chest had tightened in a single constant shiver. All I looked at was the front tyre greasing in the wet. At least the waterproofs were waterproof. Mobile indifference at 50 kph in the rain. I aimed for a place on the map called Diana. I can remember nothing about the journey there. Only the snatching handfuls of rain, the sogged map and the steaming slug-mounds of silage outside a bunker-grey cow house in a field of mud, surrounded by a continent of weather.

But miles short of Diana I was stopped by a tractor across the road. The driver would not let me pass. I couldn't understand what he said. The rain was hanging in a gauze over the tarmac. He shouted at me through the smeared perspex of the cab and waved me back over the noise of the engine. I know now that I was on the edge of the forbidden zone, to which access was illegal without the permit. He was trying to be helpful. But at the time it seemed like Herr Gummisch in Berlin. Bland obstructionism, wilful dirty hostility from an envious man in Finnish overalls. As Herr Kundt had warned, I had failed to stand back from the accumulated details. I had forgotten, oddly enough, that I couldn't get to the Iron Curtain from the backside, that the easy voyeurism from the west was part of the West itself and of the difference I was trying to explore.

Domažlice (Taus) was soaked. Wet people in the cafés left grey outlines of their sleeves on the tables. Wet fingers left deformed patches near the base of stubbed-out cigarettes. The ash clotted in the aluminium trays. Women coming in shook their hair out of hats and then pushed at it once or twice from each side.

Domažlice must be lovely on a real spring day. The long main market square is arcaded in stubby provincial arches and the houses above them come to curly Dutch gables and theatrical pediments. Although a few miles back now from the frontier with Germany, it is famous as a frontier town, the capital of a people now called the Chods and known to the Romans as the Quadi. They were a Germanic tribe, later absorbed by the Slavs – the Czechs – who came into Bohemia in the sixth century from the east. Augustus had made client arrangements with the Quadi to buffer the northern frontier of Upper Pannonia and Noricum, which ran along the Danube about seventy kilometres to the south. Emasculation by alliance, frontier as cushion not crust, Curzonian pass-control. In the fifteenth century, in the struggle for power between the Hussites and the German Catholics, the castle at Domažlice, called Chodenburg, was manned as a frontier outpost for the Czechs by the Chods. In 1428 the German crusaders were so frightened by the reports of the zealots in the castle, led by Prokop Holý the Shaven, that they fled without a meeting or a fight. It was a setback, as the overegged guidebook said, 'to the expansionist policies of the Holy Empire of the Germans', a classic bit of Làčplèsism. The castle now displays a collection of Chod napkins.

But today on the 8th the Chodský hotel was full. The Slavia and Koruna were full. The Tourist Hostel: full. And it rained. The sick children of city schools had been given time off in the fresh air near the Česky Les mountains and were sleeping in every bed. They screamed upstairs after a day indoors from the rain and the teachers felt hot. Go to Babylon, they all said. So I went to Babylon. It was six kilometres. But in Babylon the Praha was full, the Magda full, the Cerchov closed and the rain intolerable. The school-children leant out of third-storey windows and pointed. The cook ran over from a low building opposite with a tray of frozen chips and into a banged swing door. Limp puddles dripped from the chalet eaves. I drove at random up into the hills. Rain barred the headlight beam. It still felt cold.

I looked for a site where I could pitch the tent. A yard or two beyond one of the notices marking the border zone the road edged out on to a bit of meadow. In the beam from the headlight, its severe lights and shadows, I put up the tent in the rain. I was beyond caring about the regulations. I tried to sleep until the headlights of a car swung across the nylon. I listened to its tyres on the gravel. It stopped and whined up in reverse, stopping again with the lights fixed on the tent. I scrabbled out expecting guards. But it was an old man, outlined in black against the headlights, with the collar of a coat pulled up around his neck and his hair sticking out sideways. He spoke German. I shouldn't stay here. We packed my stuff up roughly and I followed the tail-lights of his car for a few miles through the forest, the Böhmer Wald, saturated with the rain.

He was the cook in a hotel. The yellow light from the windows leaked out on to the scabby pine trunks. He took me into the kitchen. The hotel was full with the children from the cities, but I could sleep in his office. Josef's hair was as white as his clothes, as his white cook's sandals. The only colour was in his tanned face. He sat me down among the chipped enamel and scrubbed boards of the kitchen and gave me hot chocolate and white soft cheese which he prodded into shape on the plate with his fingers. 'I love England,' he said without prompting. 'I love democracy.' The border had sheared away the details, the necessarily scurfy details, of political democracy and had left in his mind a shining totalitarian ideal, an elixir in the chalice of England, still presided over in some way or other by the Churchill who had wanted to save Central Europe from Communism. 'I love England too,' I said. We didn't mention Churchill's 'naughty document', nor Munich.

Josef had been to Chicago, where his brothers lived, but had come back to the Šumava, these forest hills. He preferred them to the Dwight D. Eisenhower Expressway. His brothers left in 1938. He rolled up his white sleeve. A number was tattooed on the thin strip of hairless skin along the underside of his forearm. The blue figures were imprecise, as if they had spread a little in the time. Josef had been in Auschwitz-Birkenau for four years. His natural weight was 84 kilograms. When the advancing Russian armies arrived at the murder camp he weighed 36 and was unable to stand without help. He said his legs were like chair legs. As though 48 kilograms, eight stone, was a measure of what had happened there.

In the top of a cupboard he had the blue and grey striped trousers he had worn and a cap like Casey Jones's. He put it on to show me and grinned under the peak, a boy in photographer's fancy dress. He then rummaged in the back of another cupboard in the bedroom. There were some posters of 1960s racing cars on the walls. Jim Clark smiled in a green helmet. Josef then came up with one wooden clog. It had leather uppers and another number – different from the one on his arm – burnt into the sole. He washed his face with both hands in the basin and then rubbed away at the skin with a towel.

The border ran within a few minutes of his hotel, but Josef was indifferent to it. The experience of Auschwitz already occupied any mental space which a closed border would have taken. He was actually free to come and go now, but coming and going now had a terrible irrelevance. He had already known the most dreadful manifestation of the closed frontier in the parody-colony, the racial island of the death camp. Any new one meant nothing next to it.

I wanted to ask him about everything, about Auschwitz, about the Stalinist anti-Semitism in Czechoslovakia after the war, when Gottwald had hanged prominent Jews, the anti-Semitism now. But the first questions were rebuffed. The fact was enough, the fact and the situation. One only had to be shown the objects and his brand. I helped him spoon out cocoa for the children. '*Arbeit macht frei*,' he said. We watched black and white television in the dark of his bedroom. The metal light picked out the hollows in his cheek. There was a film to celebrate May the 9th. It switched between scenes of the Russian armies coming westwards and of a Nazi labour-camp. '*Dass ist richtig, Dass ist richtig*,' Josef kept saying at the apocalyptic episodes enacted in the studios. We looked together at the striped, capped cadavers being whipped and tortured. *Dass ist richtig*. At the foot-high, foot-wide cots in banks like the niches in Italian cemeteries. *Dass ist richtig*. And in silence at the studio postures of the Russian soldiers in the switched-on flash of electric grenades. 'The Russians never came here,' Josef said.

Towards the end of the film he put his hand on my leg. But I said good night, went to his office, turned the lock and slept there on the floor.

It snowed on Liberation Day. I curved south in the foothills of the Šumava. Snow thickened the blossom on the cherry trees which braided the salted road. The sheep were yellow beside it. In Klatovy it was still too early for celebrations and the woman in the café thought I was German. She would take no tip. On, south and east, lining the border, burrowing towards the Balkans, casing the single tunnel.

In Stachý the village band blocked the downhill street. The tuba had slipped in the snow and the bass drum was banging out the dent with a hammer.

'You miss the postilion,' one of the band said to me in English. A handsome and very white man in a leather jacket. I did indeed. 'Today we are here to celebrate the occupation of Czechoslovakia by the Russians,' he said. I looked into his face. Not a millisecond of a smile. He combed his curly black hair with his fingers. 'Or is that your word?' he asked. 'Is it *liberation* you say in English?' And then we did both laugh. 'We sing the songs today and in August. Czechoslovakia is the only one to have a Liberation Day in the spring and a whole Liberation Week later in the year.' In the window of a pub a photograph of a Russian soldier smiling with a smiling child. It was taken in 1945.

The pub was steamed up. Aproned waitresses carried six two-litre jugs of Budvar at a time, orange and frothing, sliding them down uninvited on to the white plastic-clothed tables, the cloth held on with a chrome clip at the side. We sat in the basket-backed chairs, sponging Budvar. The band loosened up at the tables for an hour and a half before anyone began to unpack the instruments. Budvar is very good. Only a table of firemen in the corner, ready in their uniforms, were unable to share in the general consumption. They sat unhappily in front of half-drunk half-pints while the citizens expanded and sweated around them. A trayful of *borowič* in ranks of glass thimbles followed a tray full of slivovitz plum brandy, one shot each. Pork and dumplings floated up, 'the national eat'. We sat there tunnelling for oblivion. A long joke about a farmer's wife hinged on the difference between *kladný* (cold) and *chladný* (positive), or was it the other way round? We would only have folk-songs today, songs about woodmen in love with farmer's wives, the mountain with the valley. No swing, no Glenn Miller on the National Day. The second trumpet – a butcher – said he had swing. Yes, said the first, about two centimetres. It was solidarity like I had never known, real alcoholic socialism, in which we could delight on May the 9th. It was Olivia's birthday.

The arrival of the Ukrainian units in Prague had been a great day in 1945, a guarantee of the national boundaries created only a quarter of a century before. The Russians had been the only constant wartime allies of the Czechs. Beneš recognized that Czechoslovakia could survive any future German threat on their guarantee alone. The welcome they had been given was as ecstatic as any in Europe. When genuinely free elections were held a year later, with a scrupulously secret ballot and no interference in the campaign, the Communists received more than twice the number of votes (38%) of their nearest rivals, the Beneš-Masaryk National Socialists. Until 1948 the coalition government, with Beneš as president and the Communist Gottwald as prime minister, supervised a liberal regime in which there was genuine parliamentary freedom and a critical press. But this ideal moment was destroyed by the coming of the cold war and the geography of Europe.

Czechoslovakia is a corridor from West to East. It is the hyphen between Bavaria and the Ukraine. Bismarck had warned that it was the key to the continent, which should be left in the hands of the

Czechs, 'who have no lust for dominion'. The Czech acceptance of Marshall Aid in June 1947 was too much for Moscow and three days later it was refused. Czechoslovakia had been unoccupied since December 1945 and the country separated the Red Armies on the Vistula and on the Danube. If Moscow was to preserve its eastern European crush zone intact, the gap had to be blocked. This was the argument publicly used twenty years later after the August invasion. Capitalist Czechoslovakia would become a cancer in the middle of the Socialist community.

In February 1948 a crisis over the packing of the police force by the Communist Minister of the Interior, Nosek, led to the resignation of most of the non-Communist members of the coalition. Within four days Gottwald's substantially Communist government had taken power. Even then, at the May elections, in which voters decided for or against a single Communist list, 90% of the Czechs and 86% of the Slovaks registered their approval.

'There is work to do,' my friend Radomír said. He looked like Alan Alda. He was a customs officer down the road at Strázný. Just a job. He fixed up the clarinet. The band shufflingly assembled its instruments and played a few windy trial notes. Nobody stood up and another round arrived. We talked about my destination. I always said it was Bratislava. And where then? Hungary. Madarsko. And where then? Rumunsko. And where then? Řecko? Greece. *Řecko*. Always the same reaction, the same disappointed envy in their faces, the border in their faces, a generous envy in their certain knowledge that any movement would end like one of those toy cars that reverses when it comes to the furniture, snuffling the edges of the room, until at last, after tracing its configuration, it begins to repeat the pattern. 'You are lucky to be a free boy,' Radomír said and drained another empty thimble of the *borowič*. I told him that this was a nicer place to be than Greece, but he said that was absurd.

The chairman of the Stachý Village National Committee swung in through the door. A shaved, boss-eyed bullet head. The brown suit was stained in the thigh-high creases. Suddenly there was business. The band stood to. The firemen straightened their tunics and brushed away the bun crumbs. I sat up. The concert master hurried in buttoning up too much of his jacket. He was followed by one of the serious waitresses. The band stumbled into a jolly number and their director started conducting them from half-way across the room. He squeezed his buttocks between the firemen's chairs, held out two fingers horizontally in a V and made rhythmic gestures with them. The other hand tugged at the chairbacks and then at his tie, round behind the knot, flattened his hair, which sprang back up, and then touched his zip. The Village National Committee chairman smiled as if on the May Day mausoleum. He tapped a biro on his teeth in time, swung his appalling eyes around the room and jokingly grimaced at the wrong notes. It was chaos. The head of the tuba player was asleep between two full jugs of Budvar. His hair was weed in the spilt beer and his doughy face had oiled up like lava. The chairman made a request and we had more of the clumping merry-go-round rhythms, more foresters carving midnight hearts on the gateposts of lowland farms, more sawing down of rival maypoles, more hobbling of cuckolds' donkeys, more baking of children into pies. There was no dancing, just the swaying of empty jugs and of half-smoked Spartas. The chairman left. 'Liberation Day, Species Three!' Radomír said and hugged me around the shoulder. I had a cup of black coffee. Radomír gave me the address of a friend in Bratislava – and then sang a bit of a song. 'It's about thunder and the Tatras,' he said. We had a last thimble of *borowič*. 'Here is to the foreigners now in Czechoslovakia!' he said, we clinked the thimbles and I shuddered the drink away.

The road I had taken began to run out into mud and ruts. The rain had been sobering and constant. I was deep in the forest. A logging truck had soaked me in swilled puddle water. The puddle slopped on the banks after the lorry had gone through. Another passed. Its claw-grip was dug into the poles it carried. Five in the afternoon on a dark grey day. I suddenly arrived at the border fence. This was a mistake. It was only the 'back-border', not the frontier with Austria itself, but to have arrived here at all I had already come deep into the forbidden zone. A small wooden watchtower stood behind the fence. Its legs were straddled. It was a crude amateurish thing compared with the airport technology used by the Germans. The Czech tower looked like something an assiduous father might have built at week-ends for his blasé children. They would have played on it for twenty-five minutes. An empty truck, littered with the shards of bark and rubbed hawsers, waited at the gate in the wire. I tried to turn the bike around in the yellow mud. A young guard came to the door of the weatherboarded farm building that served as the border post. He hooked the top of his tunic together, made me switch off the bike and took my passport inside. I waited in the rain. The truck drivers made sympathetic faces. Nothing happened for an hour except the lumber trucks came and went through the barbed wire gate, the drivers handing over their identity cards as they went in empty and collecting them as they came out full. I sat in a patch of wet grass in the rain, next to a new tractor with green Russian markings, half unpacked from its crate and with the boards skewed.

The drivers made bad-luck faces from their cabs. It was getting dark. An angular jeep arrived, and an officer got out. He was the only man I have ever seen whose forehead was fat. There was a little cupid wrinkle between his eyebrows, repeated lower down as a mouth. His brown leather gloves were fat little hands and he wore leather puttees. He had been unable to bend over that morning and only one buckle on the side was done up. He looked at me as he walked over to the building, but said nothing. I had my helmet on for warmth and wrapped a scarf around my neck. A dirty white Lada turned up. Its driver wore large rectangular sunglasses in the dusk with silverized frames and a rabbit-lined parka. His hair was combed down to meet his eyebrows. The fringe jogged as one. He too went into the building, but according to training kept his face firmly to the front.

Another threequarters of an hour. The rain let up, but it was cold. The working day was finished and the trucks stopped coming through. I tried to go over to the doorway, but the guard on the gate told me in Czech to stay where I was. I tried to get a light for a cigarette from the driver of the jeep, but he looked ahead across the bonnet and wouldn't open the window. I put on more clothes for this strange outside incarceration. It was life inside closed frontiers. Was my position any different from the loggers' who gave away their passes at the fence? I could wander around, but I couldn't move. I did 1930s gym exercises like *The Great Escape*. Henlein. The place had contracted through the absence of my stained passport. And but for the cold and the wet it was oddly enjoyable. There was nothing I could do, no decisions to be made. It was, in its way, a sort of absorption. It was better than sitting listening to the rain in the tent.

The officer came out into the dark. He spoke German badly. Where had I come from? Where had I stayed the night? Where had I eaten? Where had I drunk? What sort of map did I have? What was I doing? Why was I here? Who was I? I got out the road atlas to show him. My toothbrush fell out of the saddlebag into the mud. We went under the light by the door. It was a Czech atlas, and I had bought it in Cheb. To my horror I remembered that in the pub in Stachý I had drawn my route to show Radomír. A solid blue incriminating biro line bobbed in and out of the frontier zone, looking for weak spots, some of them circled, some underlined. At least no spy, I realized, would be that incompetent. 'What is this?' He pointed at the line with a brown leather finger.

'It is my way.'

'Why do you stay with the frontier?' I looked at the map. It was green in large blobs.

'I love the forests. The mountains, the Šumava, you feel so free in a piece of Nature.'

He produced the passport. 'This is disgusting.' *Schlecht.* Helmstedt. He folded it back. The cheesecloth in the spine was visible through the rotted paper. Her Britannic Majesty was brown and bendable. Why did I have two Hungarian visas? What were my connections with Hungary? Ancient suspicion of another would-be master race. The Magyars had destroyed the Great Moravian Empire in 906. But he was not a cool interrogator. He repeated questions when he should have left silences. I told him I especially enjoyed the small Hungarian ponds. I was a professional environmentalist with an interest in the life forms of transitional zones.

'For example?'

I looked at him carefully. 'Frogs, salamanders, aquatic lizards.'

He shook the rain off his cap and asked for the names of places I had been in Czechoslovakia. He went inside again and while he telephoned I sat down on the grass. In a story, you couldn't be sure if I was a spy. I thought I might be a spy, sitting there. . . .

The young man eyed the border guard, who turned away up the track as he had done twenty times before. This was it. Adam raced for the woods, hurling himself blindly across the stream and into the bracken on the far side. He heard a shout behind him and a dog throw itself into a convulsive, desperate barking. Then, as he knew they would – he had noticed the transformer at the side of the hut where the guard had offered him a 'Sparta' – a bank of glaring spotlights burst into life. *'God!'* Adam thought to himself, 'this is a pretty fine old mess!' and struggled through the dense undergrowth which seemed to want to hold him back, as if the guards even had the brambles on their side. He noticed that Czech brambles were just like brambles in Leicestershire – why was the world so cruelly divided? At last he was in a clearing, belting for cover. He thought his chest was going to split with the agony until at last he chucked himself down in a pile of leaves – of course he knew that funny musty smell – and lay there listening to the pounding of his heart and the raucous, insistent rhythm of his breaths. . . .

The officer gave me the passport back. 'Here is a small guide to first-class routes in Czechoslovakia, *Schnellverkehrstrassen.* Remember, not more than sixty kilometres in the built-up zones!' He reached up to pat the top of my helmet. I heard it like sea in a shell. And then the seat of the Honda. 'As a matter of fact,' he said, 'how much does the Honda cost?' He saluted as I left.

I saw the man with silver glasses twice again: once in a shop in a tiny village called Pohorská Ves and once in Znojmo, where he may have been on some other business. It was a hot afternoon and the parka was zipped up to his neck. He was smoking in a bar, somehow contriving to make the smoke curl up between the dark glasses and his eyes. Perhaps it was an exercise in self-control.

Flowering chestnuts arched the road where passing lorries had clipped them. Some of the recently brushed-off petals lay on the side. The villages began to whiten as I emerged from the border mountains of Bohemia. Tiles replaced slates and the roofs settled into the plateau with scalloped eaves. The country flattened and emptied and the roads straightened towards Znojmo through the low green cornfields. I had crossed the watershed. All the streams until now, all the rain, had run down towards the Elbe and the North Sea. From here everything would flow, eventually, into the Danube. It was the great division of the continent. I didn't notice it at the time. I must have been doing 55 mph, half a minute between two culverts.

The line marked the end of Bohemia and the beginning of Moravia. Both are now Czech provinces but Moravia is the stub of empire in the borderlands of West and East. For nineteenth-century Czech nationalists the Great Moravian Empire was a model and a summons. The first Slav state flourished in the eastern Marchlands of the Carolingian empire. Like imperialists before and after them, the Franks employed vassal magnates to pad out the boundaries of power. The Morava River, which runs into the Danube just west of Bratislava, is still called the March by the Austrians.

Marches are structurally unstable. Their situation between power blocs is an impediment or an opportunity. They can either be imposed on by empire or impose themselves on the disintegrative fringes of the blocs which surround them. Finlandization and Balkanization hold hands in the crush zone.

The Moravian princes made the best of their opportunities. From 814 until the end of the century they expanded the empire up into Polish Silesia, pooling out into Bohemia and western Slovakia. It was a great cultural moment. Archaeologists have found beautiful scabbards. The Moravians were famous for worked pewter. Churchmen from Byzantium and Rome competed – sometimes violently – for their allegiance. By the 890s vassaldom to the heirs of Charlemagne was nominal.

In 892 the Carolingian emperor Arnulf, to control Sviatopluk, the Moravian Duke, sent an embassy to the western steppes, inviting the Magyar hordes to come over the Carpathians and colonize the plains on the far side. They crossed the mountains *en masse*, probably in 896, easily subjected the farmers there and ten years later destroyed the Moravian empire in a battle near Bratislava. The Magyars themselves became the threat most feared in Aachen.

I slid down into Znojmo. The silos by the grain wharves pumped up above the brown roofs. Each an engorged polished glans. Every one of these places a target. Yellow smoke from a chimney on the northern edge. Stratified lavatory bowls in the stockyards, gaping in polythene. Modern Znojmo is a centre for ceramics manufacture. Down into the brown paved streets and dusty baroque brown walls. Fine for violating a traffic-free zone. One hundred crowns to one gold canine and a sliver of a moustache (dyed). Escorted two miles out to Hotel Družba, sterilized corruption. Two crowns extra on the price of cigarettes. Waitresses doubled as whores. Everything doubled: service, duty, honour, chins. Everything its flipside. Waggled buttocks in the face of the apparat. Russians in the hotel. Brandy at breakfast in indulgent-apologetic smiles to themselves. Islands of the state. Accidents with outcrops. Craven attitudes to a man with swing. No gaiety with corn in the coop. Spy-holes in the bedroom door, magnifying fish-eyes from the outside in. The cramming of the short wave and trilled blipping of the larks. The first vines. Straggled fences in the ill lime soil. In the verges the familiar Leicestershire weeds. There was convolvulus and poppy in Iron Age Hampshire. Some strip farming: 7% of the land now owned by the state. Giles Winterbourne on a horse-drawn wooden box, wife in its window, turned down moustaches in the rain. A constant temptation to Austria across the homely wooden barbed wire fence. Lobotomized discontinuity. The first remains today of the 1930s 'Czech Maginot' made useless by Munich. Pillboxes with rounded corners like loaves, the camouflage paint worn off by weather, 'distressed'. The downstairs doorless doorways stuffed with brambles and old leaves.

I walked out of the hotel into the new-block fringes of Znojmo. A pair of rollerskaters holding hands one backwards one forwards skated downhill past me, the hair of one blown up and away, the hair of the other blown over her face.

As the town broke at the edges into lots between the vineyards and isolated garages where a dog licked at the pool in a disused tyre, it tightened again into a village. One-storey houses set back across wide verges hemmed with limes. A straight unkinked street and the grass between the trees marked diagonally where people came up to cross the road. One or two Skodas parked in the dust.

I sat on the steps of the war memorial. Brown enamel ovals on the stone and an angel above them holding a corpse. These men had died on the eastern front alongside the Russians. 'What are you doing there?' an old woman shouted at me in German. 'Do you know where you are?' The fringes of her plaid fell down her arms and bosom. She had big pink hands and forearms in which you could see the muscles. The hands must have weighed a pound each. The tapes of a white apron were tied in front under the bosom. 'Do you know where you are?' She took me by the hand. Lumpen where her fingers joined the palm. And led me over to her house. Like the others it was pantiled and rendered with heavy iron grilles on the windows and a big yard at the side and back where a wheel-less Skoda had its axle-ends on bricks and five chickens sat on the bonnet fluffed up. 'It is not Vienna,' she said as we walked over the patted-down mud. Her hair was pulled back like a dancer's and her face had been tightened with it.

A large painting of the harbour at Trieste hung over the stove. Two red gas cylinders stood next to it and fat had spat up from the frying-pan in spots on to the brigantines and quays. A panel of twelve Delft tiles let into the wall showed another grey sea-scene. It was marked with the dried opaque smear from a dirty cloth. 'We once had so much,' Elizabeth said. The place was coming apart. The flecked paper bulged and browned near the skirting, the cloth-wrapped wires to the light-bulbs were stained rusty at the hooks. The Bakelite radio was in the shape of a hive. It had been chipped and was mended with green insulating tape. She turned the radio on at the wall and we waited for the warming up. She pushed the loose plug in again to make sure and it fell back. The house had been there three hundred years, her family since 1870. A foxed photograph wiped off with a cuff. An ancestor in the recognizable street, in her apron, her galosh mouth.

The radio warmed on: why in these circumstances the intellectuals are under pressure ... she turned the knob. The Socialist community ... had in its common interests ... Jordan and the Arab world ... militating against hereditary chieftaincy ... Meridian ... mainly English, Twi, Ewe, Ga, Nzima, Hansa and Dagbani ... until at last Huddie Ledbetter (Leadbelly himself) and Blind Lemon Jefferson oozed out between the beehive bars. '*Vienna*,' Elizabeth said through the Storyville rhythms and sat back with hands in her lap, crossed at the wrist and her fingers drumming the starch.

She loved the radio. It was something 'out of control'. She had heard an Austrian journalist say: 'What is all this? We are gnats in the evening.' 'Do you understand me?' 'What is Gagarin if you look from the stars? He makes a short little hop up from the tablecloth and down.' She may have heard this remark a quarter of a century before.

But Elizabeth was no quietist. She was angry. Jan had been fined for doing moonlight repair work on the Skoda at the back. Someone in the village had heard the banging of the hammer and it was reported. The family had been independent builders until 1948. Now look at it. Look at the brown on the walls. The village was divided half and half, those who were for and those against, and each knew who the other was. They had to live with each other, but you always knew the difference. It never came into the open. She had heard the children coming back from school, and now her grandchildren, saying 'The Russians are good to us.' 'Every night I used to teach them again.'

I made a slight reservation about the golden age and the absolute evil of socialism, but with Leadbelly Elizabeth got louder. She started walking round the room, improvising, picking up dirty pans as evidence of Communist iniquity, pointing at her forty-year-old bachelor son now at the table, still in his anorak and fur hat, eating fruitcake with oily fingers, as the prime symptom of what had happened to western civilization. She was accelerating out of control. Joe 'King' Oliver was feeling unhappy in Chicago. Jan was licking gearbox oil off his thumbs. The wire to one of the lights had shorted.

'Does the frontier mean much to you?' I asked. The torrent changed direction. There was no frontier. Not before the war, the First War, and in the Dual Monarchy, that was something. They all learnt German and Magyar. She said something in Magyar. The village had four names – Czech, Slovak, German, Hungarian. So much for frontiers! They were intolerable, ugly, foreign, modern, Russian things. Haven't you seen the Russians in their white cars? Fountains of hatred while Jan ate the cake. Do you understand? Do you understand? Why didn't I have a car? In a car you could carry everything. The Frenchman had a car. Jan could fix it. Jan smiled molasses. You could be quite alone.

She suddenly blessed me. Another piece of cake. *Ganz traurig.* Never drive by the woods, she said, always by the fields. You cannot be safe in the woods. And could I send a packet of Dutch cocoa from England?

Immer bei den feldern. In Mikulov a gilded and painted baroque hall in the castle now exists only in the grey reproductions of a pair of photographs. It was destroyed in 1945. Next to them a picture of Hitler reviewing a Sudeten welcome in 1938 on the wet cobbles. The photograph smiles. Through the rusted wrought-iron doorways of the church behind him in the picture an ash and willow scrub wood now grows in the roofless nave. The semi-deities are headless in the pediment and some early oats had seeded between their legs.

The road to Bratislava was the best in Europe, miles of seamless tarmac between the poplar blocks. The great affair is to move, to feel the globe tarmac under the tyres. The pipework in the natural gas fields was the structure of seatless metal chairs.

Across the Morava south of Breclav into Slovakia, another Russian tank on an uphill plinth marks the last breakthrough of the Ukrainian armies on the long numbing road from Stalingrad. Chestnuts braid the verges and a driver stands in relief between the cab and the crane in tartan trousers, waving with the other hand. Byelorussian machinery in the carrier-deck fields, food production platforms, in which any sort of rural romance has changed its clothes, transferring the pastoral back again from industrial shock-work to the twelve-share ploughs. Nearing Bratislava, the Little Carpathians rise in the east, ridged in vines and spotted with self-built wooden villas. The construction of these tiny country chalets has boomed since 1968. It too is a Czech pastoralism, channelling the energies of that Spring, 'contained by the icecap', as one man said to me, into a new sort of quietism. It identifies, in a familiar pattern, the rural with the non-political. A nation building wooden separate nests. What a fate. These bungalows can cost as much as four to five hundred thousand *koruny*. A doctor earns about 4,000 a month plus tips, a student doing a menial job maybe 1,600. That is a measure of the retreat into self in Czechoslovakia, the retreat from state: in English terms about £100,000 for a two-room pre-fab.

Bratislava began to pile up around the eight-lane highway, thickening in ageing skins, baroque onions seen past the cinemas, the tram parks, the green spires on fifteenth-century churches and on *Jugendstil* department stores, the brown Bauhaus cuboids, the acres of white *forbidden* stripes painted at intersections, until you come to the stone embankments of the slow brown river, eased between the bevelled shores, where barges and white-swept cruise boats are sparsely moored.

Pressburg, Pozsony, Bratislava is an ex-traveller. It meets you at first with the indifference of a cosmopolitan, his early life spent between the salons of various cultures, but now interfered with and confined to a nicely furnished but *intolerably* circumscribed corner of the world. Vienna is only 35 miles away, Budapest a little more than two hours. But these places are cut off. The Austrian frontier is only three kilometres west, the Hungarian about eight on the other side. The city is snug in this corner, at the point where the Carpathians, reduced to downland, cross the Danube. Celtic, Roman, Great Moravian, Magyar, Habsburg and Turkish citadels like consecutive graffiti have occupied the hill over the river. Now above the city, where the materials of Europe have slumped into structures, the sterilized restoration of a castle, ruined by fire in 1811, coldly presides. It is like the hotel at Tintagel, an ergonomic cube with four cream turrets piped on at the corners. The Slovak National Council, the distillation, the endpoint of history, the bogus remains of 1968 plans for regional autonomy, made ridiculous by the invasion, but still employing the defunct language of a previous nationalism, now meets there.

The old town beneath it has variety in a big-limbed concrete way, but all the multiplicity and inventive catalysis of a border town has come to a stop. There are big empty attempts at architectural bottom lined up along the Danube – the huge single-cantilever bridge over the river is only the most recent – and the osmotic complexities of border life have given way to the dull existence at the bottom of a bag. Closed society – the Husák icecap – and closed frontiers are mutual reinforcements: the airtight jar and the formaldehyde it contains. Neither can preserve without the other. A closed frontier is a closed society. The freedom to come and go is the heart of all freedoms.

There was an exhibition of history in the museum. Until 1948 everything on show was political: maps with little explosions in Brezno and Poprad to mark discontent in 1848, red flags for centres of the uprising in the war, boots to mark strikes and then suddenly, in 1948, history finishes. Slovakia becomes the zone for wheat-quota smashing, for building bridges of 431 metres span, for providing unprecedented maternity leave and bulk chemical storage. The past is sheared away from the present, here from there, government from politics. All the straightforward conviction of the frontier is smeared over a country that has been deprived of its own borderland status. And this makes Bratislava, where the Dubček government thought it had come to some political understanding with the Russians only a week or two before the invasion, a sad betrayed place.

Jirí Anderle's graphics were on show in a gallery on a nook-street in old Bratislava from which cars had been excluded. The bookshop next door had 'no Kafka for the time being'. Anderle drew brutally dismantled people from an imperial age, with a sort of love–hate exactitude in his draughtsmanship, stripping them down to a horrible vulnerability. Many of his paintings had a small brown photograph, pasted to the bottom right-hand corner, of the subjects before his treatment of them. They were imperialists from 1911, complete, dressed heroes to themselves, with horse to hand or wife, baby and picnic. Anderle dismantles not to the skeletal but to flesh and weakness. *Übermensch* moustaches shorn off show receding lips; naked shoulders slope forward like hangers; knees are ridiculous, rumpled pre-tear baby faces. It is the vision of themselves in the mirror, emerging from drink back home after a party. But they rot too and disintegrate, and he leaves the medals hanging from their clammy breasts. In another series one of Piero della Francesca's beautiful girls decays from the vertical into crabbed senility, a terrible progression from the quat-trocento to Francis Bacon – or Diane Arbus – in one wall. In the most recent work, a series called 'Imperator', Neronic Sheldonian heads undergo the same catastrophic degeneration. One of them wears the kind of glasses fashionable in the 1950s, squarish open frames on the Roman face over veined eyes. One scarcely needs this prod to slip 'Imperator' two millennia or even thirty years. Perhaps, one is encour-aged to think, it betrays the real subject? Are these pictures of Rus-sians? But absolute legislators are not so stupid. There is weakness in analogy. Only specifics can hurt. Drawing these awful Romans and self-important Austro-Hungarians is essentially *not* describing the Russians. To universalize a complaint is to emasculate it. The anger is turned into commentary. 'This is how things are,' it says. 'Imperial-ism, like decay, is part of the structure of things.' Anderle is famous. His pictures have been to Los Angeles and Toronto. The bait is to think of him as a demonstration of tolerance and liberalism in Husák's Czechoslovakia, a regime which allows clever criticism of itself. But that is nonsense. The pictures are self-censored luxury articles in which the quality of the draughtsmanship distracts from any radical meaning. They are love-letters to power. One recurrent omission reveals their true nature. Anderle never draws the genitalia. The disgusting naked bodies of the imperialists, so exact in every facial wart and nipple hair, become sketchy in the groin. One or two lines map out the self-censorship, where brown cocks and bunched pudenda would have clinched the argument. Anderle leaves them out because that kind of radical shock and revelation would have been too disgusting and too subversive for comfort.

'He is at the hard end,' Stano said. 'He is with the police, very right. He says: Look at me. Such things are possible here too. I can do it in this system that people say is tyranny, and I am great.' Stano hated Anderle for this betrayal of a gift. 'He is a clever sailor,' he said.

I met Stano at the café in Devín. My guidebook had told me to go to the village. High above the confluence of the Morava and the Danube, it said, perches another ancient frontier landmark. There was even a photograph in an official brochure labelled: 'A castle site, highly dear to the historical Slovak nation against the Teutonic threatens.' It also happened to be right on the modern frontier with Austria, which runs down the Morava (March) and at Devín (Theben) turns west along the Danube. Here, for once, I could visit at leisure an exact mapping of ancient on to modern frontiers and – without suspicion – look at the Iron Curtain from the backside and close to.

I should have known better. The Austrians had occupied Devín after Munich and it was sensitive. As I emerged from the new blocks of flats which surround old Bratislava in giant stubble fields of concrete and red plastic – the population of the city has grown by more than quarter of a million, trebled, since the war – the thick wire of the back border came up alongside the road. I ignored notices I could not understand. A guard in a tower picked up a phone as I went past. I zigzagged through the poor, narrow streets of Devín. Pink colour-wash walls and the tarmac mottling out into weeds. Children arranged broken bits of the tarmac in patterns, squatting next to them like poor arabs. The white walls of the castle circled a bumpy lawn of pure limestone turf. It had been deserted in 1635, ruined by the French in 1800. I came to the car park, where guide books should have been sold and a pre-season ice-cream kiosk should have been boarded up. But neither was there. The car park was fringed on two sides by the first of the barbed wire fences, isolating the castle and lining the bank of the Morava. The castle hill and the riverside trees blocked any view into Austria or of the frontier rivers themselves.

The telephone call had prepared the guards. Six soldiers and three machine-guns were there waiting for me. Sniffer dog next to the jeeps. The dog was brought up to sniff me. Every sniff an arrival. There was a cage on its face made of shiny wire, cushioned against its nose with a bit of green baize padding like part of a snooker table. The balk end. The cage was big enough to allow him to bark and I thought of Anderle. They told me to go away, the usual passport business. I had become as blasé as a fifth former with a house prefect. I asked them to have a cup of coffee with me in the bar. But they went away and I met Stano instead.

I spent a few days with Stano. He always wore a red Canadian anorak and blue jeans, and sloped about in a slow, shaggy and effortlessly charming way. He was much taller than most Slovaks, about six foot two, and his hair fell down into his eyes. He was twenty, worked as a car park attendant outside a tourist hotel and earned 1,700 crowns a month. I followed his Simca back into Bratislava from Devín.

He lived in his grandfather's house – the grandfather was not there – with turquoise mosaics in the bathroom and unfinished plasterwork in another, in a nice suburb north of the city. Dubček lived three streets away. He works for a timber business nowadays. Stano had once shaken him by the hand in Obchodná Street, like an old pop star, he said. Dubček had a Simca like Stano's. I went to look at Dubček's house. It is on the side of a hill which overlooks the city. A patch of the rough grey stucco-crust had fallen away from the house where the guttering had leaked. There was a small balcony and the garden was precise, as undemonstrative as a suit. A policeman stands outside the gate and he moved me on.

It only struck me afterwards as odd that Stano should have stayed with me for the rest of the time I spent in Czechoslovakia. He never went off to look after his car park. Nor did I think it odd until later that, with his terrible job, he still had the Simca, the longed-for foreign car which constituted – along with the country cottage – the petty bourgeois dream. How could he have paid for it? These suspicions did not crystallize at the time. He was too nice a man to suspect. It was only later, when I came to the frontier between Bulgaria and Turkey, that what happened in Bratislava appeared in another light. I now think Stano might have been a sort of policeman latched on in Devín to insulate the frontier. But I can't be sure.

We visited his girlfriends, lovely girls with long hair in poor flats – sixty crowns a month, with loos on the next floor, up the open stairwell – where corrugated mattresses were beds and sofas. None of them liked Bratislava. They called this ancient city of more than 400,000 inhabitants 'a small town' and they were right. The frontiers had shrunk it and the ubiquitous police presence tightened it up, provincialized it. But they all loved Stano. You couldn't help it. There were some Poles rather politely drinking in one of the flats. They were visibly poorer than the Czechs, dark worried men, hunched on the floor. They were all working on the enormous building site across the Danube. It was a little slip of territory awarded to Czechoslovakia by the 1920 Trianon Treaty as a 'demilitarized bridgehead' against Austria and Hungary. The new building scheme is packing the old Magyar area with upwards of 80,000 Slovaks. One of the Poles said: 'Where the money is, there you must go.' And another, drinking the *borowič*: 'When in Rome, you must do as the Pope does!'

Stano had forgotten to bring his papers one afternoon. We were stopped by an unmarked car on the edge of the city. 'Police,' Stano said and got out. He went over and chatted through the wound-down window. The man in the back seat of the police-car turned round to look at me. Stano was soon in the Simca again, smoking a Sparta, pushing Leonard Cohen back into the tape deck. No fine, just the promise of a can of strawberries next time he came back from Prague. This omnipotent charm.

Back in the house Stano turned the lights off and lit a candle. Hungarian anis and easy listening called 'Outerspection'. Stano said he had escaped for a year. At about three o'clock in the afternoon late in May 1982 he walked over the border from Bulgaria into Turkey. 'By some trees, where there was no army. A normal frontier with no fences.' He showed me the place on my map. From there to Greece, Yugoslavia, Italy, France. He was sixteen, working as a builder and a waiter. He never rang his family or asked them for money. He crossed every border illegally and his passport was clean. On the anniversary of his leaving he rang his mother. She cried on the telephone and so he came back. The day after arriving in Bratislava he was arrested on the street. A neighbour had told the police. 'What is duty?' he asked. 'Duty is money.'

He was in custody in Bratislava in the State Security Block for four months. He usually weighs 85 kilograms; he came out at 55. It was mostly nerves that took off the weight. 'If you were like this, they wanted you like this, if like this, like this.' He went through puppet motions. 'Five of us all day walking in the cell, in and out of each other, all day walking, walking.' He had told many lies consistently. He said he only did tourism. They asked, five at a time, what he did in Istanbul, where he had never been. What particular drugs did he manage? But they could fix on no criminal offence. They were friendly like a father and then they were cruel. He was only beaten once. They told him that he was a political prisoner. At the Helsinki Conference the Czech delegate said that there were *no* political prisoners in Czechoslovakia. Did I understand people who could lie so cleanly?

His mother came to the prison and cried. He had two trials. He was sentenced to two years suspended for eighteen months. He must have charmed them too. He was now, he said, in police control. There was nothing he could do without them. He had no passport.

We talked about money on the black market. He knew the rates of every capitalist currency like a jobber. He had a plan to export two second-hand Tatras to the United States. Nostalgia for the Brylcreem innocence.

'What is Czechoslovakia? Czechoslovakia is what I have in this room. You are a free boy. Your Honda is the passport. I will be Australian. You will say not a true Australian, a Slovak in Sydney. You can say, I am English, I am free, I am myself. What can I say? I cannot be me and here. I am in the West. Only my body is here. I have no friends, only comrades. People with me are also under police control. And people would like not to be my friend rather than to be under the police. But how can you understand? I am no nationalist. I want no country, no places. I do not like places. Places are nothing. Prague is the same, Bratislava is the same, Leicester is the same if there is no policing. I want to live nowhere. Devín is the worst place. I hate Devín and everywhere is Devín. I hate myself for loving my mother. I love my mother.'

The fountains in front of the State Security Block were empty on the two square lawns. At the back, metal gates filled the archway behind a closed-circuit camera. Nothing to be seen beyond the repeated blinded windows. Stano had called Czechoslovakia a Hitler *Lager*.

Madame Suippes had bought a pair of plastic beach shoes for Eucrate. The Czech customs man picked them up and smiled affectionately. '*Mon fils*,' she said in Belgian. '*Verboten*,' said the Czech. Capitalists, like the English with waiters, are too nice to border guards. They should be treated with a contempt and familiarity they can recognize. But Rodolphette shrank from the *faux pas*. The guard gave her a brown bit of recycled paper, half-way to cardboard. A deer jumped in the *broussailles* of the frontier zone. Among the onions, tinned fruit and tinned vegetables, bed linen, all kinds of underwear, socks and stockings, almonds, sultanas, currants, candied lemon peel, coconut flakes, curtains, wallpaper paste, babies' wraps and pearls, in the 'category of goods the export of which from the CSSR is not allowed within the framework of tourist traffic', appeared *footwear*. Mme Suippes was *désolée*. She *bowed* to the customs man, her lovely corsage marshmallow in suspension, and the roots of her hair-do more visible. '*Ah, non*,' M. Suippes said *en brosse*. '*Ça ne fait rien. Nix*,' and wobbled his pursed lips. He handed over the offensive footwear. Eucrate would be going without. Here was the moment for the Napoleonic gesture. The officer closed his eyes and pushed the orange shoes back towards the chaotic Suippes suitcase with the knuckles of his hand. The grace of it! It was Casals at the UN, a President avoiding impeachment! Belgians have never felt such gratitude.

Mme Suippes made conversation in the hour's wait that followed. There was something like this in Ireland?

'Quite like it,' I said.

She understood me and moved her nose. '*Ah . . . point de boom boom par ici!*'

8

Borderland

I had not noticed how grubby I had become. In Stano's grandfather's house and the various camp sites of Bohemia I had felt respectable enough, not too pungently below the level of hygiene around me. But cleanliness came with the frontier. As I changed up through the gears into Austria, leaving *la famille* Suippes behind me – '*Il faut avoir de la liberté,*' she had said on hearing of Olivia and Thomas in Leicestershire – a sense of dirt, a travel-stain, leaked into me, lit up by the bright day. Austria was *clean*. The customs men in their smoked glass booths and loden capes, their enamelled ex-imperial badges, their trimmed and buoyant moustaches, their little scalloped plates of cake on the boothside shelf, some grains of the *mille-feuilles* still sparkling on the moustache-end overhang – all this turned me into a tramp. I was a dirty smalltime bike boy on a shrivelled Honda, worming in Europe, as grubby as the passport and its stained rhetoric about Britannic Majesty, as used as the map.

The tarmac had been hoovered. A woman in Hainburg was washing the pavement on her hands and knees. The pharmacy was filled with shelves of scents and international unguents, an endless chromatic fugue on beard treatment and scalp preparations. I oiled into a café with a view of the lovely limestone hills that come down to the Danube here, as foreign to the overall chic as the Leningrad train in Helsinki. It was exhilarating. I was the model refugee, the Dickens waif let loose in the toyshop, entranced by *matériel*. I bought Austrian money in an air-conditioned bank from a girl who had made full use of the pharmacy. I asked for the largest notes she had. The Austrian money was tennis-courts after the dusty Czech *koruny*. The Communist notes had slopped into suppleness after a lifetime of folding but the schillings cracked like new flags. I bought an electronic alarm clock and a new shirt, spreading the seventeen pins, the cardboard chest and plastic neck across the width of the pink cloth café table like a poacher. The pins were beautifully made with oval heads and inch-long shafts and I threw them all spinning down the streetside soakaway.

There were conservative women in the café drinking *cappuccini* in the sunshine. Their warm newspapers smelt smoky and sweet and they had pushed the sleeves of their lambswool cardigans up past the elbow. Behind us all on the smooth dense limestone someone had sprayed *'Atomkraft? Nein danke!'* in green with orange punctuation. But the wealth of these women – I was seeing it with foreign eyes – creamed past the question and its answer with a sort of luxuriated bathtime ease, soaping their limbs with indifference. Devín was four miles away across the river, hidden from us by a boutique and a sweetshop, as forgotten and unregarded as any other memory. In my conscious dirtiness I belonged to the other side, the squeezed-out spot from a dirty skin.

My clothes went into a launderette and I paid too much money for a room I wasn't going to use. The point was the bath. I lay in a midday lather, not needing to wash, but letting the Hainburg water do it for me. Through the open window I could hear the bells of the clock tower dung-danging at the quarters and now and then, much deeper, the hooters of the Russian tugs on the river, shoved up against their barges and the current, the bass notes blown in over Hainburg like a conscience or another smell.

Outside the town, to the east, the hills come to a nose above the valley of the Danube. I walked up there along a spiralling road and then on the warm turf. It was the best day of the year. The breeze blew up between the new shirt and my skin. The air had been washed free of any haze and there were other people on the hilltop looking miles east over the great flat expanse of the Kis Alföld, the Hungarian plain, over the thick dropped silts of the Danube as it slows into Hungary. You could see it all: the toy outline of the castle in Bratislava, the stump-stalks of the new estates in Petrzalka, where the Poles would now be working, the ruins at Devín and the barge-trains on the river, drift-swinging downstream on the bends, and others working grindingly back up them, their flags hardly stirred at two miles an hour. On the other side of the valley the Little Carpathians moved off to the north-east, laden with vineyards and Czech chalets. These nations *en brosse*.

On the downland nose of the hill, where it dropped to the valley, there was a monument, a single shelly slab. It said:

ZUM GEDENKEN
AN DIE HEIMAT DER
KARPATENDEUTSCHEN
DIE IN 1945 AUS DEM

PRESSBURGER- HAUER-
UND ZIPSERLAND
VERTRIEBEN WURDEN*

It had been set up in 1980, as a golden *Rückblick*, a blue view to a perfect past in which there and then had been mashed together into one hyphenless peopleplace.

A man with a face like a gas fire told me that this was the last mountain in Austria. There was thyme in the turf and he sniffed a sprig, tickling the hairs in his nostrils.

'But it's the same stone as over there.' The lit panels of his face fluttered a little.

'Let us not talk geologically. This is the last national mountain.' He knew a couple of *Karpatendeutschen* who lived in Hainburg. There might have been two or three hundred of them there, but in the great Beneš expulsion most of them had gone to their uncles and cousins who were farmers in Austria, mopped up into the landscape. They were country people – they would not have liked Hainburg. I knew what he meant.

I rode south into the Burgenland. The roads followed dykes above the fenny fields. This was one of the classic European borderlands. The Roman frontier had run along the Danube and its fringe of marshes, the meeting of the Mediterranean and the northern worlds, but in post-Roman history the border had turned through ninety degrees, as the great succession out of Asia met the edge of a western Christendom. The last mountain in Austria, the tail end of the Alps and the first of the great flatlands of the east, that is the shape of the Burgenland. In the eighth century AD the plains of the Alföld and the Alpine rim were ruled by the Avars, plunderers with an *untermensch* population of Slavic vassals. Charlemagne and the Lombard Pepin destroyed the Avar federation in two crushing campaigns in 791 and 795. The Franks established another border Mark here, parcelled out among the nobility and brought under the spiritual jurisdiction of Salzburg and Passau.

The Magyar attacks began in 896 and pushed the edges of the Carolingian empire far back into western Europe until their utter defeat at Augsburg in 955. The pendulum swung again and by 987 the boundary of the East Mark was back at the Wiener Wald. By the year 1000 it had come to rest on the River Leitha, which runs a few miles south of Hainburg and into part of the Danube at Mosonmagyaróvár,

---

* In memory of the homeland of the Carpathian Germans who, in 1945, were expelled from Pressburger-, Hauer- and Zipser-land.

now in Hungary. I crossed the reedy Leitha at Gattendorf. It was swirled up against the concrete cutwaters, with a sofa on the bank. For more than nine hundred years the river marked the great division of central Europe between German and Magyar, between the Holy Roman Empire and the people from the east.

The Leitha was the great symbol of the Hungarian nation and its limits, but the divide was not linguistic. The medieval idea of the state rested more on simple ownership of a place over time, on a union of place with tradition, than on any identity of place and language. The great king St István of Hungary ordered that foreigners should be considered as guests, *hospites*, in Hungary, and from the beginning the Hungarian kings promoted German settlement of the areas east and south of the Leitha *inside* their own borders.

The Magyars had come from the East and in the tenth century had laid waste this western edge of the Alföld. In 1241 the Mongol Horde did the same. In 1529, 1532 and again in 1683 the Turks repeated the process, devastating the country and killing the people there. After each invasion and wasting new people were invited in. The Magyars brought Pechenegs from the steppe north of the Black Sea to settle alongside islands of their own people. In the thirteenth century, after the Mongols had come and gone, Germans were tempted down from the mountains by the promise of royal Hungarian protection, their own pastors, and some sort of local autonomy. Again in the sixteenth century, after the Turkish invasions, the Magyar overlords, deprived of their German workforce, invited other Germans from further west to come down into the plains. But the prospect of renewed Turkish attack made them reluctant and large tracts of what is now Burgenland (the name was invented in 1918) were settled by Croats from around Zagreb. For them it was an invitation to safer fertile land closer to the protective umbrella of the Habsburgs. The final recolonization of the rich flat lands around the Neusiedler See occurred after 1683 when the Turkish threat appeared to have gone for ever, and Germans again came down from the mountains.

From the first treaty between Austria and Hungary in 1048 until the Treaty of Trianon in 1921 Burgenland was, at least in theory, part of the kingdom of Hungary. But the fluidity of the borderlands, the uncertainty of life on the principal avenue of attack from the east, ensured a less definite role for the country. Central authority diminishes in a borderland and in the Middle Ages the Hungarian magnates here, some of whose holdings were enormous, regularly allied themselves with the Austrian Duke against the Hungarian throne.

The Treaty of Pressburg in 1491 complicated the situation. The

largest feudal estates in the borderland were transferred to the Habsburgs and their revenues to the Vienna treasury. Nevertheless these
estates continued to be part of the kingdom of Hungary, but incor-
porated into the feudal holdings of the Austrian Habsburgs. The ac-
quisition of the Hungarian crown by the Habsburgs in 1526 smoothed
over these difficulties without resolving them. When in the seventeenth century some of these Habsburg estates were given to Miklós
Eszterházy, a Hungarian magnate, this complex legal and territorial
geology was given another twist. A Hungarian magnate owned land
which was theoretically part of the kingdom of Hungary but which, by
the Treaty of Pressburg, was under the final control of the Austrian
crown, whose wearer also happened to be king of Hungary. Most of
the people living in this muddled land spoke German, but when it
came to choosing they had no doubt on which side they belonged.
In the great rebellion of 1848 the Germans of West Hungary
(Burgenland) sided almost unanimously with Hungary against
Austria.

After the Compromise of 1867, by which a separate Hungarian
national state was established within the Habsburg Empire, a policy of
rigid Magyarization was enforced right up to the Leitha, reaching its
apogee in 1907 when a law was passed by which *all* teaching in *all*
primary schools in Hungary, including the Burgenland, was to be in
Magyar. This Apponyi school law, spitting in the face of the loyalties
of 1848, began to stimulate the first separatist movements among the
Germans of West Hungary, whose distant ancestors had been wel-
comed as guests by István and his descendants.

The conflict surfaced in the Peace Conference after the war. It was,
in effect, an argument between linguistic and territorial nationalism.
The Hungarians had all the economic arguments on their side. The
territory of West Hungary was divided by two spurs of the Alps which
pushed into the Hungarian plain and had no good roads across them.
It had never been one political unit, but the western ends of three
Hungarian provinces. Nothing but the preponderance of German
speakers (75% of the population) linked its three sections together. Its
markets, except for Sopron (Ödenburg), lay to the east in unquestion-
ably Hungarian territory. The connections westwards into Austria
were paltry. To award Burgenland to Austria on linguistic grounds
would be to isolate it on both sides: from Hungary by an international
frontier and the tariff wall that would come with it, from Austria by
the virtual absence of communications. It would be to consign the
place to poverty and – emotively but importantly for a defeated and
mutilated country – it would slice away part of the 'lands of St István'

which had been one body, one sacred integrity since the beginning of the millennium.

The Austrians argued that on the basis of language and for the welfare, even the survival, of the citizens of Vienna and Graz, who ate its meat and drank its milk, Burgenland should become part of Austria. The discussion was muddled by a rather eccentric scheme which envisaged a Slav corridor between the two new states of Czechoslovakia and the kingdom of the Serbs, Croats and Slovenes. The corridor might restrict the spread of pan-Germanism to the east, it was thought. Some absurd self-determinist claims were made for the Croats of Burgenland (15% of the population in 1920) and Harold Nicolson thought the idea 'just'. But the Italians squashed it: they had no interest in a strengthened Yugoslavia.

On 11 July 1919 Britain, France, the United States and Japan voted for the transfer of West Hungary to Austria. Italy voted against. There was to be no plebiscite. Figuring largely in the decision was a desire to compensate Austria for the loss of so much territory elsewhere; to push Hungary – at that moment Communist under Béla Kun – eastwards and out of artillery range (about 48 kilometres) of Vienna. By strengthening Austria any spectre of an *Anschluss* with Germany would also, they hoped, recede. A weakened Hungary, whose record on the treatment of racial minorities was the worst in Europe, would make life easier.

The decision did not come into effect until 26 July 1921. When the Austrian gendarmerie tried to occupy the towns and villages of Burgenland on the allotted day, 20 August, they were shot at by bands of Hungarian volunteers. A small sniping war continued for a few days, as one idea of the nation contested with another, until the Austrians withdrew leaving a state of anarchy.

Udders were cut and vineyards destroyed. Grudges were acted on and the government in Budapest denied any responsibility. The Czechs, who had absorbed hundreds of thousands of Hungarians east of Bratislava, threatened to march on Buda. The Austrians pusillanimated and the Italians summoned the parties to Venice. It was in Italy's interest to see a weakened Austria, unable to champion the rights of the quarter million German speakers in the south Tyrol, and, by the Venice Protocol, issued on 13 October 1921, Italy arranged for an amnesty of all the Hungarian terrorists who had murdered gendarmes and prominent German speakers; the retention of Magyar officials in the transferred territory; and a plebiscite in the only large town, Sopron/Ödenburg, hoping perhaps to fillet the province and make its return to Hungary inevitable. Chancellor Schober was vilified in Austria for accepting these terms.

The Sopron plebiscite was corrupt. The Hungarians drew up the list of voters. The Austrian commissioner was withdrawn. The dead voted for Hungary in droves. Trainloads of bogus Hungarian voters were brought in from further east and the vote went 65/35 in the expected way.

Burgenland was cored by the removal of Ödenburg. The great peninsula of territory around the town comes at one point to within three miles of the old border. The new boundary cut through lifelines and both Sopron and Burgenland suffered. There was mass emigration. Shipping lines set up offices in Eisenstadt. Their advertisements offered another life in the New World. For those that were left it was a time of great hardship. The provincial parliament of Burgenland was forced to pass a law specifying the limits below which a piece of land could not be subdivided: arable and meadowland fields were to be a minimum of twenty feet wide and one fifth of an acre in area, vineyards thirteen feet wide and one ninth of an acre. This side by side with vast Hungarian estates (26% of Burgenland in 1928), most of whose owners never visited them. A cross-border arrangement was made in 1926 to alleviate the difficulties of the Burgenland peasantry, but more than anything its provisions describe the poverty of the people here, deepened by the crassly insensitive drawing of the frontier. In a zone fifteen kilometres wide bridging the frontier the peasants after 1926 could transport goods duty free up to a limit of three kilos of meat, two litres of milk, grain and vegetables up to three kilos, bread and pastry up to three and a half.

I came down to the shores of the Neusiedler See at Rust. The gradual hills were stiff with vines, the lake nothing more than tan reed beds as far as you could see. Andrew Baberton was in the Hotel Stadt Wien, a pub, holding a *Stein* of lager. He had come to buy reeds. Half the thatched houses in England now were roofed from the shores of the Neusiedler See. It was an excuse to get away. He didn't need to come, but he always liked Rust, the cleanness of the place. It made him feel ashamed. He couldn't believe that Burgenland had ever been poor. A stuffed heron stood on a barside corbel.

Andy was drinking with Hans Winkel, his contact, a man of substance, twenty years older than Andy, and wise with it. His parents always used to talk about the poverty of Burgenland. It was always a *Stiefkind*, a step-child, not properly loved by its half-parent in Vienna, as if it were an autistic child, stuck with its own hopelessness. Hans wasn't keen on this idea, but I pressed him about it. It joined up, I think, with something in his own experience, which had pushed him into dealing in anything, reeds for English cottages, used tyres for some environmentalist group, tour-cassettes to regions of Austria. He would say something definite and then look at me to see if I reacted sympathetically. His mother always used to say that the Austrians from 'Old Austria' treated Burgenland as their own little old piece of the Balkans, a charming backward little *Stück*, where geese walked about in the streets, poverty was charming and children had holes in their shoes. They had cousins over in Fertoböz, lost with the plebiscite for Ödenburg, and then the Russians and the fence. 'We have already suffered so much!' she always used to say, and Hans and his brother used to joke about it when the dinner she gave them was hardly worth eating. There had been some terrible rejection here.

'But the *Stiefkind* has grown up,' Hans said and belched. There were new roads. The constitution of Austria had poured money into the Burgenland. 'Look at this town now. Is there poverty here?' Exploitation had turned on its head and Burgenland feeds off Austria now.

In Rust, at least, what Hans said was true. The 'Free City' was sheened in a sort of National Trust patina and little plaques remarked on the age of the buildings. Travel agents advertised trips to Budapest and Disney World. And everywhere this hygiene.

'We have forgotten this borderland business,' Hans said. 'There are three-hour queues at the week-end of Austrians going to buy cheap beer in Sopron.'

'But isn't that borderland business?'

'It is the plus side,' he said. 'Borderland in the black, if you like. In all your grand historical,' he went on, 'you have dazzled. Absurdly! This is a holiday rest-home. We have campings, a *Romantika Feriendorf*, honeymooning, *ornithologisches* holiday watching.' Andy sipped lager. 'So what if in 1956 all those Hungarians slipped over in the Seewinkel? So what if Burgenland was in Hungary for a thousand years? You have a complex about this. But the history is skin thin. It is the shallow skin on the places. My mother always used to talk about the stealing of Ödenburg. Who cares for Ödenburg? It has one eye.' We had more beer, and the heron on the corbel looked stuffed. 'I can get to Vienna in forty minutes.' Andy said he thought history was very interesting. 'But look at this guy,' Hans invited him. 'But look at this guy. He is taking his Honda round Europe trying to find little problems, little people with complexes about whether they really *are* who they are, he feels really good when he finds someone who is really unhappy because their sister is living "on the other side". Do you know you really are the dangerous sort of guy? Do you want to be a politician? I hope not. You know it's people like you who make a mess of the world?' Hans went on to describe the marvel of markets and the unity of commerce. He sold reeds to the Hungarian National Board for the Protection of Historical Monuments, for which they paid in *dollars*. Dollars sequined in the dusk. 'Get out of your mind that this is a neurotic place. You know I think you've got problems yourself!'

Andy was a little bemused. He took off his tweed jacket and slapped a mosquito against his cheek. It sprawled in blood there. Hans went off to the loo. 'I'm sorry about all that,' Andy said. 'Must be a pretty touchy area.' But the three of us had trout from the metre-deep lake and Neuberger white wine, and Hans gave me the name of a woman in Siegendorf, a Croatian, who would interest me. This was generous: sugarlumps for the criminal. And then, to my amazement, he offered to take me on a little tour the next morning, to see something of Burgenland. Andy was red and shiny, delighted that something had gone right.

We left him in the morning to bird-watch in the reeds, sitting in a punt on the sedgy canal with waders up to his groin ('my Hunters'), three handbooks and a notepad. Hans had changed out of the seersucker and looked ready for golf. I bumped along behind him on the limestone vineyard roads. He pointed out of the window at calvaries and then a snipe that shot out of a little bog. My mouth clogged in the dust. Hans was touring the estate. He took me to the *Rathaus* in Eisenstadt and went on about the Eszterházy court and Haydn, the great Hungarian period for Burgenland. But in the *Rathaus* – that is why we had come here – there wasn't a mention of all that, the seigneurial grandeur of eighteenth-century Eisenstadt. Instead, dreary murals about Hallstatt Iron Age folk, Romans, the settling of Germans here by Charlemagne, the Free City status (1648), the provincial capital (1925). All this was a symptom of exaggerated border-consciousness, Hans thought. Why had the Burgenlanders of the 1920s and 1930s not dared admit that Eisenstadt was *founded* in Hungary, reached its quasi-royal peak under a Hungarian prince, had spent virtually all of its existence as a Hungarian town? All that had been sanitized out in the *Rathaus* murals and conveniently forgotten. In front of them a yellow xeroxed notice on a peg-board advertised 'Music for Peace and Joy of Mankind'. A series of trans-border concerts. 'Songs transcend frontiers', it said. Hans thought both equally sentimental.

Then on to Frau Szmudits in Siegendorf. She had a flaring red mouth and carpet on the walls, a cherry red voice and a laugh like a lawnmower. Her husband was an electrician on the trams in Vienna. She and Hans shared a past. Hans said I was interested in oddities and the room was filled with the noise of her starting up from some-where deep in the bosom. She must have been at least sixty-five and wore an apron embroidered with black and red dancers, with black and red appliqué wavelets across each breast. She popped a boiled sweet into Hans's mouth and then one into mine and then one into her own. She said she was Catholic first, Croatian second, Burgenlan-der third and Austrian fourth. I asked her what she thought about a Slav corridor coming down from Bratislava to Yugoslavia. Wouldn't it be something to live in a Slav country? She put another sweet in my mouth and said something to Hans I didn't understand. She had never been to Yugoslavia and would never bother with Pressburg. Zagreb had nothing to do with her. Hrvatska – the Croat for Croatia – was four hundred years away from her house and her family, from her clothes and from Hans. Hans smirked. But if I was so good at arrang-ing things, why not bring Vienna down to Eisenstadt? That would be more convenient. This was terribly funny and she rocked in her seat with her chin in the air. Yugoslavia was a disaster, anyway. The Serbs were a disaster. Tito wanted the Burgenland Croatians returned to Yugoslavia after the war. And some of her friends had taken their children away from the school – the Croatian school – in case the government expelled them, like the Germans who had come in out of Hungary. But what was more stupid than that? No. She was *zufrieden* – satisfied – where she was, and ran a hand up the carpet beside her.

But I wasn't to think that they all thought like that. The Croatians in the south of Burgenland were another matter. They had their little farms and the men didn't go to Vienna. Hans took another sweet and Frau Szmudits smacked him playfully. The priests down there had very strong ideas. The *Kroatische Kulturverein*. Dancing and cakes. 'And they want us to speak like the people in Zagreb. They want us to forget that we are Burgenlanders. No German words. They would have policemen coming into the kitchen to listen if you weren't cook-ing with little German thoughts, or talking to Hans with little German words.' This was a bit direct and Hans didn't respond, but flicked through a magazine. She told me about the Croatian schools, where they teach in the language, but not in this purist form, and that, she thought, was the best joke of all.

She had no friends among the Croats in southern Burgenland. They sometimes went dancing in Zagreb, but that was ridiculous. 'They would like to put us in a pie,' she said, thinking of chickens. 'But I like walking around and sometimes laying an egg.' I thought of Frau Szmudits laying an egg. Hans was cockahoop at this vindication of everything he had said in the Rust hotel. She gave us coffee with

Schlagobers floating about on the top, the cream diminishing and sinking at the hot edges. Why did she have carpet on the walls? 'It makes my husband comfortable.' At Mass they sang the hymns in Croat, but the lessons were read in German. I remembered Donne: 'Who hath divided Heaven into Shires or Parishes, or limited the Territories or Jurisdictions there?'

9
Eclogues and Corruption

It was Saturday when I crossed into Hungary at Klingenbach. The road ran down by the wood towards the 1921 line. The queue of cars, a necklace of schillings and empty boots, shone in the sun over Hungary. An hour's wait on the Hungarian side, and like a train stopped at a country signal we emerged from our cubicles and chatted. Nils from Oulu, ignoring the 2,000-year gap in their ancestries, hoped that Finno-Ugric solidarity might mean an extra-special welcome from the Magyars, bridging the millennia which divided him from the man with the Kalashnikov. No, he couldn't recognize any of the words in the customs declaration form. I thought of a man from the South Bronx trying to whisper little nothings into a cloth-capped Wallsend ear. Or an interview with Vercingetorix.

Sylvie was effortlessly voluble.

KISS MY ASS

I'M ON VACATION . . .

her breasts said. A little heart was asterisked into the corner of her sunglasses, a fraction inside the violet frames. She leant up against the wheel arch of a juggernaut with Hungarian plates, one high heel resting against the steel wheel rim. Its driver leant over the steering wheel himself smoking, his bearded armpits exposed for ventilation and brushing on the spokes.

'Do you speak English?' I asked Sylvie and smiled up at Ferencz in the cab. Ferencz stared into the Alföld. 'Do I speak English!' Sylvie said. She was from Miami Beach and had emigrated there ten years ago when just eighteen. Now she was back to see her mother in Sopron. But it wasn't nice. She pushed her finger into the pot of peanut butter and licked at the curl. It was *three* times more expensive than when she left. Neil, nine months, fathered on her by a 73-year-old Rolex salesman in Miami Beach, was right now in the Sopron apartment. Not a single room had been baby-proofed for his arrival. Her mother put her cottons in with her blue jeans. Into the jar again for a glob of putty. People spoke nasty. It wasn't like she remembered it. But one thing really got through to her. The cloth diapers? There aren't any disposables in Hungary? Her sentences began to warp at the end like plywood left out in the rain. And the cooking? Her mother cooked in pig fat? With all this paprika? She'd just been over to Vienna with Franky here. Franky went on with the Brando bit. 'We got cosifits and ten jumbo sunpats. And some nice babyfood? With the pop-up freshness guarantee?' I knew all about it. Her mother had put eight dollars' worth of Smurf in with the washing. No wonder Neil had come up in rashes. And Sylvie had lost all her colour. She told me to look at her. She used to have such a nice colour. Now she was yellow. Sunpat dob from the half-scooped pot. And the men had told her to get dressed when she went jogging in the streets. All she wanted was to get back to the poolside with Neil in the proof-pen and she could get some of the colour back.

I asked about America. 'I don't want to hurt your feelings but the States is really, I think, the best place there is. OK, so there are good blacks and bad blacks. I had one of Jose's Rolexes torn straight off my wrist. Just like you're there. But it wasn't real. I only have one real Rolex. They say that people walk past a guy lying in the street. OK, I've done that. But people are busy. They've got jobs to get to.' She must have had a bad time from the family about this. There was no doubt anyway that walking past people in the street was better than no hot water in Sopron until three in the afternoon, or the boring aggression of paprika in every damn bit of one's fatted up food or the obscene recurrence of nappies in the joggingless Pan Am trap of a town destroyed by nationalist territorial ambitions. Sylvie would never return. She would ditch Sopron like she'd ditched the used cosifits now stacked on the shelf at the back of Franky's cab. Her mother wasn't worth it. Her mother's suspicions and that ziggurat of stained cloth with all its antique paraphernalia of buckets and pins and indescribable chemicals, as grim and grubby as peasant farming. All that would be junked *wholesale*. Infant faeces and men in the gutter belonged to the chute side of life. Sylvie wanted her colour back and once she'd got it she'd stick with it.

Sopron peeled. Travel agents advertised Burgenland for 2,800 forints. A woman stood at a dusty windowsill in a street eating sandwiches as though at a bar. The whole place had atrophied. Bright expresso cafés pushed at street level into leprous houses. The upper storey windows had been blocked out with hardboard. For the first time an eastern dustiness, where the concrete pavements had cracked and shifted a little, leaving inch-high scarps in the surface, where dust and wrappers collected. Through an open window on the street I watched Toto-Lotto papers being counted under slow ineffectual fans. Five rows of men and women scanned the numbers, a pile of read on one side, unread on the other. A man had won two and a half million in Miskolc the week before. A teller two back in the third row was tiring. Her yet-to-do still outweighed her already-done. She read a number not knowing what it said. She read it again and again and the digits did nothing. She sat up from the desk and rubbed her eyes and looked out along the row and the rubber-bound piles. She was behind. She set to again. The number, not a winner, was flipped over with licked fingers.

Sopron had lost its purpose in 1921. It had been won back for Hungary because Italy wanted a weak Austria, and the traffic in the stock market declined from nearly 30,000 cattle and over 70,000 pigs in the year before the plebiscite to half that number in 1922 and less than a quarter by the 1930s. Sopron had lost both its catchment area – in Burgenland – and its outlet – in Vienna. A sealed-off, baby-proofed place. In 1956 thousands of people crossed the open frontiers for good.

I rode out of Sopron into the wide soft landscape of the Kis Alföld. The great flatness of Hungary, the endless invitation of it to the east. I drove the bike for days eastwards to the Russian border, baking where I stopped on the verges wrapped in my English oilskins like a potato.

First at Nagy Cenk only a few kilometres outside Sopron. A place which bypassed all the agonies of 1956 and the diminishments of the Trianon Treaty and joined up with the great reforming expansive liberal days of the nineteenth century, when Hungary began at last to break away from the dominance of Vienna. Nagy Cenk is a modest château. It lies back a hundred yards or so from the main road in a simple white range confronting the geometries of its French garden. Little yews pimple the axes and box lines the spaces. It is a model of discretion and lightness in which the one big splash is the swanky baroque coat of arms in the central pediment, curving out as much as sideways, the badge of the Széchenyis. On the other side of the road children skipped in and out of the shadows of a long lime avenue, along the dusty wavering path that had been worn into the turf between the trees. I lay in the shadow of an old copper beech to one side and soaked up the moderation and sweetness of this seigneurial place. There were violets and speedwell in the clover hay.

Count Ferenc Széchenyi and his son István created Nagy Cenk in the first decades of the nineteenth century. The father was a scholar and collector, but István was, as Kossuth said, 'the greatest

Hungarian'. He was the bravest and the most imaginative of all those Hungarian magnates who began in the 1820s to push their country towards the modern world. He recognized that the ancient privileges of the nobility, which had been protected by earlier generations of nationalists, were no bastion but a prison, confining Hungary to a static and outmoded way of life. To maintain the peasants as slaves, forced to labour for their alien and distant masters, was both humanly degrading and economically inefficient. In 1828 he divided the fields at Cenk between the estate and the bondsmen living there. In a letter to his bailiff he wrote: 'Let's set an example by enabling the people in the country not only to make a living but also to improve their material condition. Let us work for the public good, not only for our own profit.' He planted blackberry gardens, set up a sheep farm and a stud – the first in Hungary, with twenty English stallions and sixty English brood mares. They were all part of the model liberal estate, with this delicate and feminine house at the middle. This was not the land of paprika, of the great marauding trans-Carpathian hordes, but of Tolstoyan grasp and real nobility. István Széchenyi was the pioneer of steamships on the Danube, of chain-link bridges across it, and of railways that would make the country rich. He was an avid devotee of horse-racing and a passionate believer in the humanity of other people. All this is still there at Nagy Cenk, tended now by the State, with lovely models of railway engines and canal schemes and big-beamed paddle-steamers upstairs. One can slide around the simple rooms in free thick felt slippers, as though in a mosque; pat the fat chestnut bottoms of the horses in the stables; lie about for hours on the flowery grass under the huge plane trees in the park. There is nothing agonized or difficult about it. Despite everything, despite the terrible damage done in the last days of the war – now made good – and despite the ominous remark in the guidebook: 'The village and the house remained in the family's possession until 1945' – despite all this, Nagy Cenk is the perfect middle, away from frontiers and their confusions and exaggerations, away, paradoxically enough, from the hatreds and rivalries which the growth of national feelings engenders, replacing them with a sort of pride which goes beyond pride – that coat of arms – releasing freedoms by insisting on their exclusive importance.

Széchenyi's motto – *Magyarország nem volt, hanem lesz* – is carved into the pedestal of his statue outside the village church. It means: Hungary belongs not to the past but to the future. The terrible disappointments of 1848–9, when, with Russian help, the Austrians crushed the new Hungarian government – in which Széchenyi had been Minister of Communications – forced him into a private asylum at Döbling near Vienna. After the Imperial police had searched his rooms and confiscated his papers Széchenyi shot himself on 8 April 1860. His body was carried on the shoulders of his peasants from the station in Sopron to Nagy Cenk. The funeral was arranged for the twelfth, but the Imperial police insisted at the last minute that it should be a day early. Nevertheless six thousand people attended and in the following three days over 50,000 others from all over Hungary came to the austere family mausoleum in the village churchyard. Above the door to the crypt an inscription says in Hungarian: 'As you are, so were we; as we are, so shall you be: dust and ashes.' Near his coffin is a small, wrinkled, iron casket holding the shard of bone which the bullet tore from his skull.

On the long ride east to the Russian border, to the far side of the crush zone, the spirit of Nagy Cenk followed me. I found it in the strangest of places. It had as many sides as I cared to discover. But the point was that it seemed to embody a national idea, a pride in the place which, for their various reasons, had been absent or lobotomized in the countries I had travelled through to get here. Hungary was the arrival, the place in touch with itself, with a sense of hope and momentum that had been closed down in Czechoslovakia; invisible in the tentative movements and contradictions of the Germans; too far in the past for the Russians I had met to remember; trammelled in Finland and made bland in the far north of Norway, where climate and the padding of personal nests had shunted nationalism into a box marked 'Accepted'. Maybe it was the warmth. The Bohemian rain was on another continent. I pushed my oilskins into the saddlebags and rode in an open shirt along the edge of the Alföld on the endless trajectories of the poplar-lined roads in a haze of benevolence, in love with the flat still country. The Honda was perfect. A man in a waistcoat chased a pig across a meadow, both of them cantering in the grasses. Boys kicked a football on the far side of it, the ball arcing up above the hay and disappearing as it landed. Irises in the clotted beds along the stub-ends of village houses, running back from the street in their yards. Laburnum and wisteria arched over the road as trees. My freedom to move had seemed a taunt, even an insult in Czechoslovakia, but here it was part of the natural air, in an open southern place, where the soldiers were on spring manoeuvres and the tractors hoed the fields between the lines of maize. In Esztergom on the Danube bend I was given a *felafel*, a deep-fried ball of mashed-up chick peas, levantine food. For the first time the light was bright enough to bleach out the back of your eyes, to make the flame at the end of a match invisible. I forgot it was a Communist place. There was none of the intangible fear, the fear of writing notes in a public place, which hangs over Czechoslovakia. Hungary was no *Grenzgebiet*, but full of men kissing on meeting, the southern casualness of a jacket thrown over the shoulders, the vogue for Sztriptiz in minisex bars. The country had flowered into a disarming frankness, a sort of relish for the smallest freedoms unknown in the West and impossible in the furtive burrowings of Czechoslovakia. Hungary was on the up, coasting on a gentle dough-lifting optimism which hadn't yet soured. Or maybe it was the warmth, and the ease of the Honda, at a constant sixty, visiting nothing, unbothered with detail in the memory of Nagy Cenk.

At least that was one side of it. I had with me a book of poems by Miklós Radnóti, the young Hungarian poet who, on 9 November 1944, in a small village near Györ, had been executed by his Hungarian guards. He was a Jew and with others from his *Lager* in Serbia was being marched westwards away from the approaching Russian armies. Many of the prisoners had been shot *en route*, by retreating ss units, but when the sick, diminished column reached North West Hungary, the escort tried to find places for the weakest in a hospital. There was no room and they too were shot in a grove outside the village of Abda. Radnóti was buried in the mass grave. He was thirty-four. The bodies were exhumed the following year and a notebook full of poems was found in his greatcoat pocket.

I read Radnóti's poetry at my roadside halts, smoking on the verges, shadowing Kádár's buoyant Hungary with these intimate visions of purgatory. They are diamond views of a damaged world, in which the folding together of all its pieces, the order of reason, is broken by the careless and universal forces of barbarity. Even in the camp and on the forced march which ended at Abda, Radnóti turns away from neither side, not from the obliteration and hurt – the symbolic figure is the bomber pilot, ignorant of the bombs he drops – nor from the classical Virgilian order which, even in the worst of circumstances, he holds to as the reservoir of all humane and civilized values. It's a heroic double-consciousness, precision courage in the face of dissolution. The poet remembers in a world razed by forgetting, and in one poem, written in the Lager Heidenau in Serbia, sees himself as the root:

> Not concerned with the world – just
> With a branch hung thick with leaves –
> Still, down there, the root survives.

> This branch it adores and nurtures,
> Sending up to it good flavours,
> Sweet heavenly flavours.
>
> Now I am a root myself,
> I am living among worms –
> That is where I write these lines.
>
> Once flower above, now root below:
> Earth weighs upon me, dark and low.
> This was ordained my destiny.
> A saw is wailing over me.

This poem spent a year underground in Abda, in the folds of a coat.

'It's not like it used to be,' a man in a Paisley bow tie told me in Miskolc. He was demonstrating teletext to school-children in a post office showroom. An 1880 map showed the lines of the Hungarian postal services reaching down to the Adriatic in Dalmatia, up into Poland, way over into the mountains of Transylvania and netting thickly in Moravia. '*Immer kleiner,*' István Tasi said like an impotent. He had given his life to the post office – the national veins, as he described it – but now he was retired and his wife was dead.

'Why is it not like it used to be?'

'Monsieur Horthy is still loved by the old people. He was an aide-de-camp of the Emperor, he was a *baron* and he was an admiral. We loved him because we have had no admirals. His name spoke old Hungary, Great Hungary, of a nation with a sea coast. Trianon cut us off from that – the barbers in Paris – but Monsieur Horthy was a sort of *trait-d'union* with the past. To the young now he is nothing. They cannot remember.

> I know one ought to forget, but I
> Never forget a single memory.

But Kádár, he has to forget. He has to forget who he was in 1956, how he helped in cheating and killing Imre Nagy.'

'But isn't that to forget a wrong? To heal something? To return to something more properly Hungarian, which you should welcome, Mr Tasi?'

'This is all very well.' Thick lips. 'A growth of 12% in the agricultural sectors, a new sort of avarice in the people, in the open. But where is the frameworks? The young peoples have no morales!'

'Morals?'

'Yes, no morality. They are coming down to the Romanians for their behaviour. Everybody wants more than they can get. I have a small place down on Balaton. We – I – go there in the *haute saison*. There is a train direct. I was there two weeks ago and with the sun, of course, you see the corners again, and I wanted a man to *balayer* the place together, to cut the hays and mow the lawns. And of course I offered 500 forints a day to do it. He was younger than you. Do you know what he said to me? "I need 5,000 a day before I'm going to lift my hat to anybody." *Need*. So there you are. Where is Mr Kádár taking us? The balloon is going higher because he is throwing everything out of the box. Hungary must be Hungary to be Hungary, however many transistors there are in the houses.'

It was unadulterated conservatism: past good, present bad, a Manichaean division in which all the elisions and subtleties of nationalism and its shadings, its odd connections across political differences had been neatly sorted by the knife of time. Mr Tasi was a widower. He had teletext himself. There was not much left for him except to tie his French bow tie and demonstrate technologies to indifferent children.

> Death is racing
> Through the sparkling dust of the Milky Way
> And pouring molten silver
> On headlong shadows.

'There are the top 10,000,' Mr Tasi went on. 'They have money and they are all *épiciers*. The rest of us are poor. Even after a lifetime in the Post. I was a lieutenant on the Russian *frontière*. *Ce ne fut pas une jolie chose*. Today I have little.' That was it. He was only talking about personal decline, generalized for dignity's sake. Like Radnóti, he watched his own life as a measure of what had happened to the world. What else can one do?

> Spring flies, hair streaming loose, but the angel of past freedom
> No longer flies beside her, but is sleeping deep down, frozen
> Into yellow mud: unconscious, he lies among stunned roots.

In Pacin, on the southern edge of Czechoslovakia, I sicked up half a fish stew into the border river, the orange spew floating away on the Hungarian side in strings; and half into a ditch in the village, where I sat on the mown hay and the sick settled and dried on the swathes that were damp and warm in the middle, under the brittle crust. Of all things, a funeral passed me as I crouched there, the bier pulled by two brown horses. Feathers nodded on their foreheads and the coffin was hidden by doughnut laurel wreaths. The eighty men of the village walked behind it, led by the pastor, all of them in angular black serge suits, singing a dirge. As they went past in a low cloud of dust around their shoes the heads of all eighty, still singing, turned to watch me in the mown ditch. I thought I should apologize.

After the procession had moved off down the road, an old woman and some children came and touched me on the shoulder. I lay down on a couch in her cool house, where the lime wash had been stencilled in plum bands beside me. She gave me soda, while the children watched from around the jambs of the door. She pushed her two hogs out into the street and left her dusty mushroom dog lying by the mulberry shade in the rootled yard.

I woke up in the evening and the poison had cleared. She gave me tea and honey and in sign language we talked about children and sisters and where London was in relation to Vienna. Pacin was in the shallow basin of the Bodrog, where each house had its own well, some of them capped with little Hungarian flags on vanes, one with a toy aeroplane in the national colours and a yellow propellor which twirled. There were beautiful wheatfields, stiff with poppies and sorrel, fringing up to the oakwoods and, across the rivers, clanking antique chain ferries which used the torque of the current to judder from one side to the other. There were many levées above the flat sandy land, the dropped silts from the Carpathians where the Tisza, the great drain of the Alföld, had wandered in the past, leaving shallow alkaline lakes where it moved. And there were many gypsies. I sat at the side of a dance in Dombrád that evening, feeling ill again, watching the gypsies in white suits and ringlets, and homburgs sloped over one eye, dancing in the youth club there in effortless release.

The nearer I came to the Russian border, the slower my progress towards it. Outside Kisvarda I was flagged down by a police car with three officers and – handcuffed to one of them – a gypsy boy I had seen the night before. They came over to look at the bike. The prisoner and his escort crouched down by the side of the engine and discussed its technicalities. That was all, a casual curiosity before they drove off again.

But at last, at a village I had ringed on the map called Barabás, I came to the end of Hungary. A horse and cart in military red and green stood at the end of the row of houses, all at right angles to the street. The supply vehicle of the only horse-drawn border guards I ever met, the cobs deep in their nosebags. I rode on past them to the Russian border, three-quarters of a mile away down a straight gritty track. This, too, was a Trianon frontier, awarded to Czechoslovakia after

Beneš had charmed the conference into accepting that the Ruthenes who lived beyond it would be better off in his new 'Switzerland of Central Europe' than as part of the Ukraine, to which, ethnically speaking, their more natural allegiance lay. By the Vienna Award of 1938 Hungary acquired most of Ruthenia and in 1939, at the destruction of Czechoslovakia, annexed all of it. At the end of the war this territory became part of the Zarkaptskaya Oblast of the Ukrainian Soviet Socialist Republic, bringing the frontier of the Soviet Union down from the Carpathians and into the eastern edges of the Alföld, providing an unmediated eighty miles of frontier with Hungary itself.

Dandelion fluff floated over the maize fields in the haze. A brace of partridge got up from the grass by the border fence and flew over into the Ukraine. The fence was a simple T-bar hung with wire, in exactly the pattern of vines on the slopes around Tokaj. Lucerne crept up from the verges over the surface of the road. The sun shone on the metal dome and filigree crosses of the church in Kosino across the border and citizens scraped at the weeds between the maize. Radnóti in the sunshine on the verge.

> Can you see? As dark comes on, the barracks and the grim oak
>   fence –
> That is girded with barbed wire – dissolve: night soaks them up.
> Slowly the eye relinquishes the bounds of our captivity
> And the mind, only the mind, can tell how taut the wire is. . . .
> And the prison camp, at such times, sets off for home
> In rags, their heads shaven, snoring, the prisoners fly
> From the blind heights of Serbia to homelands now in hiding.
> Homelands in hiding!

This was his seventh eclogue.

From a mile away on the road to Barabás I heard the distant putting of a motorcycle coming towards me. In the waverings of the heat above the fields a man with a military cap and no shirt swung in and out of the potholes towards me. His neck was burnt red and he escorted me back to the village, keeping behind. Khrushchev had said in Leipzig in 1959: 'We consider that to us Communists the question of frontiers is not of major importance ... With the victory of Communism state boundaries will die off.'

We parked the bikes next to the border guard cart. Young soldiers were sitting in the garden of their quarters sunning themselves on ribbed plastic chairs. When they stood up, their naked backs were striped red and white like the thirteen states. One of them picked at his nipple hairs and then scratched a held-up elbow. They gave me a cup of coffee in which the bubbles were oil-spot rainbows. The momentum had gone. We all sat around in this end-place, indolently chewing at our lives, as the horses beyond the picket fence shuffled through the debris in the bottom of their bags.

The village vet was summoned. Dr Péter Fenes stood out among the self-forgiving border guards in their unzipped tracksuits like a manager in a take-away. A small close beard, intelligent, business-like, suspicious. It was not a good idea for a western man to visit the frontier. Why was I there?

'Touring.'

'Why Barabás?'

'The small places.'

This seemed to be good enough and he invited me home.

There was a career to be had in Budapest injecting cats and castrating dogs, but not for him. Péter and his wife – she was now a book-keeper in the 'Lenin' village collective – had come out to work among the people and look after their cows. They were both good Communists, but there was something at least in this of Torhag's self-exile to Finnmark, a sort of freedom among the simplicities. I spent the day with Péter and it emerged without his saying so that he had come to this poor eastern corner of the Alföld to improve the lot of his fellow men, to spread scientific knowledge and its well-being among those who had not been privileged enough to acquire it for themselves. He was not a naïve man. There was power in the position he had chosen. The small farmers in the village looked up to him for his science and intelligence. He was a member of the Party and had political ambitions. This was the groundwork, a constant surgery, a background he considered necessary before he made decisions for the people. He was convinced of the moral rightness of Communism and equally convinced of the economic rightness of everything that Kádár's New Economic Mechanism had set in train. Like the others in the village, he had bought a small plot of sandy land at the back of his house, ten metres by thirty-six, on which he planted vegetables and fruit bushes. He had sunk a new sort of well – no more than a thin pipe – five metres into the sand, with a suction pump clamped to its head, to water the crop and nurture his own produce. He worked an hour every day on the land. This was the self-reliant care he applied to everything he did, partly as a demonstration to himself, partly for the others in the village, the peasants, to show them the way. Six others had installed his new sort of well. Everything Péter did was this kind of amalgam of the personal and the communal, but there was a national, even nationalist, element in it too. The frontier itself meant nothing to him. Any idea of 'territorial theft' or of 'the betrayal at Trianon' was absurd. What the country now was, the country should now look to. It was a Socialist country. It was the Soviet Union's best trading partner. That was the foundation. But alongside this was the great history of Hungary. The two did not conflict. He showed his little sons – a pair of Lucifers he called them – an old picture-book history of the nation in which enemies cowered – Pechenegs, Avars, Kumans, Mongols, Tatars, Turks – and heroes triumphed – Árpád, the six *führers* of the Hordes, St István, Ladislas, Béla IV, Matthias Corvinus, Széchenyi, Kossuth, ending in the miraculous arrival from a pink *surprise* of cherub-laden cumulo-nimbus of the Admiral himself, in a simple blue uniform and the saddle of a white charger. Some of Péter thought the Horthy page laughable, some of him took it as it was meant to be. He was not interested in revanchism, an impossibility now, suspended by the absorption of the continent into a higher frame. 'How many Frenchmen want the Saarland back?' he asked me. 'No. We live in the landscapes of Yalta now.' But on the other hand, he had no truck with all those primitive Comecon schemes by which Hungary was turned 'into a Moscow suburb'. He was all for a classically generous middle way, with no exaggerations, no slipping out of control, no rigid impositions, no 1956s and no 1968s (these dates like awkward arrangements for sex). Stalinism and Nagyism/Dubčekism were equal failures on either side. The idea of neutrality was a little bomb which stayed in its box and should not be played with.

One wall of his sitting-room, where the Beelzebubs sprawled in the acrylic shag, was covered in a photograph of the Matterhorn, ten feet wide and eight high. It was the tallest landscape between here and Geneva. 'I love the mountains,' said Péter, as if the Alföld and its ponds and its wandering rivers were a measure of his self-denial. And on the other wall, much smaller, framed behind glass above his desk, a print of Holbein's 'Ambassadors'. The death's head slewed sideways at the guilty men's feet. He had bought it as a student, as 'a memory for simplicity, a lesson not to make a god of power', a weakness to which he was prone. 'Those men are the real ideologues,' he said. 'You have to look in their eyes. It is a painting about anxiety and a dirty pride. And the painting exposes them in all their furs and love of themselves. Do you know the word *hubris*? It is a picture of *hubris* and weakness and anxiety.'

Péter put on shorts and we drove out of his sandy garden in his turquoise Polski Fiat. It cost 80,000 forints or fourteen months' wages. The tyres were old and the roads were breaking up in places. He was always getting punctures. The first call was on a private pig at the far end of the village. The stewing of undigested food in her colon had made her ill. She lay the size of three people on the concrete floor of the sty, with an ignominious thermometer up her. Peter stroked the spun sugar fluff on the pork, while his thermometer cooked and the old man gave me a thimble of schnapps. The vet refused. The sow shuddered at the three injections and then jerked herself up in stages. Péter jumped out of the pen and she peed sedately on the concrete floor. A fee of 150 forints and endless gratitude.

Then on to a cow, a village away between the poplars and the rye. Péter explained his scheme to improve the old Hungarian Red with semen imported from Dutch Holsteins. It was going quite well. The lactation was up, but a drawback was emerging: more milk in the progeny seemed to go hand in hand with a partial infertility. The pattern would be clearer in a year or two's time.

He rubbered up in the farmyard like a surgeon and inseminated the poor thing. The farmer, his family and I stood around on the crusty muck, while bees dozed in and out of the shadows and the cow made one soft moo before clattering out into the yard, unaware of the change that had been wrought in her. Another private animal, and the vet as the cunning magician, miraculous powers in his kibbutznik hat and shorts among the braced and collarless peasants.

And then on to a pastor in a solid old parsonage with four huge sequoias in the garden, sprouted from seed sent in an envelope by one of his predecessor's children, prospecting in California. The pastor was a round man in a deep brown armchair, drinking Tokai cognac with us out of silver egg-cups gilded in the bowl. He was dressed like a schoolboy out for the day in white shirt, black tie and black flannels, and his hair was like the sow's. Antique peasant cloths hung on the walls. The vet and the pastor talked about the problems in family allowances: they had not kept up with inflation. There was a family in one of the villages they shared where the man drank and the children weren't allowed out to play together in the winter as they only had one coat between the three of them.

It was a scene out of Kilvert: the vet and the pastor, more united by class than divided by attitude, the only educated people in their wide soft landscapes, the two of them nursing their flocks towards an oddly shared enlightenment, both motivated by the obligations of privilege. They had both seen a film on television about unemployment in England. Wasn't that the most obvious indictment one could look for of capitalist individualism, of the inhuman market?

I asked Péter on the way back to his house in the car if the New

Economic Mechanism would cause problems when Hungary perhaps began to outstrip the slower economies of other countries in the Socialist bloc? He thought not. 'You must accept a quieter picture of these things. Do not attach so much value to your frontiers. It is possible to love the country and love the people, but not with exclusions. The same relationship between individual enterprise and an idea of community is possible between nations. Envy is the capitalist disease.'

'Envy is the disease of power,' I said.

'Capitalists concentrate power.'

'Stalin was no capitalist.'

'Stalin was an ambassador without the sensation of guilt. Let us not talk about Stalin.'

The whole family squashed into the turquoise Fiat and I followed them for twenty miles through the warm, empty plain with tall skies and kestrels over the ditches. We had a picnic next to a wooden watermill with three wheels in the race and played badminton on the bank next to it. This was all another sort of Nagy Cenk, leached of anxieties and soaked in hope. Péter caught frogs for his children. He stroked their wet backs into a trance, and we passed the leathery sleeping bodies from hand to hand.

I waved goodbye and headed for the Romanian border.

Leviathan clouds rolled in out of the east. Ridged banks of them concentrated the heat with the threat of rain. A warm gout dropped into my face, followed by a wind which held the thunder. The Alföld waited in the stirred poplars and the floodlit caramel fields, as the dust dried waiting for the rain. Relief in the change to rain like a sort of laughter, as the coiffed front moved in from Romania. The banks of black air stretched north and south for fifty miles, quiffed up and backwards by the giant movement west.

I rode towards it, towards the last of the Trianon frontiers. It was a big Euro through-route and at an Agip garage the attendant pinched my oilskins as if nobody were in them, to feel the oil in the cloth on a shop-rack hanger. The tyre rubber squeaked on the dry road and I went on through the stillness, as the doors in the villages were shut and the animals were hobbled.

The rain came in a visible barrage, edging over the barley in the cliff of a skyscraper quay. The lit dome of a church was swamped and at sixty I drove at the rain-face where the village had once been, smacking into it as if diving. Children hopped under held-up capes in towards the doors and a young woman walked slowly under a hopeless umbrella, her printed apron blotched in spreading dark empires of the wet.

I waited for the storm to go over in a village stockroom, where its guardian asked me to pick numbers for the Toto-Lotto – the luck of strangers – to win another two and a half million like that chemical worker in Miskolc. Among the flour bags and the salt licks and her ledgers, the bulb went off on and off for an hour in the electrical storm. I lay on the flagged floor and slept until the children playing on the stacks of flour sacks tore the thick dross paper of one of them and the room was filled with clouds of it. The children went silent and white and the stockwoman shrieked before dusting them off, as our tongues stuck to our floury palates.

> Felix Spa offers you Reumatism
> Treatments with the Well-K
> nown Romanian products
> * Pell-Amar
> * Gerovital
> * Ulcosilvanil
> * Boicil

flaked a notice at the frontier. House martins had spattered the boards. The amazingly beautiful Contessa di Breccia smoked on the bonnet of her Lancia, returning from her mother in Oradea. She was Magyar herself and had married an Italian. Now her bony ankles were tanned. Half a mile away, half-mile long trains eased across the frontier. There was no fence, only the ploughed strip sprouting ragwort, like a lawn waiting to germinate. A Czech tractor had harrowed part of it. Shirley Temple with a bo-peep mouth and the blue customs cap cherrywise on her curls reigned like the Virgin Queen, thinking foul scorn that any person in Europe should dare to invade her borders. Shirley pouted up and down the benches where the luggage was displayed, personally searched the Contessa, told her to put out the cigarette while she was doing so, stopped a Bulgarian truck with the flick of a single puce fingernail, and removed a thirty-gallon bottle of wine from the cab.

> Visit the 'Bears' Cave' in Chişcǎi
> A new objective in the Romanian turistic circuit
> It shelters an undeveloped gamut of stalactites

'Polack?' Shirley asked me and tapped the petrol tank. Hungarian and Romanian guards lounged together on the scuffed steel tables, and the *maitresse d'* knew this was power.

In the Visa Office – Romanesque capitals in reconstituted 'Roman Stone' – a clerk wrote out the numbers of the 100 Deutschmark notes in front of him in long tight columns with some underlined in red. I watched him through the glass of the booth. Millicent Martin spoke Romanian on the grey screen beside him. Between times he examined the beginnings of warts on his hands with a magnifying glass intended for forgeries. Seeing me look, he smiled and continued with the examination, prodding half under one of them with the point of a sharpened pencil and then with the tip of an unfolded paperclip. He gave me some lei, softened old paper, would take none of the spare forints and returned to his list of Bundesbank numbers. A spot brimmed on his chin.

Shirley was ready for me. She adjusted the cap on the curls, holding the hairclips in her teeth and smelling of scent. No sweetie. Did I have any weapons?

'No.'

'Nothing?'

'Nothing.'

'Not even a knife?'

'No.' She thought this ill-advised. Stano had warned me: the Romanians are villains.

I got out my wallet and she started fingering the papers there herself. Morgan le Fey's pointed little purple nails among exchange forms and customs regulations. She picked out the photograph of Olivia in Cazorla and mmmed at it on an upward note. Why was I alone? My notebook stuck out of the jacket pocket and she pulled it out, scattering Kleenex on to the gravel. This gratuitous intrusion, this tiny violence – I hated her for it. She told me to pick up the scattered tissues. They had blown under the steel tables and the wheels of the Lancia. The Contessa nicely gave me one that she had picked up herself. I scrabbled after them on my hands and knees while Shirley read the notes and the Contessa polished her shades on a lambswool sleeve. Looking up from the ground I noticed that the lining in Shirley's skirt had slipped. What on earth was I doing here? All I wanted was the Aegean, an end to this endless picking up of little scraps of paper and poking under cars and tables, to stand the bike at the edge of a beach and swim in the warm water of the sea. But Shirl made me get on with it. She pointed out another Kleenex with the patent toe of her shoe and went back to the notes. I crawled over.

'Who is Mr Radnóti?'

I looked up at the auburn hairs in her nostrils. 'A vet. An inseminator.'

'Is he a professional acquaintance?'

'He's dead.' I was now sitting on the gravelly concrete at the end of my tether.

'Did you know him personally?'

'Only by written communication. Letters home from when he went away.'

'Why are you visiting Romania?'

'I'm in need of treatment at the Felix Spa. Boicil.'

'Very good. And your father is Bransgore?' Shirley had not understood *lieu de naissance*.

'Yes, Mr Bransgore Nicolson.'

She wrote this down, as well as Dr Radnóti's address at Nagy Cenk, and handed me back the passport and notebook.

'Why do you write so much?'

'For memories.'

Shirley bent down and dusted the grit from my knees. She moved away towards the 1974/tenth-century Visa Section trailing sweet-smelling cyclones like a front moving through. Nothing is more frightening – at least in potential – than an arbitrary and petulant authority which is unhedged by regulation or seriousness and descends into personality at whim. Personality matches a chute into barbarity on the other side. It could not have been further from those ghostly Russian guards on the Leningrad train. Each frontier was like the dentist's: familiarity with the threat served to heighten, not diminish, it. Each crossing was another ritual mutilation, stamped smiling into the passport.

Oradea was Mexico: it was a rawer and poorer place. Young boys shovelled lignite into the basement of a building that had been sugared into pink turrets and vermilion brocade. On the pavement outside a patisserie a gypsy lay holding his groin, moaning, with the other arm folded over his face. The man who had done it returned and with a dirty high-heeled shoe kicked him there again. The victim's black and green dog-tooth suit was muddied at the flares and his jacket bagged out in shredded udders. We watched, did nothing and drank our coffee. A gypsy girl tried to sell trinkets in the café. She showed us her sister, who was blind in one eye. The waiter pushed them out on to the street, where they sat on the kerb. The older girl – she must have been about twelve – tried to light a cigarette, but a cough from deep in her lungs twitched the match away from the end of it. Her sister tried to hold her hand, but she fended her off. Another gypsy boy in a beret shuffled towards a tram, but it left before he got there and he stood with his arm outstretched holding the place in mid-air where the door rail had been.

Until the 1860s the gypsies in Romania were slaves. They had no legal personality and no civil rights. They were bought and sold like other animals. If their owner did set them free and they wandered off to another town or along the road as tinkers, someone else could simply claim them as theirs. The Nazis killed about 400,000 of these people in southern and eastern Europe, and here in Oradea they are still openly treated as an underclass, dirty and despised.

I turned south. Women lay in the shade of roadside walnut trees in bundles of calico washing, dumped in the hot and stifled afternoon. A queue of Renault Dacias outside a state patrol station was three-quarters of a mile long. It was quota day and each of the identical cars was waiting for its ration, thirty litres for the month, or about thirteen kilometres' worth a day. My tourist coupons let me skip the queue.

The Treaty of Trianon had given Transylvania and this eastern side of the Alföld to a vastly enlarged Romania. The Hungarian and Romanian populations were hopelessly intermingled, and the frontier was drawn in order to give the new Romania economic and strategic advantage over her western, ex-imperial neighbour. Over one and a half million Hungarians were shut off to the east of the border. Hungary lost the string of towns – Satu Mare, Oradea, Arad, Timişoara – which lay at the foot of the valleys running up into the Carpathians. They were the all-important exchange markets between mountain and plain, and the only railway ran between them. The elaborate drainage systems for the Alföld, which the Hungarians had constructed assiduously since the middle of the nineteenth century, were cut through by the new border, with no effective management agreement between the hostile governments. All this, and the inevitable tariff barriers, deepened poverty and prepared the way for the next war.

I rode down on the endless straight trajectories of this Romanian Alföld, between places where national identity had globbed into islands. South of Arad, in the Banat, where the terrible Turkish wars of the eighteenth century had left thousands of square miles almost literally empty of human beings, I arrived at separate villages – Serbian, Romanian, Magyar and German – each distinct in itself, separated by miles of plain. They were the scales in the skin of Europe where it had puckered at creases. The Serbians had a liking for polychrome glazed tiles packed on to the face of a building in irregular symmetries. Some Magyars tightened the chain on the bike. At Sinpetru German, a village between Arad and Timişoara, the woman in the post office frankly despised Nicolae Ceauşescu, the President and Party leader of the country. His air-brushed portrait, from which the warts and dimples had been washed away like Gary Cooper in 1948, hung on the wall, but one side of the gilt frame had fallen off and was unrepaired. The wind on the Banat stirred the dust in the wide street outside and geese huddled in the corners between the buttresses of the church. Anna, the postmistress, gave me some of the instant coffee which a cousin in the Federal Republic had sent her. 'I am not German,' she said. 'I am Swabian first and Romanian second.' She showed me a postcard of the Harz mountains. Maria Theresa had sent her ancestors here because Germans made good border guards against the Turks.

Anna said that the only reason Ceauşescu didn't get rid of all the Germans in Romania – there are 300,000 'Saxons' further east in the mountains – was because they were the best workers in the country, infinitely superior to the lazy Romanians themselves. There was a perfectly straightforward hierarchy in her mind: Germans, Hungarians, Serbs, Romanians and gypsies, each worse than the one before. And Ceauşescu himself was the prime example of Romanian corruption. He had gathered his own family around him like an emperor. His wife Elena was a full member of the Politburo. His son Nicu was given fast cars at government expense. His cousin Ilie had been made a general and was scheming to take over when the old man died. 'And look at us here. You come to see us like primitives. It has been a bad year. The leap year always brings bad weather. The wind is terrible. In the winter in the street you could sink a car. And all we have from the *Conducator* is his precious photograph.'

There was so much of a frontier between the Germans in Sinpetru and the hyperbolic, dynastic nationalism of Ceauşescu, his family of cronies and the party they dominated that the actual isolation of these Swabians in Romania, separated from West Germany itself by nearly five hundred miles, seemed relatively unimportant. Instead of dreaming of Düsseldorf they lavish care, in this flat, harsh landscape, on their peonies and topiaried box, on regilding the street memorials to God and Anna Preisach, on a domestic precision in the village (despite the municipally neglected street) which is literally cultures apart from the ragged Romanian villages across the plain.

Timişoara is a university town and the students wore T-shirts with English slogans printed across them. 'Diet Free Jogging Surf', one of them said, and another 'OK Yes Now Club 100%'. Several said 'Olympic Los Angeles 84', but they meant little more than the others. I asked a man in a café who was advertising the Olympics on his shirt if he was pleased that the Romanians had defied Moscow by sending a team. He couldn't have cared less. It was another of Nicolae's fantasies, a dream demonstration that Romania was different from the Slavs we were all meant to despise. His name was Albert Dau and he was a seismic engineer full of gloom. He had bought the T-shirt because it was written in English. He was unable to get the job for which he was qualified and at the moment was working as a technical draughtsman. His father was a farmer out in the Banat and, with no relations in the department of engineering, there was no chance of his working there. He had heard that a tip to the director of 10,000 lei or about five months' wages might get him a place. He wasn't shocked at the idea. A bribe was part of the price of most things in Romania: an international phone call, a space in the parking lot, an uninspected box or two on the Bulgarian frontier. They all demand and receive, in the currency of petty corruption, their quota of Kent cigarettes. It's a recipe for disenchantment.

Rather eccentrically, Albert traced the real decline in Romanian morale to the earthquake in 1977, when all the beautiful girls had left the country. He had been engaged at the time to a Romanian German, but she had deserted him and married a German tourist. He had an idea she was now in Brussels.

He showed me a photograph of his current girl. She was very beautiful with dark skin and long straight hair like an Indian, but Albert insisted she was as Romanian as himself. I asked him if she was a gypsy and he told me she was very clean. He would not be marrying her. There was no point, there was no future.

Every conversation drifts back to Ceauşescu. Albert thought he was going mad. He was never without two Dobermanns on short chains. The President had decided to have one castle in the mountains for every week in the year. Elena Ceauşescu was going to depose her own husband. The Black Sea Canal, half-built in the fifties with dissident slave labour, as a Romanian Gulag in which 100,000 people had died, was, on completion, to be operated by dissidents as a gesture. These crazy rumours sprang up on the underside of a personal tyranny which pumped out propaganda praising Ceauşescu as the Shining Light, Alexander of Macedon and the Supreme Judge of History. Albert didn't know whether to dismiss them. At least he knew for certain that last autumn the leaves in some of the villages outside Timişoara were sprayed green before the president drove through so that he might get a fresher idea of the state of the nation. And that the contents of an entire piggery had been slaughtered and their quarters hosed out so that the presidential nostrils should not be offended. But no one, except the power-hungry, believes in that sort of thing. Nobody loved Romania for itself. 'People will take "Romania",' Albert said, 'and squeeze it like an orange before throwing the skin away. It is something to make good use of for a moment and then dump it.We have lost all belief. Everybody is using everybody else.' He seldom read a newspaper and, when he did, it was for the football. On the other pages Romania was always great. On the sports pages there had to be *some* truth.

It was difficult not to be infected by Albert's gloom. No tractors hoed the fields of the great plain as I made my way south to the Danube. Instead, for mile after mile, I passed the farmers of Romania, men and women, wrapped against the sun while they hoed the maize fields by hand. These human herbicides picked at the earth, hunched over it and scraped at the ground as if looking for something that was hidden there, a whole nation scratching after a prize which would always elude them. I slid past at fifty. Nicolae and his paternal smile confronted me on the outskirts of villages, followed by messages calling for tighter discipline, greater efficiency and a belief in the destiny of the Romanian people.

I was no longer sure what I was looking for. The minor contradictions of frontiers had come to seem insignificant next to this painful demonstration of the distance between governors and governed. My own pleasure in the great width of the place and in simply *going*, in being able to get on the Honda and *leave*, was a constant reproach. I felt like one of Péter's ambassadors, laden with everything the world could have given me and for some reason guilty because of it. When the people working in the fields rested at mid-day, they slept in the shade of poplars along the ditches. In the evening they scythed the hay along the verges for their private cows. I was just passing through.

Most of my clothes were stolen from my saddlebags in Oravița and the wing-mirrors removed from the bike. Romania seemed a desperate country, literally without hope and disintegrating as one looked at it. At every stop I was offered double the rate for dollars I did not have. In the bank in Oravița the clerk arranged to meet me after closing hours and did a private exchange deal in which, as he said, Nicolae was not involved.

Romania, as an idea, has been distilled into the rhetoric of the government and its unconventional foreign policy, leaving the people themselves to swill about in a sump of corruption and disenchantment. It sours the landscape. The beautiful road through the Iron Gates, where the Danube breaks through the Carpathians in a series of sheer limestone gorges, was marked on the map as a good high-way. It turned out to be a rotten and rutted track, half improved and half destroyed in the process. The money had run out and rusted bulldozers lay scattered along a landscape of incompetence. I bumped and rumbled along this worse than farm track as far as Orsova and there, on a Thursday afternoon, Romania ran out of petrol. Like an old Cortina on the hard shoulder of a motorway, the whole place had come to a stop. Storks sat on a couple of gantries looking out across the Danube to Yugoslavia. Men in check caps sat on the embankment wall kicking their heels. Old willows, drowned by the joint Yugoslav-Romanian dam downstream, stood up to their waists in the water. Pink smoke pumped out of a factory on the far side of town.

I, too, was out of petrol and was instantly offered private *benzina* in exchange for my tourist coupons by the crowd of young men who gathered around the Honda. Of all the offers I accepted Barbu Nica's. He kicked his own Czech scooter in contempt. It was nothing. Barbu was a professional footballer and wore a т-shirt which said 'I'm No-body'. His hair was arranged in a flat black thatch and he had one front tooth missing, kicked out the year before.

I followed him to his flat on the outskirts of the town. The block was surrounded by nettles and there was a field of television aerials on the roof. He told me to bring all that was left of my possessions into the flat. It was on the top floor, carpeted in pink and crowded with piles of size 45 Adidas football boots. They are manufactured in Romania on a concession from the French company and Barbu had a small sideline in smuggling them to Bulgaria. He showed me his passport, the precious document, with row after row of identical Bulgarian visas at monthly intervals. Each trip lasted four days – that is what he was allowed – going out laden with Adidas, returning with pots of Brazilian coffee, quarter bottles of red Bulgarian wine, Kent cigarettes and bottles of Schweppes Mandarin Orange Drink, bottled in Sofia. The customs men were kept sweet with cigarettes. A carton of Kent was more than enough. You couldn't really give it the name of smuggling. It was just a small enterprise which paid the customs men direct instead of via the excise duty. Barbu's position as the number 5 for Orsova Chimia allowed him to do it. That is how he had the passport: for sporting contacts. His wife was a girl of nineteen. She never said anything and didn't have a passport herself. She always stayed in the flat with the boy when Barbu went to Bulgaria. He told her to cook us something and, when she was out of the room, whispered, 'Disco dancing,' to me, sighing for his four Bulgarian days. 'This is what life is for,' he said with a little toss of the head. There were plastic busts of

Schubert and Napoleon on the glass-fronted bookcase and a poster of an East German hippy band called Die Familie Silly on the wall.

Barbu pulled down the rainbow blinds over the windows and gave me a Kent. The girl was told to bring in the boy. He was about four and his right eye was strangely enlarged as if made of china. His hair was long and yellow like a doll's. Barbu made him kick a plastic football with the side of his foot. The boy turned his head on the diagonal to bring the good eye into play and tapped the ball back to his father with a bored familiarity. 'There you are,' Barbu said in the tiny flat, cramped with the spoils of all his scavengings, 'he will be in Dinamo Bucuresti one day.' Barbu's own club was sixteenth in the second division. He showed me his name in a March newspaper. 'Nico', it said in a long list of others, followed by the minute in which he had scored. It was misprinted for Nica, but that did not matter. He knew what it meant and so did I. But Orsova Chimia only paid him 800 lei a match. The strikers in Dinamo Bucuresti were getting 8,000 a match basic, more if they won. And that is what Barbu hoped for his half-blind son. 'Thank God for the border to Bulgaria. Without that we would be very poor. Thphwtt,' he said, pulling a finger across his throat.

I crashed the bike one evening watching the cropped turf between a stand of poplars near Calafat. It went down over an embankment, where the road turned sharp left, and hit a beehive, glancing off it, and then lay on the lacerated turf while the swarm recovered and I took stock. I bent back the parts of the bike that had been damaged and made sure that it worked again. A shepherd gave me water. He took the bike for a spin up the road and I sat with his sheep and the hazel stick, contemplating the luxury of my predicament. I camped there that night on the nibbled turf in among the midges and by the sleeping bees. I woke up in the middle of the night and decided to cut to the Aegean. There were two tasks left me: to find Stano's crossing-point in southern Bulgaria and to reach the sea, to complete the continent where its borders came to saltwater again. I arrived at Svilengrad, just short of the Bulgarian border with Turkey, spattered with all the muck of the Bulgarian roads. I turned west for ten miles to the point which Stano had ringed on the map. A 'normal frontier' he had called it. A column of Russian tanks was parked on the basalt cobbles. The fields were full of cornflowers and poppies, and a buzzard flapped out of an ash tree. I was not to be put off and turned in towards the line. The track towards the border suddenly enlarged to a metalled air-strip three-quarters of a mile long, with white arrows and other markings on its surface, and then shrank again to gravel. There was no doubt that this was the place that Stano had meant. But past the field-sprays on wheeled irrigation lines and the ox-eye daisies and giant thistles was the Fence, or at least a thick impenetrable barrier of three of them, with the grass growing inside. There was no way in which Stano could have walked across here. He had been lying to me. The one great escaper I had met in Europe had been no escaper at all. Had his touring in the West somehow been sponsored? All the doubts about his easiness with the policemen, his oddly comfortable house and foreign car, rose in my mind again. This was, after all, the Iron Curtain: Warsaw Pact this side, Nato the other, made more intense by ancient hatreds between Turk and Bulgar. It was the deepest disappointment on the continent, deepening the sense of failure in my own journey.

Two more border crossings before Greece, with the smoky mountains to the west. Svilengrad was on the main road from West Germany to Turkey and Mercedes heavy with belongings queued for a mile to the crossing. Lorries took a day to get through here. The cars were dense with Turks going home. My neighbour in the queue had taken two days from Mons. The boot of his car inched open in a smile above the accumulated stuff. It would be another day from here to Konya. His children listened to Walkmen, his wife slept and he picked his teeth behind a cupped hand. Nothing was searched on the Bulgarian side, but everything had to drive through a double dirt-brown water-dip, the hygiene barrier and a mutual ritual sanitizing.

Into Turkey and the structures expand. Forty customs officials in French navy-blue suits and lawn shirts like air stewards held us up for hours. Concrete balks between the lanes. Two hundred Turkish flags and the distorted music of nationalist hymns from tannoy bunches on every flagpole. Ten different banks in separate portacabin booths demonstrated the Market at work. A box of German chocolates called *Präsent* lay open on the bench next to my official, the lay-out diagram beside them. He dabbled in the box between customers and waited for further offerings. All along the row, under the noise of the foreground music, *Gastarbeitern* were taking officers aside for quiet conversations. Turk and Turk stood next to each other making inch-long gestures and hinted-at shrugs, both of them looking at the ground, shuffling peb-bles in the dust with the point of a shoe. Small deals were made, allegiances recalled, and boxes of *Präsent* and half-bottles of whisky were salted away into official metal lock-ups under the desks. The designers had provided for corruption. I gave my man a packet of Kent and he put it in his jacket pocket, where it spoilt the line of the suit.

Edirne. Thracian at first, Roman AD 125, besieged by Avars 586, captured by Bulgars tenth century, ransacked by Crusaders twice, captured by Ottomans 1362, Russians 1829 and 1878, Bulgarians 1913, Turks 1915, Greeks 1920, restored to Turkey 1922. The Selimiye Mosque was the most beautiful object I had seen in Europe. A man selling dark glasses, their insect eyes lined up in the v of his shirt, approached me and I left for Greece. A Turkish lorry had a map of Europe on the tailboard. Cyprus was an unrelieved green. Green Turkey in a yellow world. Armed guards on every bridge, dressed American, one in the Renaissance pavilion above the keystone of its arch. A peacock screamed in a cage just big enough to accommodate its fan and yellow notices pointed to Yunanistan.

The last crossing. An antique Mustafa was hung on the wall. The Greek and Turkish guards in helmets and white puttees compared the size of their children across the painted line.

The Greek officer asked me if I was going to Cyprus and gave me a cherry from a bag.

'Must I wear a helmet in Greece?' I asked him.

'No, you must not.' He looked like Anthony Quinn.

'I *must* not?'

'Yes, of course, you must *not*.'

So I didn't and with the wind in my head and the last Snagov burning itself out in my mouth, I set off down the valley of the Evro to the sea. The dusty concrete villages were daubed KKE and Pasok for the coming Euro-elections and banners vilified America across the street.

I wanted to reach the point, the southern Grenze-Jakobselv, where the Greco-Turkish border met the Aegean. I was still ten miles from the sea when I saw it from the last hill above the coastal plain. The tarmac ran out and I was on to shifting, stony roads again. 'It is a naughty road, we call it a toilet road,' a man with binoculars told me. I followed it along the levées above the maize and the flop-eared sheep. Herons gawked out of the clogged lodes. I was travelling blind – the scale of the map was too small – but I think I must have been about a mile away from the mouth of the Evros when I was stopped by a Greek Army jeep parked across the track. There was an officer and two soldiers in it. They took me back two miles to their quarters, a converted delta farmhouse shadowed by poplars, with a reed roof and a volleyball court in the garden. I waited while they telephoned. I explained what I wanted to do. They couldn't understand the motive. It was a forbidden zone. I should not have been there anyway. Was I going to Cyprus? One of the young men was told to put on his rifle and helmet and button up his jacket. He directed me out of the border zone, my ally armed and helmeted on the back of the Honda, his knees shoved into my kidneys by the awkward saddlebags and his arm around my waist. The final shut-out, the last bit of exclusive territoriality, as the frontier went uninspected to the sea.

He left me at the tarmac road, recommended Alexandroúpolis to the west and began to walk back to his supper. I rode the twenty miles to my appointed resort, and there in front of the cafés on the promenade, their chairs turned outward for inspection, as a girl in grey leather trousers and no bra bicycled slowly up and down in front of them, I arrived at the Aegean. An abandoned hippy bus said 'Pay as you enter' next to its broken door. Early in Romania I had thought of an end, and here in front of the *citrons pressés* and the ranged audience who were attending more to the braless cyclist than to any grubby new bikeboy, I performed it. It was to have been a private ceremony at the mouth of the Evros, but I was not to be put off. In the pocket of my jacket I had accumulated the small change of Europe. It was a fistful of little coins, Groschen, Bani, dinarjev, schillings, stotinki, filler, lei and a couple of forints. I went up to the parapet and together with the fluff, a few wrappers and three old matches, threw them all over into the sea.

Index

Index

Index